THE OSAGE

Tal-lee (Tally), the *Hon-ga Ga-hi-ge* of the Arkansas Osage Band. Painted by George Catlin in 1834, while Catlin was at Fort Gibson. Tally's Osage name was *Tah-hah-ka-he* (Deer With Branching Horns) or *Ta-ha-ka-ha* (Antlered Deer). National Museum of American Art, Smithsonian Institution. Gift of Mrs. Joseph Harrison, Jr.

THE OSAGE

*An Ethnohistorical Study of
Hegemony on the Prairie-Plains*

Willard H. Rollings

University of Missouri Press
Columbia and London

Library of Congress Cataloging-in-Publication Data

Rollings, Willard H.
    The Osage : an ethnohistorical study of hegemony on the prairie-
plains / Willard H. Rollings
        p. cm.
    Includes bibliographical references and index.
    ISBN 0-8262-1006-6 (pbk.)
    1. Osage Indians–History. 2. Osage Indians–Social life and
customs. I. Title.
E99.08R55   1992
306'.089975–dc20
                                                    92-22983
                                                        CIP

∞™ This paper meets the requirements of the
American National Standard for Permanence of Paper
for Printed Library Materials, Z39.48, 1984.

Designer: Rhonda Miller
Typesetter: Connell-Zeko Type & Graphics
Printer and Binder: Thomson-Shore, Inc.
Typefaces: Garth Graphic and Goudy Handtooled

This book is dedicated to my wife Barbara and my mother Luella Rollings. My life would have been empty without one and impossible without the other.

CONTENTS

ACKNOWLEDGMENTS

Many people helped in the writing of *The Osage,* and I would like to thank all of them. John Wunder, my friend and mentor, convinced me to examine the history of the Osage people, and his help and guidance in the past years has been immeasurable. John read the manuscript many times with great attention to detail and always with a critical understanding of what I was trying to accomplish. It was his criticism and observations that shaped this book. Richard White also generously read the manuscript, and his comments and questions helped me more than he will ever know.

I am also grateful to everyone at the Newberry Library for their help, and I especially want to thank Helen Hornbeck Tanner, Fred Hoxie, David and Susan Miller. These good people shared books, research, ideas, and friendship, and they helped me arrive at a better understanding of the history of Native American peoples. My life, both academically and personally, is infinitely richer for my year at the Newberry.

Many individuals helped with my research, specifically Cindy Martin at the Southwest Collection at Texas Tech University; Daryl Morrison at the Western History Collection at the University of Oklahoma; Beverly Bishop at the Missouri Historical Society in Saint Louis; and the staffs at the Archives Nationales in Paris and the National Archives and the Smithsonian Institution in Washington, D.C. I also want to thank the National Endowment for the Humanities for a travel grant that permitted me to conduct research at the National Archives.

Other scholars provided help with this book. The late Abraham P. Nasatir generously allowed me to use his extensive collection of Osage materials. Terry Wilson read the manuscript several times, and his knowledge about the Osage proved invaluable.

Elizabeth A. H. John's letters and comments were also helpful, as were Maudie Chesawall's, the Director of the Osage Museum in Pawhuska, Oklahoma.

Many families welcomed me into their homes when I was working on the book, and these vital research trips would not have been possible without their hospitality. I thank all of them: Charles and Maedell Lanehart in Oklahoma City; Melissa, Bob and Nicole Kurbis in Encinitas, California; Kent and Davetta Fry in Fort Meade, Maryland; and Arlette Gardner in Paris.

Others contributed to this book in different ways. My mother and grandmother did not live to see the completion of this book, but these two strong, independent, western women taught me the value of an education and hard work—and I needed both to finish this book. Others, both friends and family alike, helped my wife, Barbara, and me in countless ways. Their friendship and love will never be forgotten. In addition, the Osage people provided me with a constant example of strength and cultural tenacity that I grew to respect and admire.

My very deepest love and gratitude, however, goes to Barbara, who worked tirelessly typing and retyping the manuscript. Her help has gone beyond mere manuscript preparation, for Barbara has endured cold winters, dusty springs, blistering summers, and meager means while this book was being prepared. She did more than her fair share in amazingly good spirits. Barbara must share the credit for any contribution to Osage ethnohistory this book makes, for without her the book would never have been begun and surely never completed.

THE OSAGE

INTRODUCTION
Osage Images and Realities, 1673–1840

The Osage is a treacherous, cruel, thieving, and wandering nation that lives to the north of the Taovayas and Natchitoches.
—Fray Juan Morfi, ca. 1781

They are naturally amiable and friendly. . . . Strangers are always pleased with the hospitality of these people. They will divide the last meal, and never suffer one to go hungry from their village, or remain there in want, if they have to give.
—Reverend William Vail, 1826[1]

The Osage were a powerful group of Native Americans who lived along the prairie and plains margins of present-day Kansas, Missouri, Oklahoma, and Arkansas. For much of the eighteenth and early nineteenth centuries these people dominated the prairie-plains between the Missouri and Red Rivers. From the Ozark forests to the grassy expanses of the Great Plains, the Osage controlled the land. Occupying this pivotal area along the Mississippi, Missouri, Arkansas, and Red Rivers, the Osage shaped the history of the region and its people for over a century. Despite their power and their critical role, however, little has been written about these prairie people.

All native peoples who inhabited the prairie-plains have suffered an unfortunate scholarly neglect. Because their partici-

---

1. Juan Augustin Morfi, *History of Texas, 1673–1779*, 1:89; William W. Graves, *The First Protestant Osage Missions, 1820–1837*, 13.

pation in the resistance to white settlement was limited, and because they tended to avoid wars with the whites, historians, who have primarily focused on Indian-white relations, have largely ignored them. Recent ethnohistorical research, which examines persistence and change within Native American societies while stressing adaptation, has also overlooked the prairie tribes and instead focused on the nomadic tribes of the West such as the Lakota, Cheyenne, and Crow. While all of the prairie groups have suffered neglect, the Osage, in particular, have been largely disregarded. They have been the subject of limited research which lacks either significant Osage cultural content or thorough historical analysis.[2]

Those who have studied prairie people describe a people overrun by either aggressive plains tribes or unsympathetic whites. In Preston Holder's influential study, *The Hoe and the Horse on the Plains,* the prairie horticulturists are portrayed as cultural reactionaries. Holder depicts the village farmers as relics of an older world, a people unable to deal with the new conditions created by European invaders. Unable to cope with the changes produced by the horse, the gun, and the market economy, attacked by epidemic disease, mounted nomads, and Euro-American invaders, the villages remained with their declining populations as "anomalous island remnants of the old, in an engulfing sea of the new equestrian nomadism."[3]

2. Richard White, Salt Lake City, Utah, letter to author, November 23, 1983; see Terry Wilson, *Bibliography of the Osage;* W. David Baird, *The Osage People;* James R. Christianson, "A Study of Osage History Prior to 1876"; Carl H. Chapman, "The Origin of the Osage Indian Tribe: An Ethnographical, Historical, and Archaeological Study"; idem, *The Origin of the Osage Indian Tribe;* Garrick A. Bailey, "Changes in Osage Social Organization, 1673–1969"; Robert Wiggers, "Osage Culture Change Inferred from Contact and Trade with the Caddo and the Pawnee"; Gilbert C. Din and Abraham P. Nasatir, *The Imperial Osages: Spanish-Indian Diplomacy in the Mississippi Valley;* and especially John Joseph Mathews, *The Osages: Children of the Middle Waters.* Mathews's book is an intriguing study of the Osage and contains an important perspective on the history of the Osage people. No one can hope to understand Osage history without starting with Mathews.
3. *The Hoe and the Horse on the Plains: A Study of Cultural Development among North American Indians,* 136.

There are grave problems to such formulations. The Osage, one of the "doomed" prairie horticulturists, rose to meet the new challenges. At a time when most of the prairie farmers retreated and declined, the Osage advanced and expanded. During a period when the other prairie-plains societies, such as the Pawnee, remained outside the European network and retained existing political systems, the Osage enthusiastically became a part of the European exchange system and adapted the European political system. During the time when scholars such as Holder argue that horticultural societies could not adjust to challenges and opportunities presented by the Europeans, the Osage came to dominate the southern prairie-plains.

The Osage have received minimal scholarly notice, and much of the history that has been written about them is as one-sided as the conflicting observations of Fray Morfi and Reverend Vail. Historians and anthropologists who have examined them have portrayed the Osage as arrogant and bellicose. This inaccurate portrayal is a result of examining Osage history solely in terms of white society and culture. These scholars have failed to study Osage history on its own terms, and hence they have produced the resulting jaundiced view of the Osage. As a consequence of using only non-Osage historical documentation, scholars have overlooked the dynamics of Osage cultural change in the eighteenth and nineteenth centuries. They have dismissed the sometimes fierce Osage behavior as simply the result of some ingrained cultural belligerence, rather than as the actions of a people confronting powerful rivals and undergoing rapid and dramatic alterations in their social, economic, and political institutions.[4]

One cannot arrive at an understanding of Osage history relying solely on the records and documents of the Osage's enemies and rivals, yet this is what has been done in using only French, Spanish, and American documents. If one used only Fray Morfi's

4. See Din and Nasatir, *Imperial Osages.* For a similar interpretation of the Yanktonai and Teton, see Richard White, "The Winning of the West: The Expansion of the Western Sioux in the Eighteenth and Nineteenth Centuries."

or Reverend Vail's account one would indeed have a biased view of the Osage. From the point of view of the French, Spanish, and early white Americans, the Osage were often antagonistic. The Osage were hostile, but only because the newcomers threatened their way of life. The Euro-Americans came among them and brought deadly diseases, armed their enemies with powerful weapons, and encouraged rivals to move into their country and take resources vital to Osage survival. To protect their homes, families, and resources, the Osage maintained a healthy suspicion of the invaders and occasionally lashed out at them.

The Europeans failed to understand how their behavior threatened the Osage and instead maintained that the Osage were simply irrational and violent; thus their records describe the Osage as a savage people. There is, however, a rationale and design to Osage behavior, but the logic and the pattern are only evident if existing evidence is examined within the proper context. A new and more accurate perspective can be arrived at by using the records of the Osage's enemies, while being sensitive to the context of the records. This study attempts to provide such a contextual examination of the evidence in order to provide a better understanding of all the participants' behavior and to create an account that more accurately records and explains what occurred.

Obviously the methods for studying the history of a people who left no written records is different from the techniques needed to examine those societies who have abundantly documented their past.[5] In order to examine Osage history one must bring a historical and cultural perspective to the written records and include additional nontraditional historical evidence. A multidisciplinary approach is essential to understanding the

---

5. D'Arcy McNickle, review of *The Long Death*, by Ralph Andrist and *The Lost Universe*, by Gene Weltfish; James Axtell, "Ethnohistory: An Historian's Viewpoint"; William Fenton, "Ethnohistory and Its Problems"; Nancy Oestreich Lurie, "Ethnohistory: An Ethnological Point of View"; William C. Sturtevant, "Anthropology, History, and Ethnohistory"; Wilcomb Washburn, "Ethnohistory: History 'In the Round.'"

eighteenth-century Osage. One has to employ the research of archaeologists, cultural anthropologists, linguists, sociologists, biologists, and ecologists. By including information revealed by Osage oral traditions and material culture, along with the written record, one can provide a better understanding of the complexity and sophistication of these people and their history.

The Osage were originally members of a large group of Dhegian-Siouan speaking people who lived in the forests along the lower Ohio River. Sometime in the early seventeenth century the Dhegians were pushed from the Ohio to the Mississippi Valley by aggressive eastern tribes, and they began migrating west. As the Dhegians moved across the Mississippi and up the Missouri River, bands broke away from the parent group and settled near the river, establishing new homes and, in time, separate tribal identities.

By the mid-seventeenth century the Dhegians were divided into five autonomous groups known as the Quapaw, Kansa, Omaha, Ponca, and Osage. The Osage settled in the region between the eastern forests and the western plains. They established a group of villages along the prairies of present-day western Missouri. Living along the prairie margins between plains and forests, the Osage created a way of life that retained some of the older forest cultural traits, yet incorporated new elements that better suited their prairie life.[6] They continued to live in their wood-frame longhouses in kin groups established back in the eastern forests and continued to plant old, familiar crops, but they also began to form new family groups and left the forests to hunt buffalo out on the short-grass plains. In time they became a semisedentary people who planted crops in the spring at their prairie villages but spent summers and falls on the plains hunting buffalo.

Living near the Missouri, Arkansas, and Mississippi Rivers,

6. Dale R. Henning, "Development and Interrelationships of Oneota Culture in the Lower Missouri Valley," 146–48.

between the colonial frontiers of Spain and France, the Osage had early contact with the Europeans. As early as 1673 the Osage were noted by the French. They engaged in trade with the French and acquired livestock indirectly from the Spanish. French iron tools and guns were attractive to the Osage, as were Spanish horses and mules. The combination of horses, guns, and a market economy changed the Osage, but initially the changes were minor and subtle. Old patterns and lifestyles remained intact. The Osage continued spring plantings at their villages and traveled to the plains to spend the summer hunting buffalo. Horses, guns, and trade simply placed new emphasis on elements of old, familiar patterns.

Mere subsistence horticulture and hunting, however, could not supply the Osage with goods necessary to exchange with the French for guns, ammunition, textiles, and other European goods they desired. The French wanted furs, horses, and slaves, and the Osage adjusted their way of life to gather these items.

This desire to acquire manufactured products was more than Osage materialism or nascent capitalism. The Osage enjoyed the improved quality of life that iron hoes, brass pots, and woolen stroud provided, but more importantly, they needed French weapons in order to survive. Large, well-armed tribes living north and east of the Osage began raiding their villages in the seventeenth century. Without guns and ammunition they would have been defenseless against the hammering raids of the Potawatomi, Mesquakie, Sauk, and Illinois, and they would have been driven from their homes. In order to acquire the critical weapons, the Osage became large-scale commercial hunters and aggressive livestock and slave traders.

Challenged in the north and the east by the European-armed tribes, the Osage expanded south and west where the native people had little access to European weapons. They hunted further from their villages in territory that belonged to neighboring tribes. Taking advantage of their access to French trade, they expanded into Wichita, Caddo, Pawnee, Kansa, and Quapaw country. By limiting the flow of arms and ammunition into the west, the Osage maintained a weapons' advantage over their western rivals. They pushed the Caddo, Wichita, and Pawnee nations from their prairie-plains lands. Their devastating raids on the Caddo forced that group from the Ouachita Mountain forests and down the Red River. They drove the Pawnee out of the central plains north to the Smoky Hill River and the Wichita tribes south from the Arkansas Valley. The Osage, lured to the region by the abundant deer and buffalo herds and by the Wichita and Caddoan villages filled with horses and potential slaves, conquered the land between the Missouri and Red Rivers. Their Dhegian kinsmen, the Kansa in the north and the Quapaw in the south, initially challenged the Osage for control. But warfare with their neighbors and deadly epidemic disease soon weakened them, and, unable to defeat the Osage, they reluctantly shared the region and accepted Osage domination. For most of the eighteenth century the Osage controlled the prairie-plains and created a prairie hegemony.

Osage hegemony was based upon several factors: a large population, a strategic location, abundant natural resources, and an adaptable culture. The Osage was a large tribe, numbering at least five thousand people with at least one thousand warriors. They outnumbered their Native American and European neighbors, and their numerical strength allowed them to maintain a political autonomy. Able to maintain such autonomy, the Osage were able to adjust to the other demands made by the shifting circumstances of the eighteenth century. They were able to make incremental social, political, and economic adjustments. Although they indeed changed, the Osage were able to control the rate of change so that they could incorporate new elements and graft new features onto their older and more familiar cultural framework.

The Osage prairie homelands also contributed to Osage power. They lived in an area where they could take advantage of abundant game found in three ecosystems. They could hunt bear, deer, and other small game in the forests of the Ozark, Boston, and Ouachita Mountains and take advantage of prairie game at-

tracted to the forest edges. They could also hunt the great herds
of buffalo living out on the Great Plains. Not only was the Osage
homeland filled with abundant wildlife which provided ample
food, clothing, and trade goods, but it was also strategically
located, for three of the most important western rivers passed
through the heart of Osage country. Europeans on their way
west, up the Missouri, Arkansas, or Red Rivers, had to pass
through Osage territory, so the Osage were able to limit access of
European traders to the tribes living in the western interior.
Their location also permitted them to limit the arms and ammunition rival tribes living to the south and west received from the
European traders. They became the gatekeepers to the west.

Living between the frontiers of the competing Europeans also
enhanced Osage power and influence. Taking advantage of
European rivalries and playing one European nation against the
other, the Osage remained independent of European control.

The Osage were also blessed with a flexible culture which
permitted them to adjust to the demands created by the European presence. As the Osage expanded their way of life they met
the new challenges. Osage culture had always placed great value
on economic and military success. Osage men acquired status as
a result of their hunting prowess and their courage in battle.
Men who protected their people and kept their kin well fed were
respected. The increased hunting and raiding fit well within the
older social framework. Individuals who enjoyed increased status and economic success often had no access to political power
within the traditional political system; in the older system he-
redity was often more important than ability. Unless one possessed the correct family ties he could never become an Osage
leader. The Osage, however, in an attempt to limit internal strife,
created new kin groups with new positions that provided additional avenues to political power. The Osage were able to adapt
and avoid internal conflict by creating social and political compromises that recognized older patterns, yet integrated new features. The Osage changed, but the changes were always within
a familiar context. Thus Osage hegemony continued.

The French were indirectly responsible for this Osage hegemony. Economic exploitation of North America by French investment companies was a major element of French colonialism, and Indian trade was vital for economic success. The imperial and economic goals of the French companies were generally consistent with Osage goals. The French wanted bearskins, beaver pelts, horses, mules, and laborers for their trading posts and plantations. They also wanted loyal Indian allies to prevent British expansion into North America. At the same time, the Osage wanted European-manufactured goods and needed French weapons, so they usually maintained a friendly relationship with the French.

In the early eighteenth century the French established several trading posts along the Mississippi River to connect their Gulf Coast posts with Canada, and as the presence of the French grew, so did Osage trade. In 1723 a trading post, named Fort Orleans, was established by a French investment company just across the Missouri from the northern Osage villages. French traders came to trade and live with the Osage from this post, and others located in Canada, Illinois, and the Gulf settlements. Throughout the first two-thirds of the eighteenth century, French traders flocked to Osage country and armed and equipped its inhabitants.

The Spanish, who occupied Louisiana after the French defeat in the Seven Years' War in 1763, were unwilling to accept Osage autonomy and attempted to control them. More interested in controlling the Osage than profiting from them, the Spanish attempted to enforce strict commercial controls on the Osage. Hoping to bring peace and stability to their northern American colony, the Spanish halted all Indian trade in livestock and slaves, and they severely limited trade in firearms and ammunition. By closing the Louisiana livestock and slave trade and restricting the weapons trade, the Spanish thought they would end Osage raids in the interior. The Spanish plan for peace and stability was a potential catastrophe for the Osage, however, for the livestock and slave trade was critical to the Osage economy, and weapons were vital for their survival. Any reduction in trade and subsequent reduction in ammunition doomed the Osage, for British-armed Indian rivals were ready to attack and destroy them. Osage trade was so lucrative, however, that Spanish traders evaded Spanish trade restrictions and Canadian traders ignored them. Europeans continued to travel to the Osage villages with guns and ammunition, and Osage dominance in the west continued.

Throughout the eighteenth century the Osage continued to keep outsiders from hunting in their territory and from arming the Caddo or the Wichita. They stopped traders going up the Arkansas and beat, robbed, and killed intruding hunters to protect their hunting territory. The Spanish, angered by Osage attacks, attempted to control them by stopping all trade with them and finally by declaring war on them. Trade bans were ineffective, for the Canadian traders from outposts on the Des Moines River and from Prairie du Chien continued to visit the Osage, and American traders from the Illinois settlements across the Mississippi paid little attention to Spanish trade embargoes. Spain's military presence in the area was limited to less than one hundred soldiers, no match for the one thousand Osage warriors. Spanish attempts to arm the Wichita and Caddo and send them against the Osage were never successful. The Spanish eventually recognized their inability to harness the Osage and reopened their trade with them.

Both the French and the Spanish were forced to deal with the Osage as relative equals. Their numbers, strategic location, rich animal resources, and resilient culture that could accommodate change enabled the Osage to resist French and Spanish control, drive out or subjugate rival Native Americans, and maintain hegemony on the central prairie-plains.

The economic productivity that created Osage power and domination, however, eventually weakened them. Economic success and the increased warfare that accompanied it created stress within their social and political system. Initially, Osage culture incorporated the changes created by the European pres-

ence. The continued growth of the economy and continued violence, however, posed challenges which ultimately the Osage
were unable to meet. There were new opportunities for wealth
and prestige with the lucrative trade and frequent raiding. More
Osage enjoyed this new prestige and wealth, yet because of the
hereditary nature of Osage leadership positions these Osage had
no means of gaining political power. The Osage created new
clans, positions, ceremonial prerogatives, and ritual activities to
provide status to meet the growing demands for power. But the
adaptations which worked successfully in the eighteenth century would prove inadequate in the nineteenth.

Ambitious Osage, denied power within their traditional political framework, left the tribe and established independent Osage
bands where they possessed political power. At the same time
outsiders intruded among the Osage and fashioned alien political concepts that challenged older patterns. Foreign traders and
government officials became directly involved in Osage politics
and created authoritative political leaders consistent with European political conceptualizations. The combination of foreign
intrusion, especially by the Chouteau family of Saint Louis, and
increased hunting and warfare destroyed Osage political unity.
Economic success and outside interference bred political chaos.
By the late eighteenth century the Osage had separated into
three autonomous bands: the Little Osage living in the north
along the Missouri River, the Arkansas Band living in the south
along the lower Verdigris River just north of the Arkansas, and
the Big Osage remaining along the upper Osage River. This
divisive pattern continued on into the nineteenth century, until
by the 1830s the Osage were living in at least five distinct bands.

The Osage political system began to weaken at a time when
the people needed political unity to confront the challenges
posed by the United States and Native American rivals. After the
United States gained control of Louisiana, Osage trade continued to grow, and economic growth continued to weaken the
Osage social and political system. Osage hegemony was based
on Osage population, location, resources, and cultural adap-

tation. After the United States' occupation, these foundations began to erode and with them Osage power and independence. The Osage, who had outnumbered both the French and Spanish, were overwhelmed by thousands of eastern Indians who moved into Osage country. Their strategic location on the Arkansas and Missouri, which had once allowed them to limit access to the west, became simply a pathway for outsiders going west. The rich resources of Osage country attracted thousands of outsiders, Indian and non-Indian alike. Lack of Osage unity prevented them from stopping the invasion and tragically compelled them to ally themselves with their eventual conquerors.

Chickasaw, Cherokee, Delaware, and other eastern Indians, forced from their homelands by white settlement and United States Indian policy, invaded Osage country. The southeastern tribes settled along the lower Arkansas and along the White River of the Ozarks. These outsiders posed an immediate threat to the Osage. They stripped the forests and prairies of game, and they raided Osage villages for women and children. At the same time the Osage had to deal with this eastern threat, they also had to contend with a growing problem in the west. The Kiowa and Comanche began acquiring guns from American traders, and they, along with the Pawnee, became a serious threat to the Osage out on the plains. Wedged between the aggressive plains tribes and the large eastern tribes, the Osage had to have guns and ammunition to resist them. After the end of the War of 1812, however, few Canadian traders came to the Osage. The Osage, therefore, had to maintain good relations with the only trading partner that remained, the United States. Anxious to maintain trade, the Osage remained at peace with the United States throughout the nineteenth century.

The United States, eager to remove Native Americans from the east, took advantage of the Osage situation. In exchange for peace and continued trade, the United States government forced the Osage to give up their land in a series of treaties. In 1808, at Fort Osage, the Osage were compelled to give up almost all of their forest lands in the Ozark and Boston Mountains. In 1818 they ceded thousands of acres of prairie land, and in 1825 they went to Saint Louis and surrendered almost all of their remaining lands on the prairie-plains.

Despite the forced land cessions of 1808, 1818, and 1825, many of the Osage remained on their traditional homelands and refused to move to the narrow confines of the reservation. Confronted by strong, well-armed Native American tribes from the east and powerful tribes in the west, the Osage struggled throughout the 1820s to protect their villages and hunting grounds. By the 1830s the Osage, weakened by smallpox, cholera, other epidemic diseases, and the almost incessant Native American warfare in the east and west, were finally unable to resist removal from their homelands. Tragically for the Osage, peace with the United States had been more costly than war with the Native Americans.[7] In the spring of 1839 federal troops forced the Osage to leave their villages along the Verdigris and move north to the reservation. There were no gardens in 1839 and the spring plantings of 1840 were made on reservation lands. Osage hegemony was no more.

7. Richard White, *The Roots of Dependency: Subsistence, Environment, and Social Change among the Choctaws, Pawnees, and Navajos,* xiii–xix, 315–23.

1.

OSAGE LIFEWAYS

I am perfectly content with my condition. The forests and rivers supply all the calls of nature in plenty.

—Big Soldier, 1820[1]

The eighteenth and the nineteenth centuries were times of tumultuous change for the Osage. They maintained a dynamic culture that held firmly to their old, traditional lifeways, yet they accepted changes necessary for survival. Throughout these critical years the Osage demonstrated a remarkable cultural tenacity.

The Osage occupied a large region that included prairies, forests, and high plains. In their yearly movements the Osage used the prairies along the headwaters of the Osage River as a base for hunting trips into the woodlands of the east and the high plains of the west. Their homeland was rich in natural resources that provided food, clothing, and shelter. They gathered native plants, sowed crops, and hunted local animals for food. Osage hunters took antelope, buffalo, elk, deer, bear, mountain lion, wolf, otter, turkey, dove, quail, duck, prairie chicken, rabbit, raccoon, opossum, muskrat, and bobcat. They ate acorns, walnuts, pecans, hickory nuts, pawpaws, persimmons, and chinquapin roots. Pine and oak trees from the forest and cotton-

1. Ora Brooks Peake, *A History of the United States Indian Factory System, 1795–1822*, 230.

Wáh-chee-te, the wife of Clermont, and a child. Painted by George Catlin during his 1834 visit to the Osage country. National Museum of American Art, Smithsonian Institution. Gift of Mrs. Joseph Harrison, Jr.

wood, walnut, willow, ash, hickory, and pecan trees growing along the river bottoms were all used. The Osage constructed their lodges out of flexible saplings and covered them with mats made of woven marsh grasses. The fertile soils along prairie river bottoms supported the corn, bean, squash, and melon crops that Osage women planted spring after spring.

Osage people wore functional clothing made from prepared skins of native animals. Deer, elk, and buffalo hides were used, as were textiles woven from buffalo hair. Osage males wore a narrow, decorated belt made of leather or native textiles, which was later replaced by trade woolens. Wrapped over and under these belts were deerskin breechcloths. Men covered their legs and hips with buckskin leggings adorned with scalp lock fringe and gathered below the knee with leather or cloth garters. Deerskin or buffaloskin moccasins secured with leather thongs covered their feet. For much of the year Osage men wore nothing about their upper bodies, and only during the cold winter months did they wrap themselves in buffalo robes or woolen trade blankets.[2]

Osage women also wore skin moccasins and buckskin leggings. Usually the leggings were dyed red or blue and were fastened to a leather or fabric (braided buffalo wool) belt. Over the leggings women wore leather or cloth skirts or long buckskin shirts or tunics. Their children wore little clothing at all. When they did begin to dress, at about six or seven, they dressed in the style of the adults. The boys wore moccasins, leggings, and breechcloths, and girls wore shirts or tunics with leggings, skirts, and moccasins.[3]

2. Alice Marriott, *Osage Research Report and Bibliography of Basic Research References,* 62, 64; George Catlin, *Letters and Notes on the North American Indians,* 275–78; Richard N. Ellis and Charlie R. Steen, eds., "An Indian Delegation in France, 1725," 390; John Francis McDermott, ed., *Tixier's Travels on the Osage Prairies,* 275; Henry M. Brackenridge, *Brackenridge's Journal Up the Missouri, 1811,* 57.

3. McDermott, *Tixier's Travels,* 128, 138; "Many, and indeed most of their little children, are seen going abroad naked, even at this cold season of the year,

Osage men, unless they were mourning, shaved their heads, leaving only a narrow strip of hair along the top. This strip began about the middle of the head and extended back one or two inches. Hair was cropped about two inches long and was greased to stand straight up. Two strands from this tuft of hair were allowed to grow, and when long enough, scalp locks were arranged into two lengthy braids decorated with beads, ribbons, and feathers.[4]

Hairstyles distinguished married from unmarried women. Unmarried women wore their long hair braided and either brought it together in two rolls on each side of the head or wore it in one long braid decorated with beads, silver rings, and brightly colored ribbons. Married women simply gathered their long hair together behind the head and tied it with a leather or cloth tie. Until they were about ten years old, Osage children wore their hair in special kin group haircuts. Each of the Osage clans had distinctive styles of cutting their children's hair, which usually involved shaving portions of the head and leaving tufts, notched ridges, or circles that had symbolic meaning for the clans.[5] Approaching puberty, Osage children abandoned their clan cuts and began to wear their hair like the adults.

The Osage pierced and wore jewelry in their ears. They usually made a long slit along the earlobes and suspended strings of beads, beaded loops, and pieces of bone on silver hoops from the opening. An early visitor among the Osage remarked, "Their

---

notwithstanding the thermometer has sometimes stood below *zero,* and the ground is frozen six or eight inches deep" (Jedidiah Morse, *A Report to the Secretary of War of the United States on Indian Affairs,* 225).

4. McDermott, *Tixier's Travels,* 137; Catlin, *Letters and Notes,* 275–77; Lewis Edwin James, comp., *Account of an Expedition from Pittsburgh to the Rocky Mountains Performed in the Years 1819 and 1820, By Order of the Hon. J. C. Calhoun, Secretary of War, Under the Command of Maj. S. H. Long,* 16:271; Thomas Nuttall, *A Journal of Travels into the Arkansas Territory during the Year 1819,* 250; Morse, *Report to the Secretary of War,* 227; Francis LaFlesche, "The Osage Tribe: Two Versions of the Child-naming Rite," 94.

5. LaFlesche, "Child-naming Rite," 87, 94; Nuttall, *Journal of Travels,* 251; Alice C. Fletcher and Francis LaFlesche, *The Omaha Tribe,* 1:42–46.

ears, slit by knives, grow to be enormous, and they hang low under the weight of the ornaments with which they are laden."[6] Men and women wore several long necklaces made of shells, animal bones, trade beads, and metal scraps. They also wore silver bracelets and arm bands and "a profusion of rings on the fingers."[7]

Both men and women decorated their bodies with tattoos. Men who had won war honors were permitted to have a "mark of honor," a large symbolic design, tattooed on their chests and shoulders. Individuals who held certain clan positions were also tattooed with symbolic designs. A warrior could have his wife or daughter tattooed as a sign of his accomplishments, and often a woman's entire body from the neck down was marked.[8] The Osage also used body paint. Men and women alike used white, black, yellow, and green paints on various parts of their bodies. Sometimes the paints were applied according to the individual's whim, and other times the color, design, and place of application carried ceremonial significance. Every day, women applied red paint along the part of their hair, symbolizing the path of the sun. When men prepared for war they painted their faces with a black paint, made from ceremonially prepared charcoal, for they were to be as relentless and merciless as fire when they went to war.[9]

The Osage occupied three distinct environments during the year and alternated their lives between prairie farming and plains and forest hunting. They also occupied three different types of houses, with an appropriate house for each environment and economic activity. While they resided in their villages on the prairies, they constructed wood-frame longhouses like those

6. McDermott, *Tixier's Travels*, 137.
7. For the quote, see Catlin, *Letters and Notes*, 275; McDermott, *Tixier's Travels*, 138; Morse, *Report to the Secretary of War*, 227.
8. Fletcher and LaFlesche, *Omaha Tribe*, 1:219–21; McDermott, *Tixier's Travels*, 138; Francis LaFlesche, "Ceremonies and Rituals of the Osages," 66.
9. Francis LaFlesche, *War Ceremony and Peace Ceremony of the Osage Indians*, 49, 54; McDermott, *Tixier's Travels*, 137; Nuttall, *Journal of Travels*, 250.

used by Native American tribes living in the eastern woodlands. The Osage longhouse was a large, oblong shelter. Depending upon the size of the family and the availability of building materials, the Osage longhouse was from forty to one hundred feet long, about twenty feet wide, and from fifteen to twenty feet high. The Osage constructed their longhouse by first erecting a row of posts down the center of a cleared space. The center posts supported a ridgepole running the length of the building. They took long, flexible poles and drove one end of them into the ground and then bent the shafts over the ridgepole and tied them to stakes planted firmly in the ground along the opposite side. After attaching several horizontal poles lengthwise to provide strength and stability, they covered the entire framework with overlapping mats of woven marsh grasses. By the early nineteenth century they used buffalo hides along with the mats to cover the roof and walls.[10]

The Osage longhouse had two entrances, each covered with a reed mat or a flap of buffalo hide, and the floor was covered with grass mats and buffalo hides. Family possessions—clothing, food, and tools—were hung from the wooden framework or piled along the sides or at the ends of the building. These large dwellings usually housed from ten to fifteen kinfolk. The interior of the longhouse was dark and smoky, for only a portion of the smoke from the cooking fire escaped through holes in the roof. The large longhouse was only used when the people were at their prairie villages in the spring and fall.

By late May or early June they left their villages and traveled to the treeless plains to hunt the plains bison.[11] When they left for their seasonal hunting trips, they stripped the longhouse of

10. Elliott Coues, ed., *The Expeditions of Zebulon Montgomery Pike*, 2:528–29; McDermott, *Tixier's Travels*, 117; Morse, *Report to the Secretary of War*, 227; David Bushnell, Jr., "Villages of the Algonquin, Siouan, and Caddoan Tribes West of the Mississippi."

11. George F. Will and George E. Hyde, *Corn Among the Indians of the Upper Missouri*, 91; Morse, *Report to the Secretary of War*, 205; McDermott, *Tixier's Travels*, 140.

its reed mats and cached most of them in pits near the village site. Leaving the wooden frame standing, they took only enough mats and lodgepoles to use for their smaller hunting shelters. The Osage hunting lodge was a long, low affair, about fifteen feet long, seven feet wide, and four feet tall. They constructed it simply by driving a row of lodge poles into the ground, bending them over, and covering them with buffalo skins.[12] They lived in these plains lodges only until the end of July, when they began the trip back to the prairie villages. Arriving back at the village sites by early August, they reconstructed their longhouses and lived in them while they rested from the summer hunt, and the Osage women harvested their garden crops and prepared them for winter storage.

By late September or early October, the Osage again left their villages for the plains, where they once again used their plains lodge. When winter arrived and the weather became cold on the plains, the Osage returned to the familiar prairies where they erected either a smaller version of the oblong longhouse or a circular, wigwam-type shelter. Both structures were the familiar wooden frameworks covered with either mats, skins, brush, or a combination of mats and hides. The circular wigwams were about ten to fifteen feet in diameter, while the modified longhouses were about fifteen feet long, seven feet wide, and five feet high.[13] They spent the winter in small family communities constructed along the river bottoms and nearby woods where game, firewood, and food for their horses was available, and where they could escape the winter winds of the unprotected prairies.[14] As the weather warmed they returned to the

12. McDermott, *Tixier's Travels,* 186; Josiah Gregg, *Josiah Gregg's Commerce of the Prairies,* 59.

13. John Bradbury, *Travels in the Interior of America: In the Years 1809, 1810, and 1811,* 62; McDermott, *Tixier's Travels,* 134, 159; Morse, *Report to the Secretary of War,* 227; Brackenridge, *Brackenridge's Journal,* 59.

14. Morse, *Report to the Secretary of War,* 205; Coues, *Expeditions of Pike,* 2:529; Garrick A. Bailey, "Changes in Osage Social Organization, 1673–1906," 95.

prairies and by March were back in their large longhouse villages. As the danger of plant-killing frost decreased, the women cleared the garden plots and planted their crops. Then the yearly cycle began anew.

This cycle persisted throughout the eighteenth and much of the nineteenth century. It was an Osage solution to the problem of survival posed by their environment and the times. For much of the seventeenth, eighteenth, and nineteenth centuries the pattern remained relatively unchanged. In time, as the horse and buffalo became more important, and as economic and political motivations changed, the Osage traveled further west and took more game. The essential pattern endured; it was their way and worked for them.

Villages were usually located in the middle of a clearing or on an elevated prairie near a river, stream, or spring. The Osage constructed their villages on the prairies where the Little Osage, Marmaton, and Marais des Cygnes came together to form the Osage River. They remained in the general area, moving only when repeated planting depleted the soil, pasture and firewood were exhausted, or family or tribal feuds flared up. Once Europeans arrived, the Osage occasionally moved their villages to be closer to the trading posts. They sometimes moved when they were threatened by enemy tribes. For much of the eighteenth century Osage villages were large, densely populated centers with over one hundred lodges and a thousand or more inhabitants.[15] By the early nineteenth century, however, various factions left the three major village groups, and established smaller communities along the prairie river bottoms. The village had an amorphous quality as villagers moved to other villages, visited

---

15. Abraham P. Nasatir, ed., *Before Lewis and Clark: Documents Illustrating the History of the Missouri, 1785–1804*, 1:172; Anthony F. C. Wallace, *The Death and Rebirth of the Seneca*, 22; Pierre Margry, ed., *Exploration des affluents du Mississipi et découverte des Montagnes Rocheuses: 1679–1754*, 311; Mildred Mott Wedel, "Claude-Charles DuTisné: A Review of His 1719 Journeys," 150–51; Morse, *Report to the Secretary of War*, 203, 213; Coues, *Expeditions of Pike*, 2:590–91; *Annals of Congress of the United States*, 9th Cong., 2d sess., 1041–43.

relatives elsewhere, or left on hunting trips. George Sibley, a United States government factor who lived among the Osage, observed, "It is next to impossible to enumerate them correctly. I have made several attempts in vain. They are continually removing from one village to another, quarreling and intermarrying, so that the strength of no particular village can ever be correctly ascertained."[16]

In the early eighteenth century the Osage arranged their village lodges according to moiety (tribal division) membership, with *Tsi-zhu* clans in one area and *Hon-ga* clans in another, but by the early nineteenth century this pattern seems to have disappeared. When Zebulon Pike visited the Osage in the fall of 1806, he commented that "their towns hold more people in the same space of ground, than anyplace I ever saw. Their lodges being posted with scarcely any regularity; each one building in the manner, directions, and dimensions which suits him best, by which means they frequently leave only room for a single man to squeeze between them."[17] The moiety arrangement was still used sometimes, however, when they were out on the plains. For important ceremonial occasions the Osage set up their lodges in a great circle grouped according to clan.[18]

There were no permanent ceremonial buildings in the villages. Although a ceremonial structure, called House of Mysteries (*Tsi Wa-kon-da-gi*), was erected from time to time, no lodges were used exclusively for religious or political functions. Religious and political leaders customarily met in one of the moiety leader's lodges or in those of clan leaders.[19]

16. Morse, *Report to the Secretary of War*, 204–5.
17. Donald Jackson, ed., *The Journals of Zebulon Montgomery Pike: With Letters and Related Documents*, 2:31.
18. Francis LaFlesche, "The Osage Tribe: Rite of the Chiefs; Sayings of the Ancient Men," 69.
19. LaFlesche, *War and Peace Ceremony*, 51–52, 81–83. When the moiety leaders and the tribal elders met in one of the leader's lodges they were called the *Non-hon-zhin-ga Wa-thin Tsi* (House of the Little Old Men). For examples, see Mathews, *The Osages*, 26–27; McDermott, *Tixier's Travels*, 142, 172.

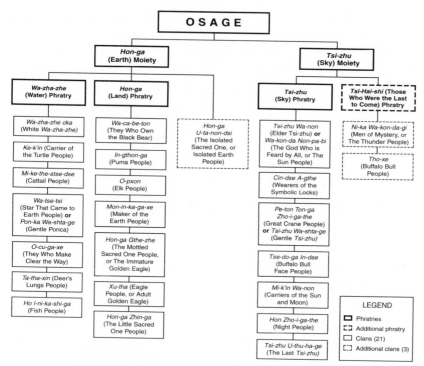

Reconstructed Osage Clan/Social Organization (Late eighteenth to early nineteenth centuries). Created by Barbara Williams-Rollings.

Another feature of Osage lifeway patterns was their social organization. The Osage organized their society according to an elaborate and complex kinship system. Every member of the tribe belonged to one of the large kin groups or clans. Membership into the clans was determined at birth as every Osage was born into the clan of his or her father. Clan members believed that they shared a common ancestor and considered fellow clan members as family. The shared clan ancestor was often an animal, plant, or phenomenon of nature, and many of the clans took their name from their common ancestor.

The Osage organized their clans in several ways. They grouped all the clans into two major tribal divisions (moieties), the *Tsi-*

zhu and the *Hon-ga*. The *Tsi-zhu* group represented the sky and peace, and the *Hon-ga* symbolized the earth and war.[20] The Osage saw a duality in nature that they duplicated in their symbolic tribal organization. Believing that the world was made up of two great parts, the Osage symbolically arranged their people into two great divisions of Earth and Sky People.

Originally the Osage were composed of fourteen clans divided equally between the *Tsi-zhu* and *Hon-ga*. Over time, however, the number of clans increased to twenty-one. It is unclear when or how this came about, for the accounts of the additional clans are recorded only in tribal *wi-gi-e* (oral traditions) and are shrouded in Osage metaphor and symbolism. It is likely that as the tribe grew larger, perhaps because of population growth, the incorporation of new peoples, or simply out of a desire to create new social groups to redistribute status and power, the number of clans grew to twenty-one. The twenty-one clan division appears to be the longest lasting social organization of the Osage, for most of the surviving *wi-gi-e* and ceremonial ritual involved only twenty-one clans. The pattern of growth continued, however, and three additional clans were later included to make a total of twenty-four clans.

The Osage grouped their clans into subgroups within the two moiety divisions. When there were twenty-one clans they were divided into three groups (phratries) of seven clans. The seven clans that made up the *Tsi-zhu* represented the sky, while the fourteen clans of the *Hon-ga* were divided into two groups of seven representing the two great divisions of the mother earth: land and water. Later, three additional clans were added to the Osage—two became part of the *Tsi-zhu,* and one joined the *Hon-ga* moiety.

The water group of the *Hon-ga* moiety, called *Wa-zha-zhe,* included seven clans: *Wa-zha-zhe cka* (White *Wa-zha-zhe*); *Ke-k'in* (Carrier of the Turtle People); *Mi-ke-the-stse-dse* (Cattail Peo-

---

20. Alfred L. Kroeber, "Cultural and Natural Areas of North America," 75.

ple); *Wa-tse-tsi* (Star That Came to Earth People, or *Pon-ka Wa-shta-ge,* Gentle Ponca); *O-cu-ga-xe* (They Who Make Clear the Way); *Ta-tha-xin* (Deer's Lungs People); and *Ho I-ni-ka-shi-ga* (Fish People).[21]

The land group was also called *Hon-ga* and was composed of seven clans: *Wa-ca-be-ton* (They Who Own the Black Bear); *In-gthon-ga* (Puma People); *O-pxon* (Elk People); *Mon-in-ka-ga-xe* (Maker of the Earth People); *Hon-ga Gthe-zhe* (The Mottled Sacred One People, or The Immature Golden Eagle); *Xu-tha* (Eagle People, or Adult Golden Eagle); and *Hon-ga Zhin-ga* (The Little Sacred One People).

A single separate clan named *Hon-ga U-ta-non-dsi* (The Isolated Sacred One, or Isolated Earth People) was considered a member of the larger *Hon-ga* moiety, yet not a member of either the *Wa-zha-zhe* or *Hon-ga* phratries. According to Osage traditions, this group came about when the *Wa-zha-zhe, Hon-ga,* and *Tsi-zhu* peoples first came to earth. The three groups, upon arriving on the earth, met a group living in a village surrounded by decaying flesh and bones of both men and animals. The *Wa-zha-zhe* invited these villagers, known as the Isolated Sacred One, to join them and to abandon the filth and decay of their village. The Isolated Sacred One group agreed, joined with the three other groups, and together the four groups moved on to a new country.[22]

The *Tsi-zhu* was made up of nine clans organized into two divisions. Seven of the *Tsi-zhu* clans, believing that they were closely related, were linked together in a group that was also known by the name of *Tsi-zhu.* The two remaining clans were grouped in a division known as *Tsi Hai-shi* (Those Who Were

21. LaFlesche, "Rite of the Chiefs," 52–55. There are several ways of representing the Osage language in written form. Generally scholars use Francis LaFlesche's method. Some Osage today, however, insist that LaFlesche's Osage is not exactly correct and contains Omaha intonation and pronunciation (Maudie Chesawall, Osage Tribal Museum, Pawhuska, Oklahoma, interview with author, July 1982). LaFlesche's stress and accent marks are omitted from this work.
22. LaFlesche, "Rite of the Chiefs," 61.

the Last to Come). The seven clans that made up the *Tsi-zhu* sub-division of the *Tsi-zhu* moiety were *Tsi-zhu Wa-non* (Elder *Tsi-zhu,* or *Wa-kon-da Non-pa-bi,* The God Who is Feared by All, or The Sun People); *Cin-dse A-gthe* (Wearers of the Symbolic Locks); *Pe-ton-ga Zho-i-ga-the* (Great Crane People, also known as *Tsi-zhu Wa-shta-ge,* or Gentle *Tsi-zhu*); *Tse-do-ga In-dse* (Buffalo Bull Face People); *Mi-k'in Wa-non* (Carriers of the Sun and Moon); *Hon Zho-i-ga-the* (Night People); and *Tsi-zhu U-thu-ha-ge* (The Last *Tsi-zhu*). The *Tsi Hai-shi* phratry was composed of two clans, the *Ni-ka Wa-kon-da-gi* (Men of Mystery, or The Thunder People) and *Tho-xe* (Buffalo Bull People).[23]

Each of the twenty-four clans was further divided into several subclans. They each possessed a distinct name and symbolic totem similar to the larger clan, and they were each assigned a specific ceremonial function. Every clan had at least two sub-clans with one always serving as *Sho-ka* (ceremonial clan messengers), but others included as many as five subclans.[24]

Despite the complexity of the twenty-four clans and numerous subclans (at least fifty-five), the tribe thought of itself as the union of the two great universal elements, the earth and sky. The ceremonial symmetry of twenty-one clans was used in most of the tribe's rituals. The addition of three clans, the Buffalo Bull and Thunder People clans to the *Tsi-zhu* moiety and the Isolated Earth People to the *Hon-ga* division, did not invalidate earlier ceremonial traditions. The Osage simply included the additional clans in the new ceremonialism and grouped them within the other clans in the older ceremonies.[25] Such a compromise was consistent with Osage behavior, for the Osage were a remarkably flexible people.

Each Osage clan possessed a sacred tribal fireplace or ceremonial position and a *wa-xo-be* (tribal bundle), both of which figured prominently in Osage ceremonies. Throughout the cer-

23. Ibid., 53–54; Bailey, "Osage Social Organization, 1673–1969," 263–70.
24. LaFlesche, "Child-naming Rite," 91.
25. LaFlesche, "Rite of the Chiefs," 54.

emonies the three groups of seven fireplaces and *wa-xo-be* were acknowledged, yet twenty-four clans and twenty-four fireplaces and bundles participated. In certain rituals the Osage recalled the older, simpler form and arranged the twenty-four clans into fourteen ceremonial clan groups.[26] During major tribal religious ceremonies, however, all twenty-four clans were represented, each seated in a specific order according to moiety and clan affiliation and ceremony.

While the Osage clans were not organized as economic or political units, they did possess social and political significance within the tribal structure. Clan members took care of their fellow members and at times acted as individual military units. In certain instances clan members provided food for ailing children of the opposite moiety. Clans also provided the framework for marriage. Osage men and women chose their partners from the opposite moiety: *Tsi-zhu* men and women could only marry *Hon-ga,* and *Hon-ga* had to choose from *Tsi-zhu.* This exogamous system insured tribal unity as both halves of the tribe were continually linked by marriage, the Sky People joining the Earth People to recreate symbolically the universe and hence the Osage people.[27]

Men and women who had reached puberty were called *tse ga non* (newly grown) and were eligible for marriage. Men, however, usually married in their late teens or early twenties, while women married shortly after puberty. Marriages were arranged by the parents of the male, and often neither of the couple knew each other. When the male's parents found a suitable wife for their son, they asked four *ni-ka don-he* (good men) to negotiate with the woman's family. The *ni-ka don-he* established that both families were indeed from different moieties and clans and negotiated a proper gift exchange between the families. The mar-

---

26. Ibid., 53–54; Louis F. Burns, *Osage Indian Bands and Clans,* 29.
27. LaFlesche, "Rite of the Chiefs," 48–51, 53–54; Betty R. Nett, "Historical Changes in the Osage Kinship System," 176; J. Owen Dorsey, "Siouan Sociology," 233.

riage ceremony was a simple affair organized around this exchange of gifts. The newly married couple settled among the
husband's family, usually within the same lodge. In time, however, the Osage abandoned the patrilocal residence pattern, and
couples began living in the bride's family lodge. Some Osage
practiced polygyny; husbands sometimes married younger sisters of the first bride.[28]

Major Osage ceremonies required participation of all twenty-
four clans. A significant portion of almost every ceremony included the recitation of lengthy clan ritual prayers called *wi-gi-e*.
Found within the *wi-gi-e* were accounts of each clan's origins,
how they acquired their clan names and totems, and how they
fit into the tribal structure.[29] The *wi-gi-e* also contained the story
of the Osage people, and although each clan's *wi-gi-e* was different, a common thread was found throughout them. All *wi-gi-e*
related how the Osage, once separate, came together to become
one people. While stressing the importance of each clan's role
within the tribe, all emphasized the importance of Osage unity.
Every clan was important and played a vital role in the tribe's
ceremonies. The Osage who composed the *wi-gi-e* insured that
unity was symbolically emphasized throughout; subclan, clan,
phratry, and moiety functions ceremonially linked the people
and constantly reminded them that although they were composed of many families, they were one people.

Upon an examination of the *wi-gi-e*, it is clear that the Osage
changed religious ceremonies and sociopolitical institutions
over time. In their *wi-gi-e* the Osage called these institutional
changes "a move to a new country," and this metaphorical phrase
is found throughout Osage *wi-gi-e*. As they met new challenges,
they made subtle alterations in their religious beliefs and incorporated them within their traditional religious framework.[30]

28. Bailey, "Osage Social Organization, 1673–1906," 16–17; Francis LaFlesche,
"Osage Marriage Customs," 127; Nett, "Changes in Osage Kinship," 177–78;
McDermott, *Tixier's Travels*, 182–83.
29. LaFlesche, "Rite of the Chiefs," 45; idem, *War and Peace Ceremony*, 202.
30. LaFlesche, "Rite of the Chiefs," 62–63.

The Osage believed that all things of the universe were manifestations of an all-powerful, omnipotent, mysterious, and invisible life force called *Wa-kon-da*. *Wa-kon-da* was everywhere and brought life to all things and created the Osage tribe by linking the Sky People with the Land and Water People. *Wa-kon-da* was manifested throughout, and the Osage saw *Wa-kon-da* everywhere, even beyond the earth. The sun, moon, stars, thunder, and wind were all parts of *Wa-kon-da*. Everything was *Wa-kon-da*.[31]

The ancient leaders created a worldview that called on the Osage to work in unison with *Wa-kon-da*. In order for the people to enjoy a good life they appealed to *Wa-kon-da* to ask for understanding and support. The people strove to work in harmony with the cosmic force. Osage religious leaders continued to make discoveries about *Wa-kon-da* which changed and expanded their beliefs. As the Osage people met new challenges, their religious philosophy changed and supported behavior that would insure tribal survival and security. The Osage wanted to live in peace and harmony with the universe, and the leaders sought to create a religious rationale consistent with such desires.

The Osage were a religious people, and they continually sought the aid and support of *Wa-kon-da*. Every day, before dawn, the Osage rose from their lodges and went outside to pray to *Wa-kon-da*. In 1820 the Territorial Governor of Arkansas reported, "These Indians have a native religion of their own, and are the only tribe I ever knew that had. At day-break, every morning, I could hear them at prayer, for an hour. They appeared to be as devout in their way as any class of people."[32] This dawn prayer was noted by other travelers among the Osage. A Protestant missionary wrote in 1821, "As a people, they are punctual, and apparently fervent in their morning and evening devotions." An unsympathetic Protestant minister living near the Osage in the

---

31. For a description of the creation of Osage spiritualism, see Mathews, *The Osages*, 26–30.
32. Morse, *Report to the Secretary of War*, 213.

early 1820s wrote, "They pray, indeed, if it may be called prayer, as we were told; and even now, as the day dawns, whilst I am writing in my house, I can hear them."[33]

Important events in Osage lives were sanctified by religious ceremonies that solicited the approval and support of *Wa-kon-da*. All ceremonies consisted of the recitation of specific clan *wi-gi-e* and the ritual manipulation of sacred symbolic objects. Each clan and subclan owned distinct religious knowledge that made up essential portions of Osage ceremonies. Clans also owned sacred objects, such as ceremonial pipes, looms, and *wa-xo-be*.

Individuals could purchase the *wa-xo-be;* depending on the nature of the ceremony, clan, subclan, or individual bundles were used. Most ceremonies required the ritual unwrapping of the bundle, revealing its sacred contents. The contents of the *wa-xo-be* varied according to clan and totem, but all contained a stuffed hawkskin symbolizing thunder, war, night, and courage. The hawkskin, along with other ceremonial symbols such as scalps, miniature pipes, or other such paraphernalia, were enclosed in a deerskin pouch, then placed in a woven rush pouch, and finally put, tightly wrapped, within another pouch of woven buffalo hair.[34]

Almost all Osage ceremonies involved the participation of all twenty-four clans with essential recitations and performances that only the specific clans could provide. Every clan arranged its religious information into seven degrees. Each degree of ceremonial knowledge required the memorization of the *wi-gi-e*, its ceremonial form, and its ritual sequence. Those clan members who learned all seven degrees of ritual information were called

33. Ibid., 219, 224. John Bradbury, on his journey up the Missouri in 1811, stayed at Fort Osage and witnessed the dawn prayer. Bradbury, upon hearing the morning prayer, left the fort and observed an Osage: "He rested his back against the stump of a tree, and continued for about twenty seconds to cry out in a loud and high tone of voice, when he suddenly lowered to a low muttering, mixed with sobs: in a few seconds he again raised to the former pitch" (*Travels in the Interior of America*, 63–64).

34. LaFlesche, "Rite of the Chiefs," 64–65, 72–73; idem, "Right and Left in Osage Ceremonies," 281–82.

Non-hon-zhin-ga (Little Old Men). The *Non-hon-zhin-ga* of all the Osage clans within a village group gathered in a council, also known as the *Non-hon-zhin-ga,* which possessed religious and secular power.[35]

Religious information was considered a real possession that the *Non-hon-zhin-ga* could pass down to clan members who were able to purchase them. Clan ceremonial knowledge was open to any clan member who could afford to buy the ceremony and pay for the initiation. Apparently both women and men could acquire a degree if they could pay for it, although it seems that in the eighteenth and nineteenth centuries only men participated.[36] Once an individual had purchased the ritual information and been initiated into that degree, he or she could participate in any tribal ceremony where that particular level of ritual information was involved and in turn could also pass the information along for a price. Ceremonial knowledge was thus limited to those who could afford it.

Thus, there existed in the Osage villages a nascent class structure. Early Osage society was clearly divided into a leader class and a commoner class. This hierarchy was based on a number of factors. Wealth was one of the most important elements, for it provided access to tribal religious knowledge. It also enabled a family to entertain the leaders and gain power and influence. Often, position and prestige of clans and certain subclans were fixed into Osage tradition, thus certain families were able to retain high status and membership in the leadership group. Individuals could also gain status and, in time, access to the leader class by excelling in battle. Bravery was rewarded by the tribe with specific warrior honors and tribal status. Throughout the eighteenth and nineteenth centuries, Osage class boundaries were fluid and the wealth distinctions usually meager.[37]

35. Francis LaFlesche, "Tribal Rites of the Osage Indians," 84–90; idem, "Rite of the Chiefs," 47–48.
36. LaFlesche, "Rite of the Chiefs," 47–48.
37. Holder, *Hoe and the Horse,* 36–37.

Acquiring clan ceremonial knowledge, however, did entail a great deal of time and relative expense. For example, the first degree of the Buffalo Bull People clan was the *Wa-xo-be A-wa-thon* (the singing of the *wa-xo-be* songs), which was a vital part of Osage war ceremonies. In order to acquire this degree, an Osage candidate had to first gather the pelts of seven animals: a lynx, a gray fox, a male puma, a male black bear, a buffalo, an elk, and a white-tailed deer.[38] Upon collecting the seven pelts, the candidate had to provide gifts for all of the participants in the initiation ceremony and ample food for the *Non-hon-zhin-ga* and others involved in the three-day rite. This system theoretically made clan knowledge, and the accompanying status, available to all, yet in reality it confined clan leadership to the more prosperous families of the tribe. The *Non-hon-zhin-ga,* those clan members who possessed complete religious knowledge, were the clan and tribal elite.

Clan ceremonies involving clan *wi-gi-e* covered all significant aspects of Osage life. Osage parents solicited the blessings of *Wa-kon-da* for their children with the child-naming ceremony. The naming ceremony was an important one, for until newborn children were ceremonially named they were not considered real people and had no place in the clan structure. During the ceremony, clan elders gave children specific clan names according to their sex and order of birth, such as first-born son or first-born daughter.[39]

The naming ceremony for all clans took place within the lodge of a member of the Isolated Earth People clan, whose members had the ceremonial prerogative of maintaining the naming house. This naming lodge was not specially constructed; it was merely the lodge of either an Isolated Earth *Non-hon-zhin-ga* or a clan member who had acquired the degree that included the naming ceremony. The ceremony required the mother of the child to plant

---

38. LaFlesche, "Child-naming Rite," 43–44.
39. Ibid. Only the first three born of each sex had distinct clan names. Those who came after did not receive clan-prescribed names.

seven hills of maize. When the maize ripened the mother hosted a feast for the participating *Non-hon-zhin-ga*. The father cut the child's hair in a distinctive clan pattern, and the child kept the clan haircut until he or she was about ten years old to insure the blessings of *Wa-kon-da*. The naming ceremony involved the participation of several clans' *Non-hon-zhin-ga*. The parents and close relatives of the newborn fed the participating clan leaders and gave them gifts for their role in the ceremony.[40]

Other important Osage events were cloaked in tribal ceremonialism; the ancient *Non-hon-zhin-ga* created lengthy, elaborate rituals to sanction important undertakings. For example, they believed that war should not be conducted without serious thought, preparation, and the blessings of *Wa-kon-da*. The *Non-hon-zhin-ga* viewed wars as aberrations and as threats to the people, as Osage attacks and raids on others prompted retaliation. They therefore created a long and elaborate ceremony to prepare the Osage for war. This ritual, called *Wa-sha-be A-thin Wa-tsi* (Dance to Possess the Dark Object), took several weeks to complete, and its central theme, expressed in *wi-gi-e* symbolism and ceremony, was an appeal for the help of *Wa-kon-da* and for tribal unity. The ceremony involved the ritual construction of war standards and preparation of the sacred war charcoal. After deliberations, the *Non-hon-zhin-ga* chose a leader of the war party who then had to leave the village to fast and pray for *Wa-kon-da*'s help.[41]

The war ceremony promoted tribal unity, and it provided the *Non-hon-zhin-ga* with control over the aggressive tendencies of tribal members. Its complexity and length, however, prevented any immediate military response, and frequently prompt action was needed. These limitations eventually convinced the Osage to change tribal rites and organization to meet new demands. In time, the Osage authorized individual clans to organize their

---

40. LaFlesche, "Rite of the Chiefs," 66; idem, "Child-naming Rite," 29–95.
41. LaFlesche, *War and Peace Ceremony*, 3–143.

own war parties within a single moiety or clan without the long appeal for help and success of the older ceremony.[42]

The easing of restrictions, as seen in the newer types of tribal-recognized war parties, clearly came about as the tribe went to war more often. Osage territorial expansion in the late seventeenth, eighteenth, and early nineteenth centuries met resistance and violence. The tribal ceremonial recognition of new military patterns represented an effort on the part of the Osage leadership to meet new situations and deal with them within the traditional tribal structure.

The return of a war party was an occasion for another series of ceremonies. Captives were frequently incorporated into the tribe. After a brief ritual, the captives were adopted into one of the twenty-four clans and were designated as clan ceremonial messengers called *Sho-ka*.[43] The Osage honored the warriors of a successful expedition in a ceremony known as Dropping the Sticks on the Hawk *wa-xo-be*. After securing the permission of the *Non-hon-zhin-ga* of the Thunder People clan, which had ceremonial control over the rite, the tribal *Non-hon-zhin-ga* gathered in the middle of the village. The *Tsi-zhu* leaders, sitting in a specific clan order, arranged themselves in a row along the north side, while the *Hon-ga* sat in clan order along the south side. The hawk *wa-xo-be* of the Elder *Tsi-zhu* clan was unwrapped,

---

42. LaFlesche records three types of war parties: "1. A war party composed of the warriors from the gentes [clan] of one of the two great divisions. 2. A war party made up of two or more of the gentes of one of the two great divisions. 3. A war party organized by one gens" ("Rite of the Chiefs," 66). He never makes a distinction between parties 1 and 2. Mathews states that there were three new types of raiding parties created. One type involved only one clan's members. Another involved two or more clans of one moiety, and the third was a war party composed of clans from both moieties who could raid together, yet could not carry the sacred *wa-xo-be* with them (*The Osages,* 76). It is unclear whether or not there were two or three new types of raiding parties. The real significance of the new war parties is not whether there were two or three types, but the fact that the Osage dispensed with the formally structured war ceremony and adopted new flexible military organizations to deal with new conditions.

43. LaFlesche, *War and Peace Ceremony,* 83–84. Adopted members were accorded respect and were called *O-xta* (favored one).

and the sacred hawk was placed on the ground between the two lines of *Non-hon-zhin-ga*. The *wa-xo-be* of the war party leader's clan was also unwrapped and placed alongside the *wa-xo-be* of the Elder *Tsi-zhu*.

Each warrior who had participated in the expedition and displayed bravery came before the *Non-hon-zhin-ga* and the two hawk *wa-xo-be*, dropped a small painted stick upon the *wa-xo-be*, and recited his war deeds. The Osage called these brave deeds *O-don*. Each *O-don* had to be unchallenged by all members of the tribe. The Omaha, a closely related tribe, maintained that if the *O-don* was not deserved the stick would fall off the *wa-xo-be* and expose the warrior as a liar and shame him before his people and eventually cause his death.[44] The *O-don* were categorized and ranked according to the act and the bravery displayed. The Osage recognized thirteen honors, with the highest *O-don* performed while defending the village and fields where the women worked. Other *O-don* honored were killing, wounding, and striking an enemy. Scalping an enemy or beheading an enemy were also worthy of merit. Ironically, scalping and beheading, both frequently noted and associated with the Osage, were among the least honored *O-don*.[45]

Attaining honors gave warriors status in the tribe. Brave Osage warriors were honored and respected, and upon obtaining all thirteen *O-don*, warriors were able to participate in a number of Osage ceremonies. They were called upon to recite these honors as an integral part of certain important ceremonies and were paid for their ceremonial participation.[46]

Thus, while attaining the seven degrees of clan religious knowledge might have been out of reach of many Osage because of the wealth required, a young man could still attain status by dem-

44. Ibid., 85–86; J. Owen Dorsey, "An Account of the War Customs of the Osages," 128–30; Fletcher and LaFlesche, *Omaha Tribe*, 2:435–37; Francis LaFlesche, "The Osage Tribe: Rite of Vigil," 67–68.

45. LaFlesche, *War and Peace Ceremony*, 228.

46. Francis LaFlesche, "Work Among the Osage Indians," 121.

onstrating bravery. The system of awarding *O-don* encouraged
the defense of the people and also provided another means of
access to the leadership class. Although the Osage consistently
honored their warriors, they never completely developed separate warrior societies as did many of the plains tribes. In 1840
Victor Tixier, a Frenchman who spent the summer hunting
with the Osage, noted that a group of young warriors had formed
a separate village and called themselves *Bande-des-Chiens* (Band
of Dogs). Little else is known about this group, but it is likely
that they were the beginning of an Osage warrior society. Other
plains tribes had soldier societies among them, and they commonly took the name of dogs or their relatives, such as the Dog
Soldiers of the Cheyenne or the Fox society of the Crow.[47]

Not all war parties were successful, and the Osage developed
ceremonies to sanctify death and deal with the sorrow that accompanied it. Death taboos were absent among the Osage. Indeed, mourning and related death rituals were important elements of Osage religious life.[48] When an Osage died, family
members daubed their faces with mud and went out alone to
fast and pray to *Wa-kon-da*. In time, however, mourners were
not content to fast and pray, and they began to seek revenge.
Tribal tradition maintained that while an important tribal member was mourning for a family member he was visited by the
spirit of his dead kin. The spirit claimed that spirit land was a
lonely place and asked his kinsman to kill someone to accompany him. The mourner raised a raiding party and sought out a
stranger to accompany his relative in the spirit world. After the
killing, the mourner scalped the victim and fastened the scalp to
a pole over the dead relative's grave.

The mourning ceremony was essentially an abbreviated version of the war rite with a designated mourner who undertook
the fasting vigil. After the vigil, ritually prepared mourners de-

47. Bailey, "Osage Social Organization, 1673–1906," 65; McDermott, *Tixier's Travels,* 128–29.
48. LaFlesche, *War and Peace Ceremony,* 86.

parted to acquire the necessary scalp. Because the ceremony involved the feeding and payment for clan *Non-hon-zhin-ga*, only those Osage who could afford it conducted the mourning ritual. Enough, however, used it to create problems for the Osage. The mourning-ceremony killing usually precipitated a series of retaliatory raids which in turn inspired still more demands for blood revenge and led to a never-ending cycle of violence and death. In spite of the violence and its attendant problems, the ceremony was extremely important to the Osage, and despite vigorous efforts of government agents, it was practiced until the early twentieth century.[49]

Another important ceremony was the peace ceremony or *Wa-wa-thon*. It was similar to the peace ceremonies of other prairie and plains Native American groups. The *Wa-wa-thon,* sometimes called the Calumet Dance, involved the preparation of sacred pipes and ritual smoking by the participants and an exchange of gifts. The Osage used it to foster peace and friendly relations among Osage clans and bands and with other Indian nations.[50]

Osage ceremonies contained evidence of a people in transition. The Osage in the eighteenth and nineteenth centuries were undergoing tremendous cultural changes brought about by the European colonization of North America. Their way of life came under attack as Europeans brought new diseases, weapons, animals, economic systems, values, and alien cultures. During this period the Osage were under increasing pressure to change their way of life, and change they did, but throughout they displayed an amazing cultural resiliency, and they forged the necessary changes within an Osage context.

Osage social institutions and traditions supported a theory that the Osage were a people in the middle. Indeed, they called themselves the Children of the Middle Waters. Osage *wi-gi-e*

49. Ibid., 86–87, 143; George A. Dorsey, "The Osage Mourning-War Ceremony." In time the ceremony was modified somewhat, and a lock of hair from a stranger was substituted for the scalp.
50. Holder, *Hoe and the Horse*, 65.

maintained that they were a forest people who lived east of the
Mississippi River and traveled west to settle in the middle on the
prairies between the wooded forests and the treeless plains.
Their culture displayed evidence of such movement, for it was
an eclectic one containing the features of eastern woodland peoples, semisedentary prairie and plains farmers, and nomadic
plains hunters.[51]

Osage clan structure was similar both to the Menominee and
the Winnebago of the upper Midwest. All three tribes maintained patrilineal clans with animal totems. These peoples all
grouped their clans into moieties representing the earth and
sky. All three grouped their village lodges according to moiety
and clan. The Osage, Menominee, and Winnebago assigned
specific clan names to their children according to sex and order
of birth. The Osage not only retained their eastern woodland
social traits but also consistently used lodges that were evidence
of their eastern woodland background. While other prairie tribes
adopted the earth lodge and plains tribes used the buffalo-skin
tipi, the Osage continued to live both on the plains and prairie in
their old-style woodland longhouses.

While retaining their woodland background, the Osage also
possessed many cultural traits remarkably similar to the semisedentary tribes found along the plains and prairie river valleys,
such as the various Caddoan groups. The Osage consistently
practiced intensive horticulture and used agricultural symbolism in their rituals; it will be recalled that the important naming
ceremony involved the ritual planting and harvesting of corn.[52]
As among the Caddo and Pawnee, Osage women played a significant role in religious ceremony. Women could acquire all
seven degrees of clan knowledge, and both the Osage and the
Caddo possessed *wa-xo-be*. The class stratification present among

51. Fletcher and LaFlesche, *Omaha Tribe*, 1:35–36, 38–39; J. Owen Dorsey,
"Migration of Siouan Tribes"; John R. Swanton, "Siouan Tribes and the Ohio
Valley"; George E. Hyde, *Indians of the Woodlands: From Prehistoric Times to
1725*, 168–70; Henning, "Development of Oneota Culture," 146–48.
52. LaFlesche, "Child-naming Rite," 58.

the village people was also found among the Osage, as status and wealth were dominated by only a few Osage families.

The complex ceremonial forms of the Osage were also those of a sedentary or semisedentary people. It would be unusual for a wandering, hunting people to maintain such a large, complex ceremonial system that required the presence of so many different people. Nomadic hunting people traveled in small kin groups for much of the year, and joined together for only a few special ceremonies conducted a few times a year. The Osage thus seem to have possessed many of the cultural traits of the semisedentary horticultural groups, yet they also added cultural elements of the newly created mounted nomad plains tribes.

Although the Osage maintained large enough groups to conduct their complex rituals, both the Osage and the plains hunters were made up of several independent bands which came together at certain times of the year. Among the Osage and the plains peoples, tribal members were allowed to move freely among bands. The sacred bundle of the Osage was similar to the bundles of the plains hunters in that Osage bundles belonged to individual clans, subclans, and individuals, in striking contrast to the riverine agricultural peoples who viewed the *wa-xo-be* as a tribal or village possession.

Hunting was a major element of Osage life, as it was among the plains nomads, and Osage ceremonialism contained a predominance of hunting and war features. Osage *wa-xo-be* contained the religious artifacts of a hunting people: miniature weapons, pipes, scalps, and other hunting symbols. Despite the agricultural elements of some Osage rituals, surviving bundles contain no agricultural goods, symbolic or otherwise. But whether more agriculturally or hunting-based, the Osage maintained their full clan participation ceremonial system into the twentieth century. Even as the Osage divided into five bands, they maintained members of all twenty-four clans in each individual band.[53]

---

53. Marriott, *Osage Research Report,* 105–6; LaFlesche, *War and Peace Ceremony,* 202.

Because of the Osage position along two major rivers that
drained into the Mississippi between two European frontiers,
they had considerable contact with European cultures in the
eighteenth century. They had early access to horses, guns, and
the new economic opportunities provided by the European
presence. Europeans provided guns and other material goods in
exchange for items that the Osage could provide, such as food,
furs, and slaves. The Osage became aggressive and expanded
their territorial control to the south and west in order to acquire
the new material possessions that insured their survival and
made their lives easier. Osage culture changed to deal with the
new world shaped by the Europeans. As the people became
more aggressive the culture adapted; the tribe retained control
and approved of the new behavior.

Hunting and war became more important for the individual
Osage, and the tribal leadership created appropriate ceremonies to sanctify these activities and retain tribal unity. War and
hunting rituals eventually dominated Osage ceremonial activities, and agricultural symbolism became only a minor part of
clan and tribal rites; the *wa-xo-be* never acquired the sacred
quality to the degree that it did among the horticultural village
people where the bundle was a holy, tribal possession. The individual nature of the Osage bundle was more closely related to
those bundles among the plains peoples.[54] By the late eighteenth
century the Osage were split into several bands and village
groups who hunted and lived separately. These band divisions
were similar to the plains hunters, yet the Osage continued to
incorporate cultural changes within the context of the older
rites and the earlier culture as each band contained, at least
symbolically, all twenty-four clans.

Tribal changes required the creation of new ceremonies, social patterns, and tribal clan organization. The older Osage clan
organization of twenty-one divisions was expanded. Signifi-

54. Holder, *Hoe and the Horse,* 76.

cantly, the Osage entrusted two of the clans added to the tribal structure, the Thunder People and the Buffalo Bull People, with the war ceremonies. It is also significant that one of the additional clans took the name Buffalo Bull. Clearly the presence of a clan called Buffalo is evidence of the change that was taking place among the Osage in the eighteenth century. As mounted Osage hunters ranged further onto the plains and the buffalo assumed a greater economic significance, the Osage acknowledged that significance by incorporating the animal into their tribal traditions and social organization. It is not certain whether these two clans were added as new people joined the tribe or were created to give special importance to groups already within the tribe who were dissatisfied with tribal conditions. It is certain that the Osage continually sought accommodation with challenges and created new institutions within their clan structures to deal with new conditions.

The entrusting of the war rites to the new clans signified the trust and embrace Osage society held for their changing culture. The lengthy weeks of the long war ceremonies of the Osage were superseded by the newer types of raiding parties that did not require such preparations and time. The incorporation of the Osage mourning rite, which gave social approval for revenge, is another example of the Osage culture attempting to incorporate new activities within the tribal ceremonial context and traditional tribal control.

Another example of the social change taking place among the Osage and further evidence of the transitional quality of their culture involved their marriage customs. The Osage were patrilineal and moiety exogamous, and they also practiced sororal polygyny. Polygyny was not widespread and may have come about as a result of a number of changes.[55] As fur trading became an increasingly prominent economic enterprise among the Osage, fur preparation also became more important. Polyg-

55. Bailey, "Osage Social Organization, 1673–1906," 16.

yny was a means of collecting the labor of several women, who traditionally prepared the pelts. The increased warfare among the Osage in the eighteenth and nineteenth centuries may have also created a shortage of eligible men and encouraged polygyny.

Clearly the aspect of the Osage marriage customs that most obviously reflected the changing nature of their culture was the peculiar combination of patrilineal descent and matrilocal residence: clan membership was traced through the father, yet married couples apparently lived with the wife's family. This combination was extremely rare among Native Americans, and it apparently represented a transitional stage as lineage descent and locality were changing.[56] Early residence patterns of the Osage were patrilocal with the husband's household. This was true of all other related tribes, and all early Osage traditions involving village lodges insisted that the Osage erect lodges in village sections according to clan. This existed only when lineage and after-marriage locality were synonymous. It was impossible in this system for a couple that was moiety exogamous, whose clan membership was traced through the father, to live in the lodge of the mother. The tradition of living in village sections according to clan would break down if the people practiced patrilineage and matrilocality, but this is what occurred among the Osage. Nineteenth-century travelers who described Osage villages failed to note any residence system or village pattern.

The rare combination of patrilineal descent and matrilocal residence may have come about as a means of dealing with new situations created by increased hunting and warfare.[57] With the creation of new, sanctioned war parties, individual clan raiding parties became a part of Osage military activity. Brothers and fellow clan members commonly hunted together and went to war together. If clan raiding parties were unsuccessful and mem-

56. Ibid.; Nett, "Changes in Osage Kinship," 180–81; Robert F. Murphy, "Matrilocality and Patrilineality in Mundurucú Society."
57. Bailey, "Osage Social Organization, 1673–1906," 16–17, 43–45.

bers were killed, entire households could be destroyed by losing their young men. Osage raiding and hunting parties ranged hundreds of miles and were gone for weeks, leaving patrilocal households without their young men for long periods of time. The households would have no one to protect them or provide them with fresh game, an important element of the Osage diet. With the increased, widespread hunting and raiding that occurred in the eighteenth and nineteenth centuries, patrilocal Osage households suffered.

Matrilocal households, however, would eliminate many of the unfortunate aspects of patrilocal residence and increased hunting and raiding. Made up of young men from different clans, the households would still have young men to bring in fresh game and protect the household when clan groups left to hunt or raid. Furthermore, if the war party was destroyed, a household would not be left without any young men. The adaptation of new residence patterns to cope with increased raiding created a more secure household situation.[58]

Thus, throughout the eighteenth and early nineteenth centuries, Osage society continued to change and adapt to the new conditions as all aspects of the Osage way of life came under attack. Class structure changed as guns, horses, and the European presence created new paths for tribal status. The expanded raiding allowed more opportunity for *O-don* and status. Increased raiding also provided increased wealth, which in turn permitted more individuals to acquire ceremonial knowledge. The seven pelts necessary for the initiation ceremony, difficult to obtain while hunting on foot with only a bow and arrow, were easily obtained with a musket and a horse. Food, required for feasting and entertaining, was easily gathered with the added mobility of the horse and killing power of the musket. Old leading families were soon challenged by new socially advancing Osage. The old social and religious prerogatives eroded as new

58. Ibid., 43–45.

economic and social opportunities became available. Yet the Osage continued to incorporate changes into their culture. They continued to bend and assume new traits and values. The Osage, a society under pressure, acted accordingly, sometimes with style and grace and at other times with terrifying ferocity.

2.

OSAGE POLITY

The chiefs are not obeyed as among you.

—Jean Lafond, 1787[1]

The traditional Osage political system was an elaborate and complex organization. Intertwined completely within the equally complex Osage clan system, the Osage political structure contained strictly defined leadership positions and distinct political prerogatives linked to specific clans. Political power was divided in a prescribed manner between two tribal chiefs, their soldier assistants, and the tribal council. Tribal chieftainships were hereditary positions, and the soldier assistants were chosen from a few elite kinship groups. Membership in the powerful tribal council was theoretically open to all, but in practice it was limited to a few lineages within a very few subclans. Both the restricted access to leadership and the formal structure gave the Osage political system, unlike Osage social and religious practices, an inflexible quality.

A reconstruction of the early Osage political system neces-

---

1. Cruzat to Miró, November 12, 1787, Abraham P. Nasatir Manuscript Collection, "Imperial Osages: A Documentary History of the Osage Indians During the Spanish Regime," 3:210. Hereafter referred to as "Nasatir Papers," this collection is an extensive repository of seventeenth- and eighteenth-century French and Spanish documents relating to the United States. The French documents are primarily from the Archives Nationales, Archives des Colonies, Série C13A, and the Spanish are from the Archivo General de Indias, Sección Papeles de Cuba.

sarily relies upon tribal oral traditions and upon meager clues found in eighteenth-century European accounts. According to Osage *wi-gi-e,* the Osage originally lived without government. In time, however, chaos and anarchy convinced the Osage to create a system of government.

The basic political unit of the Osage tribe was the village, and according to tribal *wi-gi-e,* in the beginning all of the Osage lived in a single village located along a river. One day the river flooded, and the Osage fled the rising waters. One group made it to the top of a hill, while others fled to a nearby timbered ridge. A third group escaped to higher ground and sought shelter in a dense thicket, while a fourth group found refuge at the base of hill just above the floodwaters. Some of the Osage, unable to escape, remained in the flooded village. After the floodwaters receded, the *Non-hon-zhin-ga* insisted that the people remain in the groups they had formed during the flood. They claimed that *Wa-kon-da* wanted the people to live apart and to establish five separate villages. The villages took on names based on the locations assumed during the flood. The group that fled to the hill was called the *Pa-ciu-gthin* (Upon-the-Hilltop, and later the Big Hill People); the forest refugees became *Con-dseu-gthin* (Upland Forest People); those who had escaped to the brush thicket were named *Wa-xa-ga-u-gthin* (Thorny Thicket People); those who stayed at the base of the hill during the flood were known as the *Iu-dse-ta* (Down Below People); and those who remained in the village were called *Non-dse-wa-cpe* (Heart Stays People).[2]

This division into five villages became the basis for Osage political and social organization. The five groups created by the flood were maintained throughout the eighteenth and nineteenth centuries. As the Osage expanded and moved west, the five villages splintered and broke apart, but the old group identities survived. The Osage changed their residence patterns, but they maintained their ties to their traditions. By the late eigh-

2. Mathews, *The Osages,* 143–48; LaFlesche, "Rite of the Chiefs," 45.

teenth century the five old village names had become the names for bands of Osage who lived in multiple villages, erected near one another.

Each of the five bands had its own political structure and a full complement of all twenty-four clans, insuring village cere-monial integrity and independence. Unfortunately, the date of the flood and subsequent tribal division is unknown, yet tradi-tion maintains that this was an early event in tribal history. It is also hard to interpret this history, as it is difficult to distinguish metaphor from reality. It is certain, however, that these groups did exist, for these names or close variations are found in writ-ten records, and significantly, today the Osage still maintain these same band names.[3]

The Osage chose two leaders, one from each moiety. There-after, Osage villages were governed by two leaders, one from the *Tsi-zhu* and one from the *Hon-ga*. These hereditary positions were limited to specific lineages and subclans within each moiety. The *Tsi-zhu's Ga-hi-ge* (leader) came from a specific subclan within the Great Crane clan. The *Hon-ga's* leader came from another subclan within the Star that Came to Earth clan.[4]

The earliest mention of Osage polity, contained within a 1694 report by Jesuit priest Jacques Gravier, describes the dual chief-tainship: "About the 20th of June, the French and the savages who had left here during the previous month to seek alliance of the *Osages* and *Missouries,* in the expectation of the great profits that they would derive from the trade with the latter, came back with two chiefs from each village, accompanied by some elders and some women." Twenty-five years later, a French soldier vis-iting the Osage commented, "They have several band chiefs."[5]

---

3. LaFlesche, "Rite of the Chiefs," 45.
4. Ibid., 68; Bailey, "Osage Social Organization, 1673–1906," 21.
5. "Vers le 20e de Juin les François it les sauvages qui etoient partis d'ici le mois précédent pour aller demander l'alliance des Osages et des Missouris dan l'espérance du grand profit qu'ils tiretoient de leuer commerce sont revenus avec duex chefs de l'un et l'autre village, accompagnés de quelques anciens et de quelques femmes" (Reuben Gold Thwaites, ed., *Ottawa, Lower Canada, Iro-*

The two *Ga-hi-ge* were equal in status and authority, and their primary function was to encourage village tranquillity and stability. Osage *Ga-hi-ge* were village mediators. To insure village peace, they settled disputes among the inhabitants. If violence occurred, the *Ga-hi-ge* intervened to stop it. When an Osage killed another Osage, the *Ga-hi-ge* stepped in to prevent any blood revenge and forced the murderer to give the victim's family compensation for the death. If the murderer refused, the *Ga-hi-ge* had the power to banish him from the village. If the victim's family refused compensation and sought revenge, the *Ga-hi-ge* could also exile them. In extreme instances, if village members consistently threatened the peace of the village, refused to behave within accepted tribal guidelines, and were the source of strife, the *Ga-hi-ge* had the power to execute them.[6]

While most of the moiety leaders' functions were secular, they also possessed religious roles. The *Ga-hi-ge* erected their lodges in the middle of the village, with the *Hon-ga* lodge on the south and *Tsi-zhu* lodge on the north. Both lodges were tribal sanctuaries where all could seek refuge from abuse or attack. The *Ga-hi-ge's* lodges were sacred, and the *Ga-hi-ge* maintained consecrated fires within both of them.[7] The Osage also believed that the *Ga-hi-ge* had special healing powers, and when there was illness in the village the people sought help from them.

In most Osage ceremonies the moieties had important symbolic roles, with the *Tsi-zhu* representing peace in tribal ritual and the *Hon-ga* representing war. Just as the moieties had ceremonial associations with war and peace, so did the *Ga-hi-ge*. The *Hon-ga Ga-hi-ge* was associated with war and assumed the prominent role in time of war. In peaceful times the *Tsi-zhu Ga-hi-ge* assumed special responsibilities. When outsiders came among the Osage, they were met by the *Tsi-zhu Ga-hi-ge*, for it was his

quois, Illinois: 1689–1695, 159, 168–70); "Ils ont plusieurs chefs de bande" (Margry, *Exploration des affluents*, 311).

6. LaFlesche, "Rite of the Chiefs," 67.

7. Ibid., 68–69.

role to deal with outsiders who came in peace. Visitors always stayed in the *Tsi-zhu Ga-hi-ge's* lodge and conducted their business with the Osage through him. The *Tsi-zhu* leader had no more power than the *Hon-ga* leader, he simply possessed different obligations. As represented in their clan structure, the Osage saw a duality in nature—earth and sky, peace and war—and they assigned their *Ga-hi-ge's* duties according to this duality. Power was shared but separated according to function.

The *Ga-hi-ge* had other leadership duties. During the tribal buffalo hunt on the plains, both *Ga-hi-ge* were responsible for leading the people and insuring their safety. They shared the duties and responsibilities of the hunt, with the *Tsi-zhu Ga-hi-ge* leading the people one day and the *Hon-ga Ga-hi-ge* the next, alternating leadership during the entire hunt. Their responsibilities were great, for if any property was lost or a member was killed during the hunt the moiety leaders had to compensate the people for their losses.[8] Accordingly, the *Ga-hi-ge* had considerable power during the hunt. Because a safe and successful hunt was vital to the Osage, the *Non-hon-zhin-ga* granted them ample power to conduct it. The *Ga-hi-ge* led the people out onto the plains. They chose the camping places and sent out scouts to find the bison. Once the bison were sighted, they carefully planned the attack on the herd. Discipline was critical, for if anyone approached from the wrong direction or attacked too soon, the herd would scatter and ruin the hunt. To insure hunt discipline, each *Ga-hi-ge* had five assistants to enforce his will.

These assistants, called *A-ki-da,* helped preserve tribal harmony as well as maintain hunt discipline. The *Hon-ga Ga-hi-ge* chose his *A-ki-da* from five specific kin groups: the Puma, Bear, Elk, Fish, and Isolated Sacred One clans. The *Tsi-zhu Ga-hi-ge* chose his *A-ki-da* from the Thunder People, Buffalo Bull People, Sun People, Carriers of the Sun and Moon, and Buffalo Bull

---

8. Ibid., 67; McDermott, *Tixier's Travels,* 174.

Face People clans. The leaders chose these soldiers on the basis of *O-don* and personal ties of kin and friendship. The Osage ranked the *A-ki-da,* and three had specific titles: *A-ki-da Tonga* (Great Soldier), *A-ki-da Ga-hi-ge* (Chief Soldier), and *A-ki-da Zhin-ga* (Little Soldier).[9]

In addition to enforcing their leader's will, the *A-ki-da* were responsible for selecting *Ga-hi-ge.* When a *Ga-hi-ge* died, or when one grew so old that he could no longer function as leader, the *A-ki-da* chose a new moiety leader from the correct lineage and clan. They usually chose a male descendant of the *Ga-hi-ge,* and generally, they chose his eldest son. The *A-ki-da* could bypass the eldest son and select another male from the same lineage if the son was incompetent or did not possess the proper disposition for the office. If an heir was underage or immature, the *A-ki-da* could choose a guardian to act as a regent until the candidate achieved maturity.[10]

The *Ga-hi-ge* shared their political power with a council composed of Osage clan *Non-hon-zhin-ga.* This group of older and wiser members of the tribe was responsible for insuring the village's safety by intervening and propitiating *Wa-kon-da* and for supervising the village's relationships with other villages and nations. *Non-hon-zhin-ga* initiated cultural changes when they believed those changes were vital to Osage life. They were more powerful than the *Ga-hi-ge* and *A-ki-da,* for they represented the entire tribe (all clans were represented in the *Non-hon-zhin-ga*), and they had power to establish or change tribal policy. They also had the power to regulate warfare by controlling the tribal

9. LaFlesche noted an additional *Hon-ga* clan from which *A-ki-da* could be selected. He called it *A-hiu-ton.* This clan, however, is not identifiable according to any traditional clan names and remains a mystery. See "Rite of the Chiefs," 67–68; Bailey, "Osage Social Organization, 1673–1906," 22–23.

10. Bright to Dearborn, December 20, 1806, *Letters Received by the Secretary of War, Main Series, 1801–1870;* Harold W. Ryan, ed., "Jacob Bright's Journal of a Trip to the Osage Indians." The old *Ga-hi-ge* retained their title, but none of the power or responsibility. The duplication of title and name makes it very difficult to determine just who people are in the historical record. See LaFlesche, "Rite of the Chiefs," 68; Holder, *Hoe and the Horse,* 53.

rites that sanctioned military campaigns. The Osage village was dominated by the *Non-hon-zhin-ga,* who established rules of behavior which were in turn enforced by the two *Ga-hi-ge* and their *A-ki-da.* The *Ga-hi-ge* were concerned primarily with internal matters, while *Non-hon-zhin-ga* focused on both internal and external affairs.[11]

Individuals became *Non-hon-zhin-ga* by hosting clan leaders and acquiring the seven required degrees of clan religious knowledge. Because of the wealth involved in acquiring each degree, membership was accessible only to mature members of wealthier Osage families. Although women were assuming positions within the *Non-hon-zhin-ga* by the late nineteenth century, this was apparently a later adaptation, for no women are mentioned in early accounts as being members of *Non-hon-zhin-ga,* and clearly the name—Little Old Men—suggests that males made up the membership of the early Osage religious council.

There were other Osage officers. When the *Non-hon-zhin-ga* sent their men to war, they appointed several officers to lead the expedition. Selecting experienced warriors, the council chose several men to share the responsibilities of leading a war party. The *Do-don-hon-ga* was the official leader, but his role was to fast and pray for the success of the raid. During the expedition, he traveled with the men, but he stayed apart from them and constantly appealed to *Wa-kon-da* for support. The actual leadership of the groups was held by the *Xthe-ts'a-ge Wa-ton-ga* (Chief *Xthe-ts'a-ge*) who was assisted by several other *Xthe-ts'a-ge* (war captains) chosen from both moieties. These men established the strategy for the expedition and directed the attack. The offices were temporary, and the men's power lasted only for the duration of the expedition.[12]

Other notable positions among the Osage were the *Xo-ka* and *Sho-ka. Xo-ka* were ceremonial leaders who were chosen to lead

11. Bailey, "Osage Social Organization, 1673–1906," 27.
12. LaFlesche, *War and Peace Ceremony,* 76–79.

certain rituals. The only power they possessed was to direct ritual behavior during tribal rites. They could not initiate the rituals, and their power was limited to the specific ceremony. *Sho-ka* were captives adopted into specific subclans and employed by the tribe as clan messengers. Since all of the messages were oral ones, the *Sho-ka* were skilled speakers who had prominent roles in Osage ceremony, but they possessed no significant political status.[13]

It is apparent that little coercive power existed among the Osage. They had several band chiefs, although those chiefs had little authority, reported French soldier Claude-Charles Du-Tisné in 1719. In 1724, as Etienne de Véniard, sieur de Bourgmont departed for his expedition to the plains, he took with him sixty-four Osage led by six war chiefs. In 1751, a French officer reported that the Osage had lost twenty-two of the chiefs in a recent attack.[14] All early reports of the Osage mention several Osage chiefs. These chiefs were either *Ga-hi-ge, Non-hon-zhin-ga, A-ki-da, Do-don-hon-ga, Xthe-ts'a-ge Wa-ton-ga, Xo-ka,* or *Sho-ka.* These early French observers, while unable to distinguish between the leaders' responsibilities, were able to pick out those individuals who seemed to possess some political power or play a prominent role within the tribe.

Early accounts do not record specific chiefs in action; therefore, the actual authority of the chiefs is conjectural. Throughout the eighteenth century, Osage chiefs frequently remarked that they could not control their young people. French and Spanish colonial officials consistently refused to believe the Osage, but in truth Osage political leaders never possessed direct coercive authority over their people, except in a few limited circum-

13. LaFlesche, "Rite of the Chiefs," 52, 74; idem, *War and Peace Ceremony,* 4–5, 11, 204; "Journal of Mr. Vail, During a Preaching Tour," *Missionary Herald* 29 (October 1833): 367.

14. "Soixante et quatre Osages commandes par quatre chefs de guerre de leur nation" (Margry, *Exploration des affluents,* 311, 398); Theodore Pease and Ernestine Jenison, eds., *Illinois on the Eve of the Seven Years' War, 1747–1755,* 358.

stances.[15] The conceptualization that the Indians had one supreme leader who maintained direct authority over his people was European, not Osage. The Europeans made assumptions based on their experience and worldview and tried to impose them upon the Osage.

Only in a few instances did tribal leadership possess direct authority over tribal members. During tribal-sanctioned war parties, the *Do-don-hon-ga* and *Xthe-ts'a-ge Wa-ton-ga* had power over their followers. Membership in a war party, however, was voluntary, and the leader's control was temporary, lasting only until the raid was over. Also, during the tribal hunt the *Ga-hi-ge* and their *A-ki-da* had direct control over the hunters. Only in these vital, sometimes dangerous instances were leaders given direct authority over tribal members. Once the attack—either on Osage enemies or the buffalo—began, the Osage behaved as they saw fit. Furthermore, in those circumstances where warriors gave up their independence, their leaders had the responsibility of compensating for all losses.[16] The concept of political authority of the Osage was completely different from that of the European.

The Osage had an elaborate political structure, one with formalized positions and functions, yet it seems clear from early accounts and Osage tradition that political power was shared and limited. Direct political control was only necessary in certain instances where activities required group participation and coordination. Just as political positions were designated, so was political power. Within certain circumstances, specific behavior was necessary and the weight of Osage experience and tradition enforced the proper behavior.

The tribal council, traditionally more powerful than the dual *Ga-hi-ge*, had little direct authority. The *Non-hon-zhin-ga*, made

15. James A. Clifton, *The Prairie People: Continuity and Change in Potawatomi Indian Culture, 1665–1965*, 55–62.

16. LaFlesche, *War and Peace Ceremony*, 5, 13; McDermott, *Tixier's Travels*, 174.

up of members of all tribal kinship groups, worked for una-nimity and consensus. The tribe symbolically met when the *Non-hon-zhin-ga* met, and decisions were made only after consider-able discussion and only if most of the *Non-hon-zhin-ga* agreed, for if a number of the council opposed a particular act or deci-sion it could not take place.

The village remained the central base of Osage political or-ganization prior to the nineteenth century. Identifying and ver-ifying the villages, however, has proved somewhat of a prob-lem for historians, because tribal tradition has not completely meshed with historical evidence. The earliest written record of the Osage is from 1673, when their name is noted on Father Jacques Marquette's map. With the exception of fabricated reports from Father Anastasius Douay, who noted seventeen Osage villages on the Osage River in 1687, all other early reports of the Osage make mention of only two Osage villages.[17] In 1714, the first true written account of any Osage villages came from coureur de bois Etienne de Véniard, sieur de Bourgmont, who traveled up the Missouri River. He noted two Osage villages: "The first river that falls into the Missouri is 30 leagues along on the left side as you go up, called the Ausages [Osages] River on account of the tribe which lives there who bear the same name."[18] After noting this first Osage group on the Osage River, he went on to describe another group along the Missouri River: "This Mis-souri river runs to the north and northwest. I shall not give a description of this river. I will only tell which tribes occupy its banks, to my knowledge. There are the Missouri, a savage nation whose name is like the river; who are allies of the French. There are also the Auzages [Osages], another savage nation, allies and

17. Chapman, *Origin of the Osage*, 96–97.
18. "La première rivière qui tombe dans le Missouri, à 30 lieues à gauche en montant, est appelée la rivière des Ausages [Osages] par rapport à la nation qui y demeure et porte le même nom" (Baron Marc de Villiers, *La Découverte du Missouri et l'histoire du Fort D'Orléans (1673–1728)*, 60); Marcel Giraud, ed., "Etienne Veniard De Bourgmont's 'Exact Description of Louisiana,'" 15.

friends of the French."[19] Five years later Claude-Charles Du-Tisné visited the Osage villages. DuTisné noted one village along the Missouri River near the Missouri Indians and another along the upper Osage River.[20]

In time, the French began to distinguish two groups of Osage: one living along the Missouri River, the Little Osage (*Petits Osages*), and those along the Osage River, the Big Osage (*Grands Osages*). Tribal tradition explains that the Little Osage were merely the Down Below People. Unfortunately, the Europeans were not always consistent in references to the Osage; usually they made distinctions between Big and Little Osage, but at other times they only wrote *Osage* or *Aus, Os, Osages, Ozage,* or *Ossages*. Further complicating the issue was the presence of divisions among the major groups. Apparently, kin groups occasionally left the major divisions and camped apart, yet retained band affiliation.

Because of the nature and paucity of eighteenth-century records, it is difficult, if not impossible, to distinguish between villages and bands. Although throughout the French period only these two groups of Osage were mentioned, there was one brief reference to two villages of Great Osage made in a letter written in January 1752.[21] Years later, in March 1773, Spanish documents revealed that there were at least two groups of Little Osage along the Missouri. A French Canadian trapper, trading illegally

19. "Cette rivière de Missouri court au Nord et au Nord-Ouest. Je ne ferai point la description de cette rivière; je dirai seulement les nations qui occupent ses bords qui sont à ma connaissance. Il y a les Missouris, nation sauvage du nom de la rivière, lesquels sont alliés des Français. Il y a aussi les Auzages, autre nation sauvage, alliés et amis des Français" (Villiers, *Découverte du Missouri,* 60); Giraud, "Bourgmont's 'Exact Description of Louisiana,'" 15.

20. "Ils ont à une lieue de chez eux, [Missouri Indians], au S.-O., un village d'Osages, qui n'est esloigné du grand village que de 30 lieues" (Margry, *Exploration des affluents,* 310–11).

21. Mathews, *The Osages,* 147–48; Bailey, "Osage Social Organization, 1673–1906," 19, 30; "Les grands ôsages des deux Villages' . . ." (Pease and Jenison, *Illinois on the Eve,* 448).

among the Little Osage, was captured by the Spanish, and during his interrogation he testified that "they have been in the tribe of Little Osages . . . this tribe is divided into two Bands, one above the other along the banks of the aforesaid river [Missouri]."[22] This is the only mention of two Little Osage villages, but archaeologists have found the remains of several possible Little Osage village sites along the Missouri River in present-day Saline County, Missouri. Yet in a description of the Indians of Louisiana written by Governor Kerlérec six years later in 1779, only two villages were noted, one 140 leagues up the Osage River and the other 40 leagues above the mouth of the Osage River, one league from the Missouri.[23]

Existing French reports suggest that the Osage were divided into two or perhaps three villages, which is difficult to reconcile with Osage accounts of five villages. Osage scholar John J. Mathews, however, claimed that the Down Below People moved to the Missouri River, but the Heart Stays People, Big Hill People, Upland Forest People, and Thorny Thicket People all remained in four villages close to one another at the forks of the Osage River.[24] These villages may have been mistaken by Europeans for one village because of their close proximity.

In addition to the two noted village groups, there were early reports of Osage Indians traveling along the upper Arkansas River. In 1719, Jean-Baptiste Bénard, sieur de la Harpe confronted a band of Osage just south of the Arkansas, and in 1722 a Frenchman who had been up the Arkansas complained of

22. Abraham P. Nasatir, "Ducharme's Invasion of Missouri: An Incident in the Anglo-Spanish Rivalry for the Indian Trade of Upper Louisiana," 251.

23. Chapman, *Origin of the Osage*, 104–25; Brewton Berry, Carl Chapman, and John Mack, "Archaeological Remains of the Osage"; Robert T. Bray, "The Missouri Indian Tribe in Archaeology and History"; Nasatir, *Before Lewis and Clark*, 1:52.

24. Father Douay's report is apparently an outright fabrication; thus his report of seventeen villages seems to be either an account of Osage hunting camps or an exaggeration. Douay did not visit the Osage people. See Chapman, *Origin of the Osage*, 75–76; Mathews, *The Osages*, 147–48.

being pillaged by the Osage.[25] Throughout the French period, reports continued of Osage activity along the Arkansas River.

Also during the 1770s, reports began to appear that a number of Osage had moved to the Arkansas River. Athanase de Mézières, at Natchitoches in the fall of 1774, wrote that "the rumor is spreading among the Indians that the Osages have abandoned their ancient village in order to form another far distant from the first, and far up the Rio de los Arkansas." In 1776, Clermont, an important Big Osage *Ga-hi-ge,* complained to the Spanish in Saint Louis that half of his nation was along the Arkansas River and claimed that they would be "the ruin of his Nation."[26] Reports such as these continued throughout the period.

In the summer of 1784, a letter from Francisco Cruzat, Lieutenant Governor of Upper Louisiana, to his superior, Esteban Rodriguez Miró in New Orleans, revealed that the Big Osage were divided into three groups:

> All the aforesaid nation [Big Osage] was divided in three parties, one of them—which was that of the two said principal chiefs—remained to trade with the traders who were sent to them; the second, at the head of which was the referred to new chief *Cuchechiré,* went to winter on the Arkansas river about one hundred and seventy leagues from the indicated Fort Charles III, . . . the third party penetrated further into the prairies to be able more opportunely to make war on the Panis Piques [Wichita].[27]

By 1785, clearly a distinct group of Osage stayed along the upper Arkansas. A December report in that year stated, "Along the course of the aforesaid river (Arkansas), about one hundred leagues above, live the Little Osages." It continued, "The village

25. Glen R. Conrad, ed., *Historical Journal of the Settlement of the French in Louisiana,* 147, 209; Mildred Mott Wedel, "J.-B. Bénard, Sieur de la Harpe: Visitor to the Wichitas in 1719."

26. Herbert E. Bolton, ed., *Athanase de Mézières and the Louisiana-Texas Frontier, 1768–1780,* 2:110; Ríu to Ulloa, November 12, 1767, Nasatir Papers, 1:20.

27. Cruzat to Miró, June 23, 1784, Nasatir Papers, 3:81–83.

of the Great Osages is situated 120 leagues in the interior on the river bearing their name. . . . The village of the Little Osages, of which those who have settled upon the upper waters of the Arkansas River are a part, is situated eighty leagues from the mouth of the Missouri on its right bank, one league inland."[28]

It is impossible to account for all of the Osage villages throughout the eighteenth century. During this period the Osage were moving west and conducting raids over a wide range of territory. They ranged south of the Red River in present-day Texas to north of the Des Moines River in present-day Iowa. Contemporary accounts did not distinguish between Big Hill, Thorny Thicket, Heart Stays, and Upland Forest Peoples—only between Big Osage, Little Osage, and the Arkansas Band. The nature of most accounts failed to provide evidence to discern village units, and the Osage's seminomadic existence has further complicated any archaeological investigation. By the middle of the eighteenth century, the Osage spent most of their time traveling in small groups and hunting across their wide territory; these groups cannot be linked with specific band names. Still, by the late eighteenth century the Osage were located in at least three bands, one along the Arkansas River, another at the Osage River, and another along the Missouri. Each of the three major bands was made up of several villages.

It is difficult to determine accurately the Osage divisions even during the nineteenth century, for the Osage were still expanding and dividing into more village groups. Unfortunately, those travelers who visited the Osage almost always arrived among them during the summer, when they were hunting and when their large villages were abandoned. Those travelers that did find the Osage in their horticultural villages seldom saw all of the Osage. They either visited Osage bands living in the south

28. Clearly, by the 1780s the Osage were dispersed into at least three or perhaps more groups. Again, the information that exists is fragmentary and from non-Osage and oftentimes, particularly with De Mézières, hostile sources. See Lawrence Kinnaird, ed., *Spain in the Mississippi Valley*, 2:160, 164.

along the Arkansas or those groups in the north along the Osage, Neosho, and Verdigris Rivers. Few encountered both groups. Although it is claimed by some that by 1806 there were four villages, Zebulon Pike, who began his well-known trip to the Spanish Southwest in the fall of that year, counted only two villages among the northern bands, and when James Wilkinson left Pike and descended the Arkansas, the southern bands were still dispersed in several small hunting camps. George Sibley, the government trader at Fort Osage, went hunting with the Osage in the summer of 1811, and he visited three groups of Osage living in three large hunting camps: the Little Osage, Pawhuska's Big Osage, and Clermont's Arkansas Osage. In 1815 and 1816, Jules de Mun and Auguste Chouteau, on their ill-fated journey west, passed through the northern Osage country and described three Osage villages (perhaps four, De Mun was not clear) along the northern Neosho and mentioned the Arkansas Osage in the South.[29]

In 1820, George Sibley, still living among the Osage, described the Osage in the northern part living in two villages of Big Osage, three villages of Little Osage, and half the tribe living with the Arkansas Band. A map prepared in 1822 showed three villages of Little Osage, one village of Arkansas Osage, and two villages of Big Osage. In 1831, Protestant missionaries living among the Osage noted six villages. Louis Cortambert, who visited both the northern and Arkansas Osage bands in 1835 and 1836, named six villages, four in the north and two in the south. Five years later, Victor Tixier visited the Osage and described at least eight villages.[30]

29. Jackson, *Journals of Pike*, 1:306–13, 2:4–6; Thomas D. Isern, ed., "Exploration and Diplomacy: George Champlin Sibley's Report to William Clark, 1811," 96–99; George R. Brooks, ed., "George C. Sibley's Journal of a Trip to the Salines in 1811," 189–95; Sibley Papers and Lindenwood Collection, Missouri Historical Society; Thomas Maitland Marshall, ed., "The Journals of Jules De Mun," 167–205, 311–25; Morse, *Report to the Secretary of War*, 203–4.

30. Morse, *Report to the Secretary of War*, 203–4; Clarence E. Carter, ed., *The Territorial Papers of the United States*, 19:392–94; "Letters of Nathaniel B. Dodge

Again, it is difficult to correlate Osage tradition with historical records, as even the early nineteenth-century records are fragmentary. Some of the Osage bands were identifiable in the eighteenth century, and by the early nineteenth century all five were noted. In 1815 a group called *Gros Côte* (Big Hill) were mentioned, and by 1835 Heart Stays and Thorny Thicket People can be distinguished. Louis Cortambert visited the Osage in 1835 and described six villages. Five of the villages noted by Cortambert clearly corresponded to Osage tradition: the Down Below, Heart Stays, Thorny Thicket, Big Hill, and Upland Forest People. The villages of the Big Hill and Upland Forest bands were along the Verdigris River, but the others were all along the upper Neosho River. The sixth village, named Maurinhabatso, was the site of the American Fur Company trading post and was made up of members of Pawhuska's Thorny Thicket village. Although the number of identifiable bands are not distinct from existing records, it is certain that after 1714 the Osage dwelled in at least two or three villages, and that by 1839 there were as many as eight. Osage claims of the five distinct village groups seem as plausible as European guesses.[31]

With the division of the Osage into various band groups, the Osage duplicated their initial political organization, claiming that each band possessed a full clan representation with com-

---

and William F. Vail," *Missionary Herald* 27 (September 1831): 288–89; Carl H. Chapman, ed., "Journey to the Land of the Osages, 1835–1836, by Louis Cortambert," 215–16. Perhaps there were only seven. Tixier states that there was a Little Osage village, yet when he described and named each Osage village he did not associate one directly with the Little Osage. He did mention a separate village led by Belle Oiseau that might be the Little Osage village, which would make the total seven. If it was not the Little Osage village it would be an addition to the named seven and make the total eight. This is particularly confusing, for a Belle Oiseau was a noted Big Osage warrior who was often associated with the Little Osage Band. Mathews claims seven villages and Bailey lists eight. The author, after examining Tixier closely, is inclined to agree with Bailey. See McDermott, *Tixier's Travels*, 126–29; Bailey, "Osage Social Organization, 1673–1906," 60; Mathews, *The Osages*, 596–98.

31. Marshall, ed., "Journals of De Mun," 311–25; Morse, *Report to the Secretary of War*, 203–4; Chapman, "Journey to Land of Osages," 215–16; McDermott, *Tixier's Travels*, 126–29.

plete *Non-hon-zhin-ga, Ga-hi-ge,* and *A-ki-da.* It does, however, seem doubtful that when they lived in as many as eight villages that each one possessed the full complement of clans and required officials. It is more likely that with the separation of bands into smaller and smaller villages the ceremonial functions could only be carried out if all of the villages belonging to a single band came together. Although there is no evidence of any ranking of bands or overall tribal organization, it seems that the dual *Ga-hi-ge* of the Upland Forest Band were the recognized tribal leaders. This, however, is only assumed because later principal Osage chiefs, recognized as such by Europeans, were members of this group.[32] The tribal *wi-gi-e* speak of the political organization in the ideal state and do not always describe real conditions.

Europeans were conditioned because of their political experience to assign supremacy to one leader, and when they went among the Osage they were prepared to deal with a single leader, not two. The French noted clearly that there were many chiefs among the Osage, yet they also ranked them, describing them as first and second chiefs; this ranking is not accounted for in Osage tradition. The *Ga-hi-ge* were theoretically equal, but the *Tsi-zhu Ga-hi-ge,* because of his role as peace chief, would have been most directly involved with non-Osage. The Europeans came looking for a single leader, and consistent with their preconceived notions, they were met by the *Tsi-zhu Ga-hi-ge.* It is only reasonable, therefore, to assume that the first chiefs referred to were probably the *Tsi-zhu Ga-hi-ge.* There is some evidence that because of the increased contact with the Europeans by the late eighteenth century, the *Tsi-zhu Ga-hi-ge* became more powerful than the *Hon-ga Ga-hi-ge.*[33]

Again, the true nature of tribal political organization is not absolute. It seems that all band *Non-hon-zhin-ga* could meet to-

32. Mathews, *The Osages,* 143–48; LaFlesche, "Rite of the Chiefs," 45, and *War and Peace Ceremony,* 202; Bailey, "Osage Social Organization, 1673–1906," 19.

33. Bailey, "Osage Social Organization, 1673–1906," 19.

gether as a tribal *Non-hon-zhin-ga,* but the extent of these powers is lost. In 1808, an overall tribal organization was mentioned when a group of Osage complained about an approved treaty: "The chiefs who were not present when this treaty had been entered into, declared that the White Hare, and the chiefs who had signed it, had no right to dispose of their lands without the general consent of the nation being first obtained in council, among themselves."[34] Here perhaps is evidence of a single Osage tribal council, but the evidence is sketchy, for the Osage complaining in Saint Louis were members of the two northern groups, and they did not include the Arkansas Band. If there was any tribal political organization, it probably played a more significant role when the different villages were close together. With the passage of time, as the Osage abandoned traditions of the semisedentary peoples and began living further apart in small, distinct villages, any overall tribal political organization weakened and eventually disappeared.

The transitional nature of Osage society and culture in the eighteenth and nineteenth centuries can be seen in their political organization, the eclectic features of which can best be observed within a chronological framework, for the Osage system changed over time. In the eighteenth century the Osage possessed a political organization much like the Indian people of the eastern forests and prairie river valleys. By the early nineteenth century, however, they began to display some political traits of the plains peoples. Historical accounts and tribal *wi-gi-e* document these changes and reflect Osage attempts to deal with rapidly changing social, economic, diplomatic, and environmental situations.

The formalized political system of the Osage, with its hereditary leadership and clan ties to political position and function, was strikingly similar to several eastern hunting tribes. The Menominee and Winnebago of the eastern woodlands possessed

34. Indian Claims Commission, *Commission Findings on the Osage Indians,* 224.

intricate clan structures and linked specific functions and positions to various kinship groups, as did the Osage. A principle responsibility of the Winnebago chief was to preserve internal tribal peace and settle internal disputes. Further, his lodge was considered a sanctuary where wrongdoers or even tribal enemies could find safety and refuge. While the Osage chose two leaders from the dual moieties, their leaders' principle function was to maintain peace within the village, and their lodges were tribal sanctuaries.[35]

The traditional Osage political system also shared traits with some sedentary southern tribes and bore a striking resemblance to most semisedentary horticultural plains-prairie peoples. The Osage moiety divisions and dual leadership associated symbolically with war and peace was very similar to several southeastern tribes, such as the Creek and the Choctaw.[36] The hereditary nature of tribal leadership and its connections with specific clans was common to the plains-prairie peoples. The close ties between the tribal priesthood and the tribal political leadership was found among the Osage and the plains-prairie people. The class stratification and accompanying political power was also common to both. Political function and office were tied intimately to particular clans and subclans in both the Osage and plains-prairies people, such as the Wichita, Pawnee, Mandan, and Arikara. In both groups, the primary function of the tribal chiefs was to maintain the internal tribal peace and stability; political powers were strictly defined and the tribal council and chiefs had control only over specific activities of the tribal membership. The political systems of the Osage and northern and southern Caddoan groups were highly structured and contained firmly defined functions and positions that permitted little flexibility or political autonomy outside the tribal framework.

35. Robert F. Spencer and Jesse D. Jennings, et al., *The Native Americans,* 396–97; Robert H. Lowie, *Indians of the Plains,* 94.

36. Fred Eggan, *The American Indian: Perspectives for the Study of Social Change,* 17–18.

For most of the eighteenth century, this complex political system worked for the Osage. The specialized and intricate sociopolitical structure of the Osage was well suited to their stable, semisedentary existence. When the Osage spent most of their time together in their large agricultural villages or on common tribal hunts in the immediate area, their formalized system proved satisfactory.

As the nineteenth century progressed, however, the Osage's rigid political system came under increasing attack by new forces that challenged the traditional structure. These new forces primarily resulted from the European presence. Europeans, directly or indirectly, introduced horses and firearms to the Osage and encouraged trade. The combination of horses, firearms, and new economic opportunity produced dramatic political changes among the Osage. The Europeans provided the means—horses and guns—and rewarded the results—increased hunting and raiding. These rewards convinced the Osage to rearrange their individual, and subsequently their local and tribal, priorities. The Osage gradually abandoned their semisedentary agricultural village life and became a seminomadic plains hunting people.

As the Osage changed their economy, they changed their social and political system to meet their new needs. Along the way some features were discarded and others adopted. With the increased hunting and raiding the Osage spent more time away from their village bases. The possession of horses allowed Osage hunters to roam far from their villages, and their possession of firearms allowed smaller groups to successfully hunt and raid. Mounted, armed Osage raiding parties could range far from their Osage River village bases and successfully exploit the resources of the forest, prairie, and plains. These smaller bands required a flexible political system that granted a great deal of autonomy.

Confronted with this new way of life, the Osage leadership attempted to change some of the tribe's political features to adapt and yet retain the essential qualities of traditional Osage life. The Osage granted more autonomy and independence to clans, and sacred bundles were created for bands and individuals. The *Non-hon-zhin-ga* authorized smaller clan war parties which did not require the elaborate tribal ceremonies. Matrilocality came into use and was accepted by the Osage as a means of dealing with the new conditions. Apparently, the Osage social system was flexible enough to bend and change to deal with the changing situations and still retain the familiar features of Osage culture. New clans might be created, men might go to war more frequently, newlyweds might go to live with the bride's family, and a husband might marry all his wife's sisters, but the Osage culture was not fundamentally altered. The Osage continued to respect the traditional systems, and the structure remained intact. But the elastic quality of the Osage social structure was missing from the political system.

Traditional leadership was challenged by the Osage themselves. Individuals who enjoyed status and economic success as a result of the increased hunting and raiding often had no access to leadership positions. A great warrior or hunter could never become one of the chiefs unless he possessed the correct kinship relationship with them. Within this traditional system, ancestry was more important than merit in determining leadership, and this created resentment within the tribe.

There is, however, evidence that the Osage might have been able to adapt their structured and stylized political system to recognize the new importance of the warriors and hunters and open up the leadership positions. A successful hunter or warrior could acquire enough wealth to purchase the requisite ceremonial knowledge, entertain the clan leaders, and gain membership in the *Non-hon-zhin-ga* or tribal council. Purchase was an acceptable means of gaining tribal council membership and within the traditional system the council had more political power than did the two chiefs.[37] Therefore, the Osage had a

37. LaFlesche, "Rite of the Chiefs," 65–70; Bailey, "Osage Social Organization, 1673–1906," 23–25.

way of incorporating the ambitious and aggressive new Osage within the older political structure. Furthermore, the introduction of matrilocality, while not opening up political channels, would at least allow the old tribal elite to marry their daughters to the aggressive, up-and-coming Osage warriors. Marriage would provide some traditional status to the young man and link his fortunes with those of the older Osage kinship households. The Osage tried to merge the conflicting life-styles into a tribal political compromise that would recognize the traditional elements, yet integrate new features.

3.

OSAGE ECONOMIES

I see and admire your manner of living, your good warm houses, your extensive fields of corn, your gardens, your cows, oxen, work-horses, wagons, and a thousand machines, that I know not the use of. I see that you are able to clothe yourself, even from weeds and grass. In short you can do almost what you choose. You whites possess the power of subduing almost every animal to your use. You are surrounded by slaves. Everything about you is in chains, and you are slaves yourselves. I hear I should exchange my presents for yours. I too should become a slave. Talk to my sons, perhaps they may be persuaded to adopt your fashions, or at least to recommend them to their sons; but for myself, I was born free, was raised free, and wish to die free.

—Big Soldier, 1820[1]

Living on the prairies between the western grasslands and the eastern forests, the Osage created a successful subsistence economy. By skillfully exploiting the abundant animal and plant life of the forest, prairie, and grassland ecosystems, the Osage gathered ample resources to feed, clothe, and shelter themselves.

Though the Osage changed village sites only when supplies of wood were depleted or when the garden plots would no longer support the crops necessary to feed them, they were a mobile people, moving throughout the year to take advantage of the seasonal cycle of plants and animals near them. Keen observers

1. Peake, *History of Factory System,* 229.

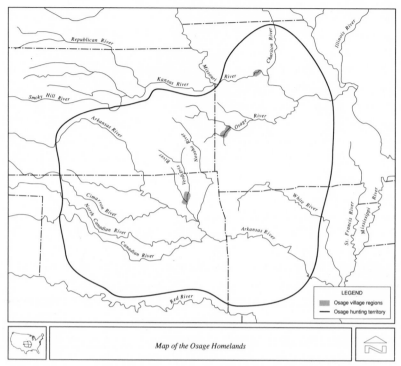

Map of the Osage Homelands. Drawn by Barbara Williams-Rollings.

of their surrounding environment, they moved frequently to secure food where it was concentrated and abundant. The Osage chose to live in an edge habitat, for doing so allowed them to exploit the diverse forms of wild game and plantlife of the three ecosystems: the forest, the prairie, and the plains.

In the eighteenth century, the Osage prairie villages were located on stretches of high ground in the area where the Marais des Cygnes, Little Osage, and Marmaton Rivers came together to form the Osage River. The three rivers, flowing from the west, meandered slowly across the prairie flatlands. Fed by creeks, streams, and springs, the rivers formed sloughs, lakes, marshes, and wide expanses of grassy wetlands. The region was an excellent habitat for wild game and was filled with fish, waterfowl, and large and small mammals from the forests and the grass-lands. The ample wildlife attracted by the rich growth provided abundant supplies of food for the Osage. The seasonal flooding of the three rivers also covered the lowlands with fresh topsoil and replenished the land, maintaining the rich, fertile soil important for Osage gardens.[2]

The Osage remained in their large villages, which contained as many as one thousand people,[3] for only a few months of the year in the spring and fall. They spent the summer on the plains and the winter in small groups near the forest edge. Upon returning to the village from their winter lodges, they prepared their gardens. Although the men helped clear and burn off the debris that remained from the previous year's gardens, agriculture was the responsibility of Osage women. Women planted their gardens near the village, along river terraces that were close to water and contained soil that was fertile and easily tilled. Working with wooden digging sticks and bone-bladed hoes, the women planted gardens that ranged in size from one-third to a full acre.[4] Individual families worked the fields, so the size of the garden varied according to the size of the family.

2. Carl O. Sauer, *The Geography of the Ozark Highland of Missouri*, 49–50. The area between the rivers is marshy. The river name *Marais des Cygnes*, translated from French, means "marsh of the swans."

3. The earliest reliable count comes from Claude-Charles DuTisné, who estimated in 1719 there were 200 warriors and 200 lodges in one village (Margry, *Exploration des affluents*, 311). In 1758, Governor Kerlérec reported 700 Big Osage and 250 Little Osage warriors (December 12, 1758, Archives des Colonies, C13A, 40, fols. 137–39). In 1777, Francisco Cruzat claimed there were 400 Little Osage and 800 Big Osage warriors in two villages (Cruzat to Gálvez, December 6, 1777, Louis A. Houck, ed., *The Spanish Régime in Missouri*, 1:140–42). Pierre Chouteau reported 1,200 Big Osage and 300 Little Osage warriors in 1804 (Chouteau to Dearborn, November 19, 1804, Pierre Chouteau Letterbook, Missouri Historical Society). Pike counted 1,695 Big Osage in one village and 824 Little Osage in another (Jackson, *Journals of Pike*, 2:40–41). In 1808, Eli Clemson reported that 1,500 Little Osage and 2,000 Big Osage arrived at Fire Prairie (Clemson to Dearborn, September 25, 1808, *Letters Received Secretary of War, Main Series*).

4. Bailey, "Osage Social Organization, 1673–1906," 22; Will and Hyde, *Corn Among the Indians*, 107.

Garden plots were used year after year as long as the land could support the crops. Several factors permitted the Osage to use the land for long periods. The yearly flooding brought new, rich soil to the gardens. The burned organic debris from the previous gardens that was worked into the soil at the beginning of the growing season also helped maintain the fertility, and the beans planted every year replaced the nitrogen. Despite the flooding, burning, and nitrogen fixing, however, the soil eventually would be exhausted, and the Osage would move on to a new site in the same general region.

The Osage women cultivated several crops, but corn was the most important. The land between the rivers was ideal for corn; the soil was rich, and there was ample water and abundant sunshine. They sometimes harvested as much as sixty bushels of corn an acre and rarely less than twenty-five bushels an acre. With such a large crop, corn alone supplied as much as half of the caloric requirements for an Osage family.[5] Combined with the squash, pumpkins, and beans from the garden, Osage women provided a substantial portion of the yearly food supply, sometimes as much as three-fourths of the total yearly food requirements for their families.

Corn's importance to the Osage is seen in its prominent role in their spiritual life. Later, as hunting became more important to the Osage economy, corn remained an important element of Osage life. Its continued importance was demonstrated by its prominent symbolic role in several vital Osage ceremonies. The child-naming ceremony used corn symbolically, as Buffalo Bull clan elders, who were always in charge of the ritual, fed kernels of corn to the infants; the ceremony ended with the planting of corn. Corn planting was accompanied by special songs and rit-

5. Will and Hyde, *Corn Among the Indians,* 107; George William Featherstonhaugh, *Excursion Through the Slave States, From Washington on the Potomac, to the Frontier of Mexico; with Sketches of Popular Manners and Geological Notices,* 73; William Cronon, *Changes in the Land: Indians, Colonists, and the Ecology of New England,* 44.

ual forms, and the first harvest was celebrated with a spiritual rite. The Osage linked corn symbolically with another food source, the bison, claiming that the buffalo bull first gave them corn. The connection between corn and buffalo was reinforced by ritual prerogatives possessed by the Buffalo Bull clan. In addition to the child-naming ceremony, they owned the rights to several other important rituals where corn played a significant role.[6]

Squash was also thought to be a gift of the buffalo; next to corn, it was the most important crop. Osage women planted a variety of squash and pumpkins amid their corn plants. Squash grew well on the terraces, and the vines covered the garden ground, its broad leaves helping conserve moisture in the soil and cutting off sunlight to unwanted weeds. Planted among the corn and squash, beans vined around the corn stalks and provided additional food for the Osage. In good years gardens provided an abundance of corn, beans, and squash. These three crops are complementary nutritious foods. Eaten alone, the three crops are nutritionally incomplete, but eaten together, beans and corn combine to create the essential amino acids humans need to live.[7]

Women of the village prepared the gardens in late April. After the plants first appeared, they weeded the garden and kept a close watch to chase away animals that tried to feed on the young sprouts. By late May, secure that their gardens were safely established, the Osage packed up their belongings and prepared to leave the prairie villages.

April and May were the earliest months Osage could plant their gardens. These months, however, were not the best time to remain on the prairie edge. The edge habitat was not a good location for food in the spring. Most of the wild plants had not yet begun their growth and provided little food. Large regional

6. LaFlesche, "Child-naming Rite," 31, 58; idem, "Rite of the Chiefs," 134–38; Will and Hyde, *Corn Among the Indians*, 251.
7. Adelle Davis, *Let's Eat Right to Keep Fit*, 35–37.

game, such as bear, elk, and white-tailed deer, were lean from the winter season, and provided little meat. Large game was also harder to secure in the spring, for the concentrated herds of deer and elk of the summer and winter months broke up during the spring, and the animals were dispersed throughout the area. The Osage were thus eager to leave the prairies, and as soon as they established their gardens, they left for a region where game would yield greater amounts of meat and be easier to hunt than the lean, dispersed, prairie game.

Such a region was the short-grass plains miles to the west, where the great herds of buffalo collected. Although there were woods bison in the nearby forests and tall-grass prairies immediately to the west of the prairie villages, the great buffalo herds were concentrated on the short-grass plains region beyond the Arkansas River.[8] The Osage packed up their villages and traveled west to hunt the buffalo. Osage villages were quickly packed when the people prepared to leave for their summer hunt. Because of their frequent travel, the Osage accumulated few material belongings. Moving on foot or on horseback further limited the number of Osage possessions. They kept little beyond clothing, small tools, and utensils. Their objects of necessity were small, lightweight, and either easily transported or easily replaced.

The summer hunts were vital to Osage survival. With little to eat on the eastern prairie edge, the Osage hunted in the west to feed their people after the last hungry days of winter and the first days of early spring. They tried to arrive in buffalo country, that region just beyond the Arkansas River and below the Great

---

8. McDermott, *Tixier's Travels*, 186–93, 257; Jeffery R. Hanson, "Bison Ecology in the Northern Plains and a Reconstruction of Bison Patterns for the North Dakota Region"; J. Albert Rorabacher, *The American Buffalo in Transition: A Historical and Economic Survey of the Bison in America*, 12–19; George W. Arthur, *An Introduction to the Ecology of Early Historic Communal Bison Hunting Among the Northern Plains*, 47–52; Isaac McCoy, *Annual Register of Indian Affairs within Indian Territory*, 18; Frank G. Roe, *The North American Buffalo*, 47.

Bend, by the early part of June, the month they named "Moon When Buffalo Regain Fat."[9]

Little information about their seventeenth-century summer hunts exists, but in 1719 a French explorer noted that the Osage were hunting buffalo in the west. In 1751, another French soldier mentioned that Osage were at the *cerne* (surround) hunting buffalo.[10] Summer hunts, prior to the horse, involved participation of the entire tribe. Only the ill and very old, those who could not keep up the pace of the arduous summer hunt, stayed behind. The Osage hunted communally. The hunts took skill, coordination, group cooperation, and discipline. Although difficult and dangerous, the hunts were usually effective. Hundreds of buffalo could be taken, providing abundant food, clothing, and tools for the Osage.

The Osage walked onto the plains searching for the buffalo. It is likely that in prehorse days they did not venture very far west. They were limited both by the distance the entire tribe could walk in a short time and by the presence of other hunting peoples inhabiting the tall-grass plains immediately west of them. During the early hunts, the Osage used a variety of methods to hunt buffalo. Most involved driving the animals into a confined area where they could be killed with hand weapons. The Osage sometimes frightened the herds of buffalo or used small grass fires to drive them off cliffs, cutbanks of a river, or into specially constructed pens. Once the buffalo were driven off a steep bluff, the Osage went among the stunned and crippled animals and killed them. All of the methods worked well, but they were hazardous, for buffalo were dangerous to people on foot.

Once the Osage acquired the horse, they continued to hunt buffalo in the west. With horses they were able to travel faster and farther. In time, the horse changed the nature of the hunt.

9. Francis LaFlesche, *Dictionary of the Osage Language,* 158, 285; Mathews, *The Osages,* 455.

10. Margry, *Exploration des affluents,* 311–12; Taffenal to Rouille, September 25, 1715, Pease and Jenison, *Illinois on the Eve,* 357–58.

What had once been an important group activity became an individualized affair. Now, small groups of mounted hunters could easily take enough buffalo to feed their people. It was no longer necessary for all of the people to hunt together in order to secure enough food. By 1840, the Osage had largely abandoned the old technique of surrounding the herds, and instead the hunters simply rushed headlong into the masses of buffalo.[11]

The summer hunt was directed by a hunt leader. This pattern was followed on the large communal hunts and later by the smaller group hunts. The leaders were in charge of the entire summer expedition. They sent out scouts to find the herds, and once herds were spotted the leaders planned and directed the attack against the buffalo.

Initially, the hunt leaders were the moiety leaders, the *Ga-hi-ge*. In time, however, the hunt was led by successful hunters who were sometimes *Ga-hi-ge*, but more often than not they were individuals who had proven themselves as skillful hunters. During early hunts, village *A-ki-da* enforced the decisions of the hunt leaders and maintained the essential hunt discipline. In time, they too were replaced by other groups of hunters who enforced the discipline necessary for hunt success.[12]

Osage men killed the buffalo, and the women skinned and butchered them. The meat belonged to the hunter who killed the buffalo, but other Osage could claim a share in the meat by helping with the butchering. Hunters gave meat away to those who failed to kill a buffalo, families that had no hunters, or hunters who had no horses. The gift of buffalo meat conferred status on the giver and insured that all Osage had enough to eat. During the hunt, everyone took advantage of the abundance and ate their fill. The Osage gorged on the buffalo meat, and they dried and smoked the surplus meat for use in the winter. Although during the summer hunt the buffalo hides were thin, Osage

11. McDermott, *Tixier's Travels,* 190–92; Brooks, "Sibley's Journal," 196.
12. LaFlesche, "Rite of the Chiefs," 68–69; McDermott, *Tixier's Travels,* 173–75, 189, 218–21.

women used the summer hides for lodge covers, clothing, rope, and other articles that did not require the thick, woolly, winter hides.

The Osage remained out on the plains usually until late July, when they left for home because the buffalo began their breeding season, which lasted from late July until the end of September. During breeding season, male buffalo, who normally remained separate from the females, mixed among the female herds. The bulls became aggressive and belligerent, making it a particularly dangerous time to hunt. The Osage preferred meat from the female, but during the breeding season they claimed the meat had an unpleasant taste. They were aware of buffalo behavior and named July "Moon When the Buffalo Breed."[13] To avoid the problems in the breeding season, the Osage returned to the prairies. Arriving in their old village sites in August, they began harvesting their crops.

During this time, plant life ripened and was abundant. Osage women picked corn and beans and hung them to dry. Squash and pumpkins were cut into long strips, partially dried, and then braided into mats. August and September was also the time wild plants produced food for the Osage. They harvested wild plums, grapes, hackberries, pecans, walnuts, and hazelnuts. Wild potatoes, persimmons, and water chinquapin were also gathered and prepared for the winter.

Late summer and early autumn was a prosperous time for the Osage in other ways as well. Their prairie village sites were located along the western edge of the Mississippi Flyway and the eastern edge of the Central Flyway. Thus the marshes and wetlands near the Osage villages were filled with migrating waterfowl, ducks and geese that began passing through the prairie region in late October. At the same time, animals in the area were fat from feeding on the summer browse. The fat prepared

13. Arthur, *Ecology of Bison Hunting,* 47–52; McDermott, *Tixier's Travels,* 194; LaFlesche, *Dictionary of the Osage,* 159, 285; Mathews, *The Osages,* 459.

the raccoons, opossums, and other small mammals for winter, and their pelts thickened. Wild turkeys began to concentrate in large flocks in the late fall.[14]

At the same time, beavers became very active. Most of the year they remained in the water, leaving it only at night to gather food. In October and November, beavers abandoned their nocturnal, aquatic life and left their lodges in streams and ponds during the day to collect food for the coming winter. These fall daytime land excursions were an excellent time for the Osage to hunt the fat, sleek animals.[15]

The fall was also an excellent time to hunt white-tailed deer. Since most of the year they fed on twigs, grass, and small shrubs, the deer preferred to live along the edge of the forest; the thick forest canopy retarded the growth of deer graze. High deer population densities existed along these forest edges where the open fields provided browse for the deer and the nearby forest offered shelter and places to hide. The Osage, located as they were along the forest edge, lived in an ideal deer habitat. To secure even more deer, they frequently set fire to prairies and forests which increased the edge areas, thus attracting more deer.[16]

In the fall, however, white-tailed deer fed almost entirely on the acorn crop. They collected in large groups in the oak forests, creating large herds in areas of acorn growth. Osage hunters were aware of these large deer concentrations and hunted the deer extensively. Not only did the deer gather in great herds in the fall, but they also changed their normal reclusive behavior. From September to October, white-tailed deer began their breed-

14. Bruce D. Smith, "Middle Mississippian Exploitation of Animal Populations," 70, 77.

15. Ibid., 82–83.

16. Ibid., 20–22, 41; McDermott, *Tixier's Travels*, 238, 249; Chapman, "Journey to Land of Osages," 213; Featherstonhaugh, *Excursion Through Slave States*, 83; Mary Paul Fitzgerald, *Beacon on the Plains*, 24; Amelia W. Williams and Eugene C. Barker, eds., *The Writings of Sam Houston, 1813–1836*, 1:273; *Arkansas Gazette*, December 9, 1823.

ing season. Like the bison, during this time the normally shy, timid animals became aggressive and belligerent. The names the Osage gave to the months of September, October, and November revealed their knowledge of deer behavior. September was called "Moon When the Deer Hide," October was "Moon When the Deer Rut," and November was "Moon When the Deer Shed their Antlers."[17] Osage observed their environment and took advantage of the seasonal behavior of the animals to secure food for their people.

Completing the harvest of their crops, the Osage packed up once again and left the villages for a second plains hunt. They returned to the short-grass plains in the west, for by late September the buffalo had completed their breeding season. The males no longer remained among the females and were no longer as aggressive and threatening as they were during breeding time. They were fat, and their hides were thick with winter coats.

The late fall hunt on the plains was part of an old pattern for the Osage, but earlier hunts may have taken place in the forest and nearby tall-grass plains. Fall was an excellent time to secure food in the forests and prairies, and the Osage did not have to go back to the plains to secure the necessary food for the winter. Once they acquired horses, it was easy for the Osage to travel back onto the plains to take the buffalo. The buffalo hides were thicker and warmer than those of the deer, and the buffalo provided more meat per animal than the smaller deer. The earliest note of a plains hunt, that of Claude-Charles DuTisné in 1719, mentioned the Osage hunting the buffalo in the winter.[18] Before they acquired the horse, they may have hunted in smaller groups in the edge and the forest, for the prairie edge and the Ozark forest were filled with game.

Depending on the weather, but usually by late December, the Osage had returned from the second plains hunt and moved

17. Smith, "Mississippian Animal Populations," 20–21; LaFlesche, *Dictionary of the Osage*, 298–99, 326; Mathews, *The Osages*, 481, 483, 487.
18. Margry, *Exploration des affluents*, 313.

back onto the prairie near their garden villages. They did not, however, regroup in their large villages. Instead, they broke up into small family groups and erected their winter lodges down off the high prairies among the trees. The winter dispersion was necessary, for forest edges could not support large concentrations of people in the winter. Large groups placed too much pressure on supplies of firewood, and after the Osage acquired the horse neither the tall grass of the nearby prairie nor the forest grasses could provide enough forage to support their large herds of horses. So the Osage remained in small extended family groups throughout the winter.

During the winter the Osage lived off their stored crops, dried buffalo meat, and food secured by hunters. They continued to hunt throughout the winter. In January and February, the Osage hunted the black bear. Although rare in the Ozark forest today, black bear were common in the eighteenth and early nineteenth centuries. The black bear did not truly hibernate, but from November until April they were relatively inactive. Feeding on the fall acorn crop, bears put on weight, their pelts thickened, and after the first snowfall they found dens and spent most of the winter sleeping.[19] After the first snow, the Osage easily located and killed the bears. They enjoyed bear meat, and the oil rendered from their winter fat was a popular feature of the Osage winter diet. Throughout the winter months, the Osage harvested the animals of the forest and tall-grass prairie to feed themselves: turkey, raccoon, rabbit, waterfowl, deer, opossums, squirrels, bear, and other regional animals were all used.

In the later winter months, it became more difficult to acquire enough food. By late February, most of the crops stored in the fall were depleted, the birds had begun leaving the area, and the beaver, now back in their aquatic, nocturnal pattern, were lean from the long winter. White-tailed deer had also lost their winter fat. By the end of the winter, the acorns were gone, and the

19. Smith, "Mississippian Animal Populations," 116–17.

deer no longer concentrated in the oak region and were again shy and difficult to hunt. Rabbits, squirrels, and other small mammals were available, but they, too, were lean by late winter and produced little meat. Although turkey put on weight in the early spring, the fall groups broke up in the spring, and the turkey remained apart until the fall.[20] As soon as the weather warmed enough for the people to begin planting their gardens and enough grass had appeared to feed the Osage horses, the Osage began gathering in their villages to begin the seasonal cycle once again.

In all phases of the pre-European Osage economy—hunting, gathering, and horticulture—the extended family was the basic economic unit. Families lived near one another in the Osage villages and camped together during the communal hunts. Male family members hunted with their clan kin while the women worked in family gardens or at the lodges. While moieties, phratries, clans, and subclans existed, there is no evidence that these groups had any major economic significance, though clans did provide a framework for group sharing. In times of need, these groups shared food with one another, but otherwise they had no economic function. Garden plots were owned by the families working them, and in the winter and spring men hunted with their brothers, uncles, and cousins, not in larger clan groups. During the large-scale communal hunts in the summer and fall, clans did not have specific economic roles, as the meat taken was shared by all participating families.[21]

Osage families were members of larger economic and social classes. Within the villages, families were members of one of two groups, either the relatively small leader group or the larger commoner class. Leader families were those whose members had displayed leadership ability and personal bravery and had maintained enough economic security to validate the position,

20. Ibid., 76–77.
21. Bailey, "Osage Social Organization, 1673–1906," 25–27. There is no evidence that leadership families owned particularly prized garden plots.

while members of families in the commoner class had not yet shown sufficient leadership ability and bravery or did not possess enough wealth to claim higher status. Well-fed and well-clothed families enjoyed status among the Osage. Skilled hunters who provided food for their families and shared with others were respected members of Osage society. Women whose gardens were productive and who were skilled in preparing skins were equally esteemed.

In time, the status given to these families became a part of the traditional Osage social and political framework. The Osage made social and economic class distinctions, and those families that consistently demonstrated superior subsistence skills became the leaders. Their positions became institutionalized and were maintained through hereditary political and religious positions and functions. To assume a high position one had to demonstrate one's economic and social worth. To become a member of the clan leaders, the *Non-hon-zhin-ga,* an Osage and his family had to present evidence of their economic skill. They had to produce a number of specific animal skins that had symbolic ceremonial significance and demonstrate the hunting skill of the initiate. Families also had to gather enough food to entertain the entire village *Non-hon-zhin-ga* during the initiation rite. These demanding prerequisites limited the membership of clan leaders to those families who had already achieved economic success.

Because of the culturally institutionalized sharing among the Osage, all commoners and leaders alike shared in the necessities of life, and thus the economic distinctions were probably meager, yet nonetheless important. An important element in establishing and maintaining social and economic status within the Osage village was through hospitality and giving. Individuals and families who either had status or sought to achieve it gave feasts and distributed gifts to their guests. Giving was an important act among the Osage. It gave status to the giver and showed regard for the recipient. Individuals gave skins, tools, or food to show respect and in turn to garner status. One gave to one's superiors and demonstrated superiority by giving. As there were typically more commoners than leaders, those families at the top received more gifts as more and more gave to fewer and fewer. Those at the top took the best and reconfirmed their place by returning most of the gifts to the people beneath them. This elaborate gift-giving effectively redistributed the village's limited wealth and guaranteed subsistence for all.[22]

The family-based Osage subsistence economy was a successful one. In good years, when the hunts were successful and the gardens productive, the Osage were well fed and warmly clothed. In years when hunters did not produce enough meat or skins, or when weather or insects destroyed the crops, the Osage went hungry and sometimes starved. Yet overall the economy worked for the Osage, and despite the occasional poor years they grew and prospered. Although the Osage eventually became involved in the market economy of the fur trade and became active traders, the essential subsistence economic pattern survived. They continued to plant their crops in the spring and hunt in large groups in the summer and fall. By the late eighteenth century, although they spent more time hunting and raiding and traveling further from their village bases, they still continued to return to them and their fields of corn. The basic pattern of Osage economic life endured.

The early Osage village was an economically autonomous unit, but limited trade with other Native American groups occasionally occurred. Trade usually was conducted in small luxury goods, those items that were not easily obtained by the respective traders. Carried out in the form of gift-giving, the Osage would trade their corn, squash, jerked buffalo meat, buffalo robes, and deerskins for salt from interior tribes, seashells from Gulf Coast tribes, and copper from Great Lakes tribes.[23] This

---

22. Preston Holder, "Fur Trade as Seen from the Indian Point of View," 134–35; idem, *Hoe and the Horse,* 36.
23. Holder, "Fur Trade from Indian Point of View," 130.

intertribal trade was generally limited to those goods that were ornamental or nonessential, for most essential goods were provided by the tribe and distributed through kinship sharing and gift-giving.

The subsistence economy of the Osage was substantially altered by the European invasion of North America. Europeans arrived armed with powerful weapons, amazing new animals, novel metal tools, and new economic conceptualizations. The Osage in time acquired the new weapons, animals, and tools, and in so doing they partially adopted European approaches to resource management and use. For a combination of social, economic, and political reasons, the Osage became active traders with Europeans.[24] As a result of their growing trade, they began to make pronounced alterations in their way of life. Change was not new to the Osage, for their culture had always been an ever-changing system. Still, they had to learn to deal with new environments, new neighbors, and the realities of new times. These changes that came about in the eighteenth century had far-reaching consequences for the Osage and their neighbors.

Living along three major river systems, the Osage were introduced to European goods through the intertribal trade system well before the actual appearance of the Europeans. One of the earliest and perhaps the most important of the European possessions was the horse. It is uncertain when the Osage first acquired the horse, but Henry Tonty reported that the Missouri Indians, close neighbors and friends of the Osage, had horses in 1684, so it is likely they also possessed them by the 1680s.[25]

The horse was an important addition to the Osage economy, but the Osage placed it within a familiar context. They called the horse *ka-wa,* which roughly translated means "mystery

24. Calvin Martin, *Keepers of the Game: Indian-Animal Relationships and the Fur Trade,* 1-21; David Wishart, *The Fur Trade of the American West, 1807-1840: A Geographical Synthesis,* 9-40.
25. Pierre Margry, ed., *Voyages des Français sur les Grands lacs et découverte de l'Ohio et du Mississipi, 1614-1684,* 595.

dog." They used their mystery dog in old, familiar ways that reinforced prehorse patterns.[26] The acquisition of horses improved the quality of Osage lives. Mounted on horses, the Osage could hunt over great distances, taking full advantage of the animal resources of two ecosystems. Osage hunters could pursue deer, bear, and other forest game deep in the Ozark forest along the White and the Saint Francis Rivers. With horses, the entire Osage village could travel to the short-grass plains to kill the buffalo. Horses permitted the Osage to travel quicker and further. Trips that had taken weeks could be completed in days. No longer were the Osage confined to hunt only as far as the weakest members could walk. Mounted hunters could travel out to where the great herds of buffalo congregated. The horse was also ideal for hunting on the treeless plains. It was far easier for mounted hunters than those on foot to kill the buffalo. Using horses, the Osage could chase the buffalo and kill enough for their people; they were no longer required to coordinate the efforts of an entire village for a buffalo hunt. Smaller, mounted hunting groups could take as much as the earlier community hunts. They could kill more, and they could carry back more meat and more hides to their villages.

Although the Osage no longer had to hunt in a single group, they continued to hunt together for many years, for they had hunted together for a very long time. The horses did, however, tend to individualize the buffalo hunt.[27] When the entire community hunted the buffalo in the prehorse times, all shared in both the work and the meat they harvested. The basic egalitarian nature of the hunt changed once the Osage acquired horses. Horses were not evenly distributed among families; without a horse, one could not successfully hunt buffalo and get an equal opportunity to secure buffalo meat. An Osage tradition of sharing continued, and hunters with horses shared their

---

26. Mathews, *The Osages,* 126–28.
27. Richard White, "The Cultural Landscape of the Pawnees," 198.

meat with those who were not fortunate enough to have a horse, but the horse did create other new pressures that challenged older social institutions. With the acquisition of the horse, the Osage prospered.

Another important European introduction to the Osage economy was the firearm. The flintlock musket was brought to North America by the Europeans, and in time it was acquired by the Osage. It is not certain when they first acquired the *wa-ho-ton-the,* or "thing that causes things to cry out," but by 1719 the Osage had several of them.[28] It is probable that they had them earlier, as French traders were dealing with the Osage in the late seventeenth century.

The gun became extremely important to the Osage, both as a means of bringing down game and as a weapon of war. Although effective as a hunting weapon, the gun had several distinct disadvantages. First, firearms were noisy; one blast from a gun would frighten an entire flock of birds, or herd of deer or turkey, and after the first shots the animals would flee. A bow and arrow, however, was silent. Osage hunters could quietly approach a group of animals and attack without creating the loud noise of gunshots which drove the animals away.

Another problem was that loading and firing a muzzleloading flintlock was an awkward process at any time, and on horseback it was even more difficult. Still, the Osage tried to make use of this technological innovation. They sometimes cut off a portion of the barrel to shorten the gun, making it easier to load and shoot from the back of a horse.[29] Yet another problem was

28. LaFlesche, *Dictionary of the Osage,* 192, 275; Mathews, *The Osages,* 130–34.

29. Osage muskets had smooth bores. Rifles had spiral grooves cut into the inside of the bore, which caused the bullet to spin as it left the barrel. The spin made the bullet travel in a straighter path, thus a rifle was more accurate than a musket. See Carl P. Russell, *Firearms, Traps, and Tools of the Mountain Men,* 34–95; James E. Knight, "Basics of Muzzleloading"; Donald Baird, "Some Eighteenth Century Gun Barrels from Osage Village Sites"; T. M. Hamilton, "Some Gun Parts from Eighteenth-Century Osage Sites"; idem, "Concluding Comments and Observations"; idem, "The Gunsmith Cache Discovered at Malta Bend, Missouri."

the fact that the gunpowder used in the eighteenth and nine-teenth centuries was very corrosive. Unless the guns were cleaned after firing, the powder ate into the barrels and en-larged them. Sometimes when the Osage ran out of lead balls for bullets, they poured small rocks down the barrel and used the muskets as crude shotguns.[30] The rocks damaged the bar-rels, and in time the muskets lost any accuracy they might have possessed when new. Guns were noisy, inaccurate, and when used as shotguns, would destroy the skin of an animal. Although the Osage eventually acquired percussion-cap muskets and shortened the barrels of the guns, the bow and arrow remained, until the mid–nineteenth century, an effective and deadly hunt-ing weapon.

Guns, however, were more useful as weapons of war against humans. The Osage could frighten their enemies with the noise and smoke of the guns. Used as shotguns, the muskets were deadly. Firearms killed at a great distance and were particularly effective against those Native Americans who were armed only with bows and arrows and only had leather armor for protec-tion. Fortunately for the Osage, and unfortunately for the tribes west of them, the French and Spanish maintained very different attitudes regarding the distribution of firearms among Native Americans.

The Spanish, intent on subjugating Indians and controlling territory through state-supported political and religious institu-tions, were reluctant to arm any of the native peoples in lands under their nominal control. Spanish colonial policy, directed by the state, worked to maintain peace and security near Span-ish missions and presidios. Consequently, the Spanish consis-tently banned the sale of firearms and ammunition to Native Americans, and until the early nineteenth century those bans were remarkably successful.[31]

30. Hamilton, "Concluding Comments."
31. Frank R. Secoy, *Changing Military Patterns on the Great Plains [17th Cen-tury through early 19th Century]*, 3–5.

The French were more intent on economically exploiting their colonial empire. Because of the relatively few French who were willing or were allowed to come to North America, the French were never able to dominate the native peoples. In order to exploit their colony, they had to rely on the loyalty, friendship, and labor of Indians. Much of the early colonial occupation was under the direction of individuals working for joint-stock companies or individual entrepreneurs eager to establish profitable trade. Native American-French contact was typically trade-oriented. The French were interested in making money in the new world, so they were generally willing to supply their Native American trading partners with guns.

The French were also engaged in fierce competition with Great Britain for control of North America, and since there were relatively few French in the interior, they relied on the loyalty of Indian people living there. In order to secure loyalty and prevent the expansion of British interests, the French used firearms and trade. Firearms, in the hands of friendly trading partners, were not a threat to the French, and were indeed useful, for armed Indians produced more furs and other goods the French traders wanted. The Indians could also keep the British or British-allied tribes out of the way of French designs. The arrangement was also attractive because it insured that the Indians participated in trade. The gun was an attractive item to Native Americans. They wanted guns to hunt and to protect themselves. Although there were accounts of the Osage digging lead for bullets, they could manufacture neither the guns nor the necessary gunpowder. The gun was something they wanted that they could not get anywhere else, so the Osage traded with the French, and the French gained a degree of influence over them.

Since the first traders among the Osage were from the French settlements in Canada, the Osage had early access to firearms. Later, because of their location near the three rivers, the Osage continued to have access to guns and ammunition well into the nineteenth century. Only when European conflicts hampered the Atlantic trade did the Osage suffer a shortage of firearms

and ammunition, and while the Osage never had an abundance
of firearms and ammunition, they usually had an adequate supply. Certainly they consistently had a greater supply than those
tribes living west of them during the eighteenth century.

The Spanish continued to ban the sale of firearms to those
Indians living west of the Osage, and the French rarely traded
that far west. This situation proved extremely advantageous to
the Osage, for as long as the flow of guns was restricted into the
interior, the Osage possessed a vital military, political, and economic advantage over their western neighbors.[32] Combined,
the horse and gun had a tremendous impact on the Osage economy. The seasonal cycle remained much the same, yet with
horses and guns they could easily take more game, which fed
and clothed their people. The Osage worked to acquire the new
European goods, and in so doing they made subtle shifts in their
economic life.

The first Europeans among the Osage were likely viewed as
new traders with novel goods. They were not seen as agents of
European imperialism and a new way of life, yet they were both.
The early trading followed the traditional gift-exchange pattern.
In time, however, with the increased European presence in the
area, trade took on new importance and was conducted in the
European, not the Native American, manner. It is important to
note that when the Osage began trading with the French they
did not abandon one way of life to embrace a new one. They
simply exchanged things they had for things they wanted. They
conducted the transactions along familiar patterns. Metal goods
simply made their lives easier; knives, razors, awls, hoes, and
needles were similar to tools that they already possessed. They
already had stone knives, shell razors, wooden awls, and bone
needles. The utensils were not new, nor were their uses—they
were just made of a marvelous new substance that was hard,
strong, and held an edge. Almost all of the European goods were

32. Ibid.

simply replacements of common Osage items with those of more durable iron. Guns and horses were completely new things, but they too were incorporated into old, familiar patterns. The Osage did eventually experience economic change, but not for a long time. The changes were gradual, and for most of the participants, subtle.[33]

The Osage first began trading for European goods not with Europeans, but with Native Americans who were in direct contact with the French. In the seventeenth century, the Osage traveled to the east to trade with members of the Illinois Confederacy. A Frenchman among the Illinois, DeGannes, described the trade: "The savages of whom I have spoken, and who come to trade among the Illinois, are the Oossages [Osage] and Missourita [Missouri], who not long ago had war with them and who, aside from their need of hatchets, knives and awls and other things are very glad to keep on the good side of this nation."[34]

As the French presence grew in the interior, the Osage began trading directly with Europeans. Most seventeenth-century trade along the Mississippi Valley was illegal trade, carried on by illiterate coureurs de bois operating in the West without licenses. These outlaw traders were either unable or uninterested in recording their activities, so there is little record of the early trade. Only hints of this late seventeenth-century illicit western

33. For further discussion of changes in Native American economies, see David Boeri, *People of the Ice Whale: Eskimos, White Men, and the Whale,* 70–79; Patricia Nelson Limerick, *The Legacy of Conquest: The Unbroken Past of the American West,* 188–90; Cronon, *Changes in the Land,* 82–107; Holder, "Fur Trade from Indian Point of View," 134–35; E. E. Rich, "Trade Habits and Economic Motivation among the Indians of North America."
34. Gilbert J. Garraghan, *Chapters in Frontier History: Research Studies in the Making of the West,* 57–58; Theodore Pease and Raymond C. Werner, eds., *The French Foundations, 1680–1693,* 389. The DeGannes memoir on the Illinois country is also known as the Desliettes memoir. Although dated October 20, 1721, Garraghan argues convincingly that it was written much earlier, for the memoir describes the Kaskaskia Indians living on the Illinois. Since the Kaskaskia left the Illinois River in 1700, Garraghan and the author are convinced that the memoir was written sometime before 1700.

trade survives. French accounts are usually terse and include little more than brief mentions of Frenchmen visiting river tribes with little description or explanation. Despite the paucity of such records we do know, however, that the French were trading with the Osage and their neighbors. In 1680, two French traders were taken to a Missouri Indian village, and in 1693, two French coureurs de bois visited the Osage to establish friendly relations.[35]

In 1686, Henry Tonty, on one of his exploring and trading expeditions, established a legal trading post at the mouth of the Arkansas River. Catholic missionaries from Quebec established a mission among the Illinois Indians near the mouth of the Missouri River in the spring of 1699, and the next year French Jesuits constructed another mission nearby. These two active French missions, located on the periphery of Osage territory, served as trading centers for the French and Indians of the region. At about the same time French priests were building missions along the middle Mississippi, other French colonists were establishing settlements near the mouth of the Mississippi River. Soon there was a great deal of European activity along the valley as French soldiers, priests, and traders traveled back and forth from the Canadian trading posts to the Gulf Coast settlements. From the outposts along the Mississippi Valley, the French sent out traders and soldiers to acquire information, trade, and potential allies. Following the great western rivers that drained into the Mississippi Basin, French traders went west to meet and trade with the Indian people living there. As early as 1704, Jean Baptiste Le Moyne, sieur de Bienville, governor of French Louisiana, reported that there were 110 traders in bands of seven and eight trading along the Mississippi and Missouri Rivers.[36]

---

35. Garraghan, *Chapters in Frontier History*, 57; Thwaites, ed., *Ottawa, Lower Canada*, 159, 168–69.

36. Margry, *Exploration des affluents*, 180. Sometime in the early eighteenth century, one band of the Osage, the *Iu-dse-ta* (Down Below People), left the Osage River and moved northeast to the Missouri River and lived near the Missouri Indians. Although the reasons for moving will probably remain unknown

The French king, eager to save money and reluctant to invest in the expensive enterprise of French North America, leased French Louisiana to a series of French investment companies. In 1717, the Company of the West, later known as the Company of the Indies, under the direction of John Law, acquired possession of Louisiana.[37] Law, convinced that large investments were necessary to properly develop the colony, created still another company, the Mississippi Company, to secure the necessary capital. He sold shares in the new company and used the money to expand the French presence in Louisiana. To promote settlement in Louisiana, Law's Mississippi Company constructed military outposts in the region and sent groups of settlers into the interior to establish farming communities. Law also dispatched agents of the company out into the west in hopes of opening trade not only with the Indians but also with the Spanish colonies in northern Mexico. In 1719, the company sent agent Claude-Charles DuTisné into the interior to meet with the Osage and Wichita in hopes of establishing trade with them and with the plains tribes living west of the Wichita. That same year, Jean-Baptiste Bénard, sieur de la Harpe, another company agent, went up the Red River and set up a trading post among the Caddo and visited the Wichita living along the Canadian River.

The company had sent Pierre Duqué, sieur de Boisbriant to Kaskaskia in 1718 to direct the company's activities in the central valley, and he began construction of a fort on the east bank of the Mississippi between the Cahokia and Kaskaskia missions. This outpost, Fort de Chartres, was completed in 1720 and served as center for further French expansion. Law's Mississippi Company collapsed in 1720, but the Company of the Indies, under new direction, continued its program of colonial

---

since it occurred at such an early date, some scholars believe the *Iu-dse-ta,* or Little Osage as they were called by the newcomers, moved north to gain access to traders ascending the Missouri River. See Bailey, "Osage Social Organization, 1673–1906," 33–34; Mathews, *The Osages,* 253–54.

37. Nancy M. Miller Surrey, *The Commerce of Louisiana during the French Régime, 1699–1763,* 159–61.

expansion. In the fall of 1723, the Company of the Indies sent an experienced French soldier, Etienne Véniard, sieur de Bourgmont, up the Missouri to trade with the Indians living in the west and to make peace with them. Bourgmont went up the Missouri River and established a fort and trading post. Located on the left bank of the Missouri River near the mouth of the Grand River, Bourgmont's post, known as Fort Orleans, was located directly across the river from the villages of the Missouri and Little Osage. For six years, while Fort Orleans was occupied, there was an active French trading post a mile away from the Little Osage villages and less than one hundred miles from the Big Osage villages on the Osage River. Although Fort Orleans was abandoned in 1729, a few years later the French established another trading post, Fort Cavagnolle, at the mouth of the Kansas River, once again not far from the Osage villages.[38]

The Osage were enthusiastic traders with the French. In addition to guns and the necessary accessories—flints, gunpowder, and lead balls—the Osage desired other European-manufactured goods. Anything made from metal was considered valuable, and textile goods, such as brightly colored Limbourg cloth, woolen stroud, ribbons, and blankets were desired by the Osage. They also wanted glass beads, metal bells, mirrors, brooches, rings, bracelets, and vermilion and other paints. The popularity of European goods is clearly evident in the remains found in Osage villages and camp sites. In the state of Missouri, which was the center of Osage activity in the eighteenth century, many of the major village sites have been excavated. In all but one, European-manufactured artifacts clearly outnumbered native ones.[39]

38. Clarence Walworth Alvord, *The Illinois Country, 1673–1818,* 153; Villiers, *Découverte du Missouri,* 79–124; Henri Folmer, "Etienne Veniard de Bourgmond in the Missouri Country"; Ed C. Hill, "Has the Site of Fort Orleans Been Discovered?"; Gilbert J. Garraghan, "Fort Orleans of the Missoury"; M. F. Stipes, "Fort Orleans, The First French Post on the Missouri"; Bourgmont to Directors of the Company of the Indies, January 2, 1724, Archives des Colonies, C13A, C4, fols. 117–25; Nasatir, *Before Lewis and Clark,* 1:28, 42, 48, 50, 52.
39. Surrey, *Commerce of Louisiana,* 357; Chapman, *Origin of the Osage,* 97;

In return for European trade goods, the Osage supplied the French with a variety of their products. The Osage, with access to horses and mules, were willing to trade them to the French. As early as 1714, François Le Maire reported that the French at Mobile possessed horses that voyageurs had acquired from the Osage along the Missouri and Arkansas Rivers.[40] In the fall of 1719, Claude-Charles DuTisné visited the Osage and acquired horses.

When DuTisné visited the Osage, he encountered a Mento chief from a village southwest of the Wichitas. The Mento were a tribe living along the Arkansas Valley and were probably members of the Wichita group. DuTisné noted in his account that he had conducted business with the Mento at Natchitoches earlier. The Mento trader promised to bring horses to the French posts in Illinois in the following spring. The presence of the Mento in the Osage village and the chief's promise to DuTisné is evidence of an active exchange system between the Osage and Caddoan-speaking tribes to the west. It is unfortunate that more is not known about this Indian trader and the nature of his business, but it is clear that the Osage were participating in a European–Native American trade network.[41]

The Illinois livestock trade was active, but records are scarce. Horses were sold in Illinois for about one hundred *livres.* However, in 1738, when horses were needed for a war with the Chickasaw, the French paid two hundred *livres* a horse. Prices decreased as one went west and approached horse country, for although DuTisné complained about the price, he paid only

---

Carl H. Chapman and Eleanor F. Chapman, *Indians and Archaeology of Missouri,* 104. Osage-manufactured goods would have been created out of organic material, such as bone and wood, which would not survive as well as the European goods of more durable iron and pottery. Little of the organic material has survived, and it is significant that in every excavated site, save one, European goods clearly outnumber the Osage-manufactured ones.

40. Marcel Giraud, *The Reign of Louis XIV, 1698–1715,* 283.

41. Margry, *Exploration des affluents,* 310–15; Anna Lewis, "Du Tisné's Expedition into Oklahoma, 1719"; Wedel, "Claude-Charles DuTisné," 162.

about thirty-three *livres* each for the horses and mules he bought in 1719.[42]

Perhaps more important trade items supplied by the Osage were the skins and fur of native animals. It is difficult to ascertain exactly how much they specifically provided, for eighteenth-century records from the far west are scarce. Those that exist often list only the area or the outpost from which the furs were derived, and specific tribes are seldom mentioned. It is certain, however, that the Osage, already fur trappers and deer and buffalo hunters, were important participants in the French fur business.

Unfortunately for the Osage, the beaver skins, which were small, easily transported, and usually demanded a good price, were not a large part of their trade. Long, cold winters were necessary for beaver to produce thick, dark-colored pelts. Winters on the Ozark Plateau were cold, but not as cold or as sustained as those in the north. Hence, the beaver skins of Osage country were never as good as those from the north. While the Osage continued to produce some beaver skins, they never were the most important trade items. Similarly, some buffalo hides were traded by Osage, but a large-scale business never developed, for buffalo hides were large and bulky, and the Osage secured them out on the plains. Despite their price, usually four *livres* a pound, they were too difficult to transport for any major trade.[43]

The principal fur the Osage became actively involved in trading was deer. There was an abundance of white-tailed deer in the area between the Missouri and Arkansas Rivers, and the skins were relatively small, thus easily packed and transported. Deerskins that included additional skin of the head and tail were

42. Surrey, *Commerce of Louisiana,* 282, 301–2. Eighteenth-century French Louisiana money was based on the *livre tournois.* There were twelve *sols* in the *livre* and twenty *deniers* in the *sol.* According to William J. Eccles, the *livre* had the buying power of about ten 1981 Canadian dollars, so a *livre* was approximately $8.30 U.S., a *sol* was approximately seventy cents, and the *denier* was worth about three and a half cents. See *The Canadian Frontier, 1534–1760,* xviii.
43. Eccles, *Canadian Frontier,* 346.

worth about twenty-five *sols* each if large, twenty *sols* if medium-sized, and fifteen *sols* if small. Deerskins without heads and tails were worth five *sols* less according to their size and condition. Prices were low, but deer were plentiful and easily taken. Twenty medium pelts with heads and tails would usually secure an Osage a musket, and one medium pelt with head and tail would buy a powder horn full of powder or two pounds of bullets.[44]

Prices also varied according to European markets and domestic competition. The Osage, situated along the Missouri system, were visited by both French and English traders. Because of the competition between the French and English, the Osage got better prices for their furs and paid less for trade goods. Since both the English and French sought Osage loyalty, they bought all the skins the Osage brought to trade, even those they did not want, in order to maintain their friendship.[45]

During the first half of the eighteenth century, the French alone exported hundreds of thousands of deerskins. In one month in 1734, 12,000 skins were shipped to France, and by 1744 over 100,000 deerskins were exported from Louisiana. The Osage were active participants in the deerskin trade, and in 1757 they provided eighty bales of deer and bearskins to the French in Illinois.[46] The Osage also traded the furs of wolves, raccoons, foxes, wildcats, weasels, and muskrats. In addition to animal furs and skins, the Osage were involved in trading other animal products. They sent tallow, bear oil, and dried buffalo meat to the French, who used the tallow for candles, bear oil for cooking, and buffalo meat for eating. Dried buffalo tongue was a particularly popular item among the French. The French also bargained for Osage corn, beans, and squash.[47]

44. Ibid., 253, 279, 346.
45. Ibid., 340; William J. Eccles, "The Fur Trade and Eighteenth-Century Imperialism," 342, 344, 346.
46. Surrey, *Commerce of Louisiana*, 350–51, 357–58; "French Report on the Western Front," *Journal of the Illinois State Historical Society* 34 (December 1941): 589; Marie George Windell, ed., "The Missouri Reader: The French in the Valley," 85.
47. Surrey, *Commerce of Louisiana*, 262; Henri Folmer, "French Expansion

The French presence in Osage country began the alteration of their economy. The Osage wanted European-manufactured products that made their lives easier and more comfortable. The French, eager to acquire Osage furs, encouraged the trade. The subsistence-scale hunting and farming of the Osage, however, could not secure enough items to trade with the French. Therefore, they began to abandon mere subsistence and became commercial hunters to secure the valuable goods.

The change from subsistence to market economy was gradual and never completed. The Osage retained much of their subsistence pattern for years. They easily adapted their economic patterns to meet the European-inspired demands. They continued to plant their crops in the spring and spend their summers and falls hunting on the plains. They spent more time on the seasonal hunts and brought back more game, but there was little alteration in the early eighteenth century. While French guns allowed Osage hunters to take more game and eat better, French knives and awls made it easier to prepare the furs and skins, and metal hoes permitted the Osage women to prepare their gardens with less toil, there was little fundamental change. A visitor to an Osage village in the early eighteenth century would have noted woolen blankets, metal pots and pans, and perhaps a better-fed people, but until more Europeans invaded Osage country, the Osage economy remained relatively stable.

Toward New Mexico in the Eighteenth Century," 146; Bourgmont to Directors of the Company of the Indies, January 2, 1794, Archives des Colonies, C13A, C4, fols. 117–25.

4.

OSAGE DIPLOMACY

When I reached the Osages, I was well received at my arrival. I explained to them your plans [for trade] which they accepted very well as far as it concerns them; but when I mentioned to them that I wanted to go to the Pani [Wichita], they were all opposed to it. . . . When I understood that they would not allow me to take my merchandise there, I asked them to let me go there with only three muskets.

—Claude-Charles DuTisné, 1719[1]

No one knows when the Osage first came to live along the prairies; their journey is cloaked in symbolism and metaphor, and as such, there is no way to date their arrival. Osage accounts of their arrival are complex and rich in detail. Although the region is filled with the remains of early cultural complexes, no one has yet been able to link the earlier Mississippian or the Oneota cultures with that of the Osage.[2] Presently, the precise date of Osage occupation of the region remains a mystery, but

1. "Lorsque j'ay esté rendu chez les Osages, où j'ay esté très bien reçu en arrivant. Leur ayant expliqué vos intentions, ils ont fort bien respondu en ce qui les regardoit; mais lorsque je leur parlay d'aller chez les Panis, ils s'y sont tous opposes. . . . Ayant connu qu'ils ne prétendoient point que j'y portasse les effets que j'avois, je leur proposay de m'y laisser aller seulement avec trois fusils" (Margry, *Exploration des affluents,* 313).
2. Henning, "Development of Oneota Culture," 146–48; James Warren Springer and Stanley R. Witkowski, "Siouan Historical Linguistics and Oneota Archaeology."

Mun-ne-pus-kee (He Who Is Not Afraid), *Ko-a-tunk-a* (Big Crow), and *Nah-com-ee-she* (Man of the Bed). These three Osage men guided the dragoon expedition of 1834. Painted by George Catlin. National Museum of American Art, Smithsonian Institution. Gift of Mrs. Joseph Harrison, Jr.

evidence suggests that the Osage were living south of the Missouri and west of the Mississippi in the general region of the Osage River in 1673. In that year, Jesuit priest Jacques Marquette recorded their presence on his primitive map of the area. This was the earliest written account of the Osage. After Marquette's map, there were scattered references from other late seventeenth-century travelers who noted the Osage presence along the Osage River.

The Osage claim that they came to the prairies from the east. This claim, couched in mythical language, provides some clues as to their origins. Their oral traditions, shared with the other Dhegian-Siouan speaking groups—the Kansa, Omaha, Ponca, and Quapaw—suggest that the Osage and the other groups were members of a single large group of Dhegian speakers living east of the Mississippi River. One version of the migration account relates that a powerful group of Indians drove the Dhegians from their homeland. Another version suggests that they left to find game. Whether they were pushed or pulled, the Dhegian group traveled west. When they reached the Mississippi River, most of them went upriver while some of them, later known as the Arkansa or Quapaw, went downstream. The upstream people moved up the Mississippi and then up the Missouri River. As they made their way up the Missouri, bands broke away and established separate tribal identities. The people who would become the Osage left the group near the mouth of the river that would bear their name. The Kansa stayed around the mouth of the Kansas River, and the Omaha and Ponca continued on up the river where they eventually made their homes.[3] While these Dhegian migration stories may differ in specific details, it is clear that the Quapaw, Osage, Kansa, Omaha, and Ponca all share the

---

3. Dorsey, "Migration of Siouan Tribes"; Fletcher and LaFlesche, *Omaha Tribe*, 1:33–41; Hyde, *Indians of the Woodlands*, 60–66, 152–75; Chapman, *Origin of the Osage*, 221–83; William E. Unrau, *The Kansa Indians: A History of the Wind People, 1673–1873*, 3–24; W. David Baird, *The Quapaw Indians: A History of the Downstream People*, 2–20; William A. Hunter, "History of the Ohio Valley," 590.

migration story. They also share the same language, common clan names, and other cultural traditions. Although the exact nature of the migration remains unknown, the pattern of a large group being either pushed from their homelands or lured to new regions is both reasonable and logical.

Elements of the oral tradition provide clues to early Osage relations with other Native American groups. Some argue that the Iroquois Confederacy's attacks from the northeast drove the Osage down the Ohio River and across the Mississippi. The Iroquois did drive the Illinois across the river in the 1650s, and some early French accounts report that Iroquois attacks had driven the Osage and Quapaw from the Ohio Valley.[4]

The early connection of the Osage with the Kansa and Quapaw helps explain their later peaceful relations, and at the same time, the early seventeenth-century migrations verify the violent relationships the Osage had with the Caddoan speakers living to the south and west of them. The ancestors of the Wichita and other Caddoan groups lived at one time in eastern Kansas near the prairie lands of the Osage. The Osage's intrusion into the prairies was resented and probably resisted. From the eighteenth century on, the Osage battled the Pawnee and the Wichita. Their seventeenth-century invasion may have only been the first round in a long struggle for control of the south-central prairie-plains.

Accounts contained in Dhegian traditions are consistent with later diplomatic patterns of the Osage. They sometimes moved to new regions to exploit new resources, and when confronted by powerful groups, they moved away from the threat and onto the territory of weaker neighboring tribes. It is not certain that the Osage were driven west by the Iroquois, but it is clear that once they were living on the prairies in the seventeenth century, Iroquois raids affected them. The Iroquois drove the Illinois across the Mississippi in the 1650s, and the presence of the Illi-

---

4. Hyde, *Indians of the Woodlands*, 60–66, 152–75.

nois groups in Osage territory increased the competition for game and conflict between those two groups. The Illinois repeatedly attacked the Osage villages in the late seventeenth century.[5]

Later, Iroquois pressure against other nearby tribes also provoked attacks on the Osage and their neighbors, the Kansa and Missouri. The Iroquois-inspired attacks were largely motivated by the presence of French, Dutch, and English living far from the Osage. Miami, Fox, Ottawa, Potawatomi, and others raided the Osage villages, killing men and capturing women and children. Even the Quapaw, living south of the Ozark Plateau near the mouth of the Arkansas River, were the victims of such attacks. The Osage, Quapaw, Kansa, and Missouri fought the raiders and tried to establish peace with their nearest neighbors, the Illinois. They had limited success with the Illinois and little with the more distant tribes. The raids continued.

The Osage tried to avoid the attacks by moving away from the threat. They may have been living along the lower courses of the Missouri River when the first attacks began, and they probably went up the Osage River to escape them. In moving west, however, they intruded into the territory used by the Wichita and other Caddo groups who were living in the prairie-plains.

The west was attractive to the Osage, for it not only offered escape from the hammering attacks of the eastern tribes, but it also offered economic opportunity. Just as they were pushed indirectly by the European presence in the east, they were pulled indirectly by Europeans living in the west. The Spanish settlements along the northern Rio Grande Valley lured the Osage west. The Spanish had traveled onto the plains and had had contact with the Wichita groups. Plains hunters engaged in trade with the Pueblo Indians before the Spanish arrived, exchanging buffalo meat and furs for the corn, beans, squash, and melons of

5. Clifton, *Prairie People*, 728; Raymond E. Hauser, "The Illinois Indian Tribe: From Autonomy and Self-Sufficiency to Dependency and Depopulation," 128, 134; J. Joseph Bauxar, "History of the Illinois Area," 594.

the Pueblos.[6] The Spanish presence among the Pueblos provided new items to the already existing trade network, and an important element in the Spanish plains trade was the horse.

The Spanish brought horses into the Rio Grande Valley, but despite their efforts to keep the horses from Indian people, the Indians acquired them: horses sometimes ran away, and Indians stole them. After the Pueblo victory over the Spanish in 1680, more horses became available to plains people. With the Spanish return to the area in the 1690s, they no longer tried to keep horses from Native Americans, and the horse trade grew.

The Osage had horses at least by the 1690s. Trader Henry Tonty, among the southern Caddo tribes in the spring of 1690, commented that "horses are very common among them" and that the Osage were raiding the tribes along the Red River. Thus, the Osage, already drawn to the west by the great buffalo herds, were also attracted by the availability of horses. Although the horse was a new animal to the Osage, the people quickly adopted it into their lives, but in a familiar context, using the animal as a dog.[7] They tied a travois on its back and used it to carry baggage, continuing their seasonal movements on the backs of Spanish horses. In time, of course, the Osage would change because of the horse, but the changes were gradual and slow.

The presence of horses posed new challenges to the old social order because horses became a new source of wealth, a source of wealth that was outside the older Osage resources framework. Prior to the presence of horses, almost all elements for survival were equally abundant and available to all Osage. Although horses were available to all Osage in theory, there were fewer of them and thus fewer opportunities for obtaining this important new asset. Capturing this large animal alive also demanded dif-

6. Waldo R. Wedel, *Prehistoric Man on the Great Plains,* 103, 107; Charles H. Lange, "Relations of the Southwest with the Plains and Great Basin."

7. Louise Phelps Kellogg, ed., *Early Narratives of the Northwest, 1634–1699,* 317; Mathews, *The Osages,* 126–28.

ferent skills than killing other game. These new factors had an effect on the social framework. The Osage had created a social order that provided status for those who demonstrated great expertise in military operations, hunting, and farming. The presence of horses created new opportunities for status and prestige that had to be incorporated into the old system. Despite the increased number of horses, their presence became a divisive element within Osage society.

Horses also affected Osage relations with tribes living west of them. The Osage could only acquire horses in the west. They had to capture wild ones or trade for them with the western tribes who lived near the Spanish. If they were unable to capture or trade for them, the Osage stole the horses. Osage trade with the western tribes was limited, because the Osage possessed little the western tribes wanted. The Wichita, Pawnee, and Caddo were farmers, so Osage agricultural goods were not important as trade items. The plains people lived close to the buffalo herds and had no need for buffalo meat or buffalo robes. The Osage could offer forest game, but there was little demand for it, so they had to round up wild horses or steal them. Stealing and capturing horses caused problems with the western tribes. The Wichita, Pawnee, and Caddo resented the Osage hunting for horses in territory they believed belonged to them. It is likely the Osage traded for horses when they could, captured wild ones when they could do it without a fight, and stole them when they could get away with it.

Once the French arrived in the area, however, the Osage acquired French trade goods which they took west to trade for horses. French traders operating from Canadian bases first came into Osage country in the seventeenth century. Their presence provided new economic opportunity for the Osage. In 1680, the Osage and Quapaw traveled together up the Illinois River to trade with Robert Cavelier, sieur de la Salle and his party. Father Louis Hennepin, a member of La Salle's group, wrote that "several savages of the Nations of the Osages, Cikaga, and Akansa came to see us, and brought fine furs to barter for our axes."[8]

Other Frenchmen visited the region and traded with the Osage. In 1683, La Salle wrote that two Frenchmen were among the Missouri Indian tribes, and Jesuit priest Jacques Gravier wrote that in 1693 two French traders had gone up the Missouri River to establish trade relations with the Osage. The traders hoped to tap the wealth of New Mexico and establish a link between the French settlements in Louisiana and the Spanish in New Mexico.[9] In 1703, Pierre Le Moyne, sieur d'Iberville wrote, "Twenty Canadians left Tamaroas [Cahokia] to discover New Mexico to exchange dollars [piastres] and see the mines the Indians have spoken about."[10] Many Frenchmen in the early eighteenth century moved into Osage country. Iberville's brother, Jean Baptiste Le Moyne, sieur de Bienville, reported that in 1704 there were at least 110 Canadians along the Missouri and Mississippi in groups of seven and eight.[11]

French penetration into the region was prompted by a combination of religious, economic, and political factors. Bringing Christianity to the native peoples was an important concern for French missionaries. Although by the late seventeenth century the earlier religious missionary fervor was gone, missionaries continued to travel west to bring the word of their God to the Indian people.[12] Economic reasons also prompted French entry into the region. French traders sought new supplies of beaver pelts and other valuable resources. Searching for new sources

8. Louis Hennepin, *Father Louis Hennepin's Description of Louisiana: Newly Discovered to The Southwest of New France by Order of the King*, 82; idem, *A New Discovery of a Vast Country in America*, 177.

9. Thwaites, *Ottawa, Lower Canada*, 159, 168–69; Nasatir, *Before Lewis and Clark*, 1:7.

10. "Vingt Canadiens sont partis des Tamaroas descouvrir le Nouveau Mexique, pour y commercer des piastres et voir ce que sont les mines dont les Sauvages leur ont parlé" (Margry, *Exploration des affluents*, 180).

11. Ibid.

12. Eccles, "Fur Trade," 345.

of wealth and access to the Spanish colony of New Mexico led the French up the Missouri.

The third element of French expansion was political. The French sought control of North America not only to exploit it economically, but also to deny its wealth and strategic location to their European rivals. French soldiers went into the interior to claim territory for the French crown. Realistically, the French could never claim real sovereignty from the Indian inhabitants, but by establishing alliances with those who possessed real sovereignty, the Indian people, they could exert some influence in the area. The French were particularly interested in preventing the English from profiting from the region, and they established peaceful relations with the native inhabitants to exclude the English.[13]

Never numerically strong in North America, the French were forced to move carefully and skillfully into the interior. Unwilling and unable to conquer the Indians, they had to enlist Native American goodwill or at least nonbelligerent cooperation. The French had to use Indian trappers to secure the valuable skins; simply put, there were too few Frenchmen and too many Indians in North America for the French to do otherwise. Because of their goals, the French had to compromise more than any of the other European powers in North America.

Because of these realities, the French never posed a direct threat to the Osage. The French did not want to force change on the Osage, nor did they want to take away their land, enslave them, or confine them to a mission farm. Only French missionaries made great demands on the Osage, and those demands were easily ignored. Most of the French, however, were content to let Indians remain Indians, albeit French Indians. Indeed, rather than force French culture and values on Native Americans, French traders adopted Indian values and culture. Typically, the French employed low-status Frenchmen as their trader

13. Ibid., 344–45, 349–50.

agents. These individuals had little to lose by adopting Indian culture, and as the suppliers of trade goods they enjoyed a higher status among Native Americans.[14]

It is likely that for the first years of the French arrival in the region, their impact was minor. For much of the seventeenth century, the only Frenchmen among them were the outlaw coureur de bois traders who had limited amounts of trade goods. The Osage region, although it contained beaver, never produced the high quality of beaver skins that were found in the north, so the Osage beaver never competed successfully against the Canadian beaver. This had a dampening effect on the trade potential for the Osage. In 1695, when the French fur market was glutted, the French tried to stop western expansion.[15] They closed off the western areas and halted all trade for beaver skins in the west. In the last years of the century, there was little market for the nonpremium Osage furs.

At the turn of the century, Louis XIV decided to reverse earlier policy, and instead of stopping the westward movement he proposed that the French extend their presence in North America. Concerned about the growing power and influence of the English in North America, the French sought to deny the English access to the interior by establishing a series of outposts linking the Great Lakes with the Gulf of Mexico. The French established a post at Detroit in 1701, and French missionaries who had already established missions among the Mississippi tribes were encouraged in their endeavors. In May 1699, priests from the Seminary of Quebec established the Mission of the Holy Family of Tamaroas, later known as Cahokia, on the east bank of the Mississippi just south and opposite the mouth of the Missouri River. That same year, Pierre Le Moyne, sieur d'Iberville tentatively established a French outpost near the mouth of the Mississippi. In the fall of 1700, Jesuit priest Gabriel Marest

14. Secoy, *Changing Military Patterns*, 7–8; Holder, "Fur Trade from Indian Point of View."

15. Eccles, "Fur Trade," 341; idem, *Canadian Frontier*, 124–25.

and a group of Kaskaskia Indians founded a mission on the west bank of the Mississippi, across from Cahokia. They remained there only until the spring of 1703, when they recrossed the Mississippi, moved south, and established a new settlement at the mouth of the Kaskaskia River.[16]

Despite this new expansion, the impact of these new French posts was limited, for at about the time they were being established, France went to war with England. For the next thirteen years, the War of the Spanish Succession limited French advances into the interior of North America, and while France fought the war there were few resources to spare for new colonial enterprises. French shipping on the Atlantic was attacked by the British navy. The western posts languished, and the Gulf Coast settlements struggled just to survive.[17]

During the war years, the missions established among the Mississippi River Valley tribes exerted little influence on the Indians. The Illinois missions at Kaskaskia and Cahokia served as bases for French traders who, despite the war, continued to venture west. The Osage, eager to acquire French goods, not only welcomed traders to their villages, but they also traveled to the Illinois missions to acquire French trade goods.[18]

The Osage wanted durable metal tools and utensils. They acquired French trade goods for their usefulness, and they also used them as trading commodities with the western tribes. The Osage, who possessed little the Wichita or Caddo wanted, could take the attractive French goods west and trade them for horses. Located between the French and the western groups, the Osage acted as middlemen. It therefore became important for the Osage

16. Eccles, "Fur Trade," 341–45, 349; Garraghan, *Chapters in Frontier History,* 60, 78–84.

17. Giraud, *Reign of Louis XIV,* 141–67, 223–45.

18. DeGannes wrote: "The savages of whom I have spoken, and who come to trade among the Illinois, are the Oossages [Osage] and Missourita [Missouri], who not long ago had war with them and who, aside from their need of hatchets, knives and awls and other things are very glad to keep on the good side of this nation" (Garraghan, *Chapters in Frontier History,* 58).

to prevent French traders from passing them and going directly to the western peoples, for if the French established direct trade with the Wichita, the Pawnee, or the Caddo, the Osage would lose their important economic advantage.

An Osage trade monopoly was not difficult to maintain in the seventeenth and early eighteenth centuries because there were few Frenchmen in the area, and with the exception of political alliances and livestock, there was little that the French desired in the west. There were few beaver there, and buffalo meat and hides were large and bulky and not valuable enough to warrant all the trouble involved in transporting them to market. Clearly the political goals of the French remained important, but until the war was over French interests were focused elsewhere; there was little political or economic incentive for the French to push beyond the Osage onto the prairie-plains.

With the end of the war in 1713, however, the French launched a revitalized effort to go west. Once the war was over, Louis XIV and his advisors revived their plans for North America. Intending to hem the English in along the Atlantic coast, the French began to renew old alliances neglected during the war and establish new ones among the western tribes. The easiest way to establish such alliances was through trade. French agents were dispatched to the interior tribes to enlist their aid in keeping out the British. The economic aspect of the Indian trade was important, but after 1700, and increasingly so after 1713, there was a strong political element involved in the French fur trade with the Indians. Trade engendered friendly relations with the Indians, and out of the commercial ties came friendship, loyalty, and military support. The French had enjoyed some success, limited only by the paucity of French trade goods. In 1712, when Fox Indians attacked the French at Detroit, Osage warriors along with other Missouri River tribes came to the aid of the French, asking for ammunition and volunteering to fight the Fox. One of the Osage *Xthe-ts'a-ge Wa-ton-ga* told the French, "We have come from a distance, and are destitute of everything; we hope you will give us powder and balls to fight with you."[19] The Osage were willing to fight alongside the French, especially if the French provided guns and ammunition and if the Osage could strike back at Indian groups that were already threats to their well-being. The Osage were thus more than willing to attack the Fox, who frequently raided the Osage.

Guns and ammunition made up the most important part of French trade with the Osage, for the Osage had only limited need for other French goods such as metal tools and woolens and other textiles; metal tools lasted for a long time, and they still used animal furs and skins for clothing. Weapons, however, were becoming crucial to the Osage. Flintlocks were useful hunting tools, but more importantly the Osage could defend themselves from enemy attacks with guns. As more Frenchmen came into the Illinois and Mississippi Valleys, they provided more arms and ammunition, which increased the violence and the demand for guns. The Osage became involved in this eighteenth-century arms race, and it became imperative for the Osage to acquire state-of-the-art weaponry.

Armed with French muskets, the Osage could defend themselves from raids by other European-armed Indians. They could also kill more game to feed and clothe their people. More importantly, they could keep the Illinois, Miami, Potawatomi, Ottawa, and Fox raiders at bay. The French, more concerned with denying land and influence to the British than seizing them from the Osage, were willing to provide both guns and ammunition to their Indian allies.[20] After all, a friendly, loyal Osage nation could help the French keep the British out of the Mississippi Valley.

In order for the Osage to acquire guns and ammunition, they had to go west to secure goods that the French wanted. Fortunately for the Osage, the political concerns of the French compelled them to pay for furs and skins that did not market very

---

19. Reuben Gold Thwaites, ed., *The French Regime in Wisconsin, 1634–1727,* 273.
20. Secoy, *Changing Military Patterns,* 7–8; Eccles, "Fur Trade," 341–45.

well in Europe. Despite the weak European demand for deer, bear, raccoon, muskrat, opossum, and small mammal skins, the French continued to take them. The Osage also traded agricultural commodities with the French. The French colonists needed food, so Osage corn, beans, bison tongues, dried meats, and bear oil were important. The French were also interested in horses and mules for their outposts. The Osage traded horses to them, and in 1714 the French Gulf colony was using horses acquired from the Osage.[21]

Another important trade item among the Osage and French was Indian slaves. Indian slaves, a marketable commodity, were taken by the Osage and traded to the French throughout the French occupation. The slave trade was conducted in a manner that was somewhat familiar to the Osage. Capturing women and children from rival tribes had long been a part of Osage wars. Captives were either killed or adopted into the Osage tribe. With the new interest in trade, the Osage continued to take captives, but rather than killing or adopting them, they traded them to the French and sometimes the English.

French explorer and entrepreneur Robert Cavelier, sieur de la Salle suggested that the French buy the enslaved Indians, return them to their native homes, and sell them back to their people. This, he argued, would establish good relations between the French and Native Americans and could possibly be profitable. Unfortunately, the results were quite different, for in offering to buy Indian slaves, the French created a new market for slaves and encouraged new Indian warfare and taking of slaves. French traffic in slaves created new alliances, but it also created increased animosity between Native Americans and the French.

At about the same time the French began participating in Indian slave trade, British traders in the Carolinas began pur-

21. Daniel H. Usner, Jr., "The Frontier Exchange Economy of the Lower Mississippi Valley in the Eighteenth Century," 180–86; Giraud, *Reign of Louis XIV,* 283.

chasing slaves from their Indian allies. The British wanted slaves, and they were keen to spread British influence in the interior. British agents were circulating among the western tribes. During the War of the Spanish Succession, because of the weakened economy in the Illinois country and Louisiana, French traders traveled to Charleston and began trading slaves to the English. English traders and newly aligned French traders traveled up the western rivers seeking trade, friendship, and slaves for the English market. The British needed laborers, and they were willing to use the slave trade to disrupt French alliances with Indian tribes. Chickasaw raiders attacked the Choctaw and other Indians allied with the French and carried off captives to sell to the English. As a result of the two competing European nations, intertribal wars were soon conducted solely to take captives that the winning tribe traded to either the British or the French.[22]

Traffic in Indian slavery was more than an element of French–Native American foreign policy, for slaves filled an important economic need in French Louisiana. The new French colony needed workers, and Indian slaves provided the needed labor. Indian slaves, however, were never an adequate supply of labor. The Native American slaves were troublesome to their European masters, for they frequently ran away. Various colonial officials in 1706, 1707, 1708, and 1714 proposed that the French exchange their Louisiana Indian slaves for black African slaves from the French West Indies colonies. The Indians, away from their homes and familiar country, could not run away on the islands, it was argued, and blacks sent to Louisiana would not run away for fear of being killed by hostile Indians.[23] Despite a

---

22. Verner W. Crane, *The Southern Frontier, 1670–1732*, 66, 111; Giraud, *Reign of Louis XIV*, 81–82; Verner W. Crane, "The Tennessee River as the Road to Carolina: The Beginnings of Exploration and Trade"; Almon Wheeler Lauber, *Indian Slavery in Colonial Times Within the Present Limits of the United States*, 26–33, 63–102; John P. Reid, *A Better Kind of Hatchet: Law, Trade, and Diplomacy in the Cherokee Nation during the Early Years of European Contact*, 27–30; Elizabeth A. H. John, *Storms Brewed in Other Men's Worlds: The Confrontation of Indians, Spanish, and French in the Southwest, 1540–1795*, 383.

23. Surrey, *Commerce of Louisiana*, 227–28.

brief experiment in 1708, when a French West Indies' trader bought several Indian slaves for the islands, the exchange proposal was never officially sanctioned.

In spite of the failure of the Louisiana–West Indies exchange, the Indian slave trade survived in Louisiana even into the period of Spanish occupation. When the Company of the Indies began promoting and developing the Louisiana colony, it sent over colonists to clear large agricultural plantations that required increasing amounts of farm labor. In 1720, the Company of the Indies complained that French traders on the Missouri and Arkansas Rivers were inciting Indian wars simply to provide slaves for trading. Indian slaves were never considered a safe investment to the company, for so many ran away. In 1726, only 229 such slaves were recorded in French Louisiana. Thus in the 1720s, the Company of the Indies began importing black slaves to supply colonial labor demands not being met by Indian sources. During French control of Louisiana (up to 1769), about six thousand black slaves were imported into the colony.[24]

Politics, economics, and warfare all pushed the Osage west. To obtain horses the Osage had to go west; to kill buffalo they had to journey west; to acquire slaves it was easiest to take captives in the west.

The Wichita, Pawnee, Plains Apache, and southern plains Caddoans had few guns, and the Osage, taking advantage of their own arms superiority, stole their horses, captured their women and children, and hunted for horses and buffalo in their territory. If the French were able to meet the western tribes directly and arm them, the Osage would not have been able to continue their trade. The Osage would have confronted strong, well-armed rivals competing for the same resources. If, however, the Osage were able to keep French traders and French guns from their western rivals, the Osage would maintain an

24. Margry, *Exploration des affluents,* 316; Wedel, "Claude-Charles DuTisné," 161–63; Surrey, *Commerce of Louisiana,* 232.

arms superiority and successfully hunt and raid on the prairie-plains.

Early eighteenth-century French records are replete with accounts of traders ascending the Missouri River, seeking silver mines, Indian furs, and a path to the Southern Sea. These Europeans visited with the Osage and exchanged their goods for Osage furs, food, and information. Louisianan self-sufficiency required tremendous investments of capital, labor, and talent, which in the early eighteenth century the French monarchy was both unwilling and unable to provide. In 1712, the entire colony was leased to Antoine Crozat, a wealthy Frenchman and financial counselor to Louis XIV. Crozat formed an investment company to develop and exploit Louisiana. Crozat's Company of Louisiana, although granted a fifteen-year charter, gave up its control of the colony in only five years. The colony had been very expensive, difficult to administer, and not profitable. In August 1717, Crozat returned the colony to the Crown.[25]

Louisiana then came under the control of the Mississippi Company, a part of the large Company of the West, directed by Scottish financier John Law.[26] Until the company collapsed, it spent large amounts of money to develop Louisiana. The company planned to exploit the mineral wealth of the area and sent agents west to find mineral deposits. The company also wanted to open trade with the Spanish colonies and exchange New Mexican silver for French-manufactured goods. Indians were an important element in the company's plans, for despite the quality of the southern furs and skins, the animal pelts remained a profitable item. Great plantations were to be established to provide foodstuffs for the French Caribbean Islands, and Indian slaves were purchased to work on them. Horses and mules were also required for the development of the colony, and the French were able to acquire them from Native Americans.

25. Giraud, *Reign of Louis XIV,* 249–56, 290–302.
26. Surrey, *Commerce of Louisiana,* 159–68.

Two agents of the Mississippi Company met with the Osage in the fall of 1719. Claude-Charles DuTisné, an experienced soldier, was sent west to meet with the Wichita and Plains Apache, two tribes who lived in the interior between Louisiana and New Mexico. DuTisné was ordered to secure peace with these Native Americans and establish regular trade with them. Out of the peace and trade, the French intended eventually to establish trade with the Spanish in New Mexico.

DuTisné ascended the Missouri River in the spring of 1719 and met with the Missouri Indians. Although he made no mention of visiting an Osage village, he did note that there was a village of the Osage near the Missouri. This was the village of a band of Osage known as the Little Osage. To the Osage they were the *Iu-dse-ta* (Down Below People), a band that had left the main body of the Osage some years before to hunt in the north and gain greater access to traders along the Missouri.[27]

Evidence of this greater access to trade is shown in the Missouri's treatment of DuTisné. He was well received, yet the Missouri refused to allow him to go beyond them.[28] The Missouri did not want their rivals armed, and despite DuTisné's threats to stop French trade with them, they refused to let him pass. Obviously, threats to withhold trade were not taken seriously by the river dwellers. Living along the Missouri River, they had ample trade, and they ignored DuTisné's economic scare tactics.

After failing in the north, DuTisné returned to the Illinois settlements, and later in the fall he set out again to go to the Wichita and Plains Apache. He traveled overland, and sometime in August he arrived at an Osage village located near the forks of the Osage River. DuTisné was well received by the Osage. He

27. Mathews, *The Osages*, 253–54; Margry, *Exploration des affluents*, 310.

28. "The Missouri are jealous that the French go to the homes of other nations. . . . " (Les Missourys sont jaloux que les François aillent chez les autres nations. . . . [Margry, *Exploration des affluents*, 310]); Wedel, "Claude-Charles DuTisné," 6.

was probably greeted by the *Tsi-zhu Ga-hi-ge,* who would have welcomed and entertained him. Although they had been trading with the French for several years, the Osage obviously desired the additional trade that DuTisné proposed. The Osage, however, also did not want him to go on to the Wichita, and they refused to allow him to continue his journey. DuTisné threatened to cut off all trade to the Osage if they refused him passage. Apparently this threat had more impact among the Osage than the Missouri, for he was allowed to go. The Osage, however, refused to let him take any trade guns. They allowed him to take one extra gun, so DuTisné and his interpreter went to the Wichita with only three muskets. The Osage were eager to expand trade with the French, but they too did not want their western rivals armed.[29]

Forced to allow DuTisné to pass, the Osage sent a messenger ahead to the Wichita to tell them that DuTisné was a slave trader who wanted to capture and enslave them. This ruse, an attempt by the Osage to prevent DuTisné from dealing with their western neighbors, failed, but the story was apparently plausible enough for the Wichita to believe. When DuTisné arrived in the Wichita village, they threatened to kill him. He finally was able to convince them that he was not on a slave-capturing mission. The association in 1719 of Frenchmen and slave-taking was strong enough for the Osage to suggest it and for the Wichita to believe it. DuTisné later revealed that at one time he had been involved in the Indian slave trade with a Mento slave trader he met at the Osage village.[30]

DuTisné eventually acquired horses from the Wichita and

29. Although there is no record of DuTisné's threat, it may have been much like Nicolas Perrot's threat to the Ottawa thirty years before, when he wanted to stop them from leaving on a raid. He reminded them that they had used earthen pots, stone hatchets, and stone knives before, and he added, "you will be obliged to use them again if Onontio abandons you" (Thwaites, *French Regime,* 159); Margry, *Exploration des affluents,* 309–15.

30. Margry, *Exploration des affluents,* 314–15; Wedel, "Claude-Charles DuTisné," 161–63.

gave them his three guns. The Wichita, however, prevented him from going on to the Plains Apache, so he returned east back through the Osage villages. There he traded for more horses and acquired some deerskins and buffalo robes. DuTisné asked for an Osage to guide him back to the Illinois settlements, but the Osage, obviously aware that he had given the Wichita his guns, refused, and DuTisné was forced to make his own way back.

The Osage could have easily killed DuTisné or robbed him, yet they did not. They allowed him to continue his journey while secretly sabotaging it. The Osage were unwilling to confront this French representative directly, but at the same time they were willing to act covertly to disrupt his trip. The Osage in 1719 wanted to continue their trade with the French and were reluctant to alienate their French trading partners, afraid that they might stop trade altogether.

The Osage fear of interrupted trade was confirmed by Jean-Baptiste Bénard, sieur de la Harpe's experiences with the Osage that same fall. La Harpe, an agent for the Mississippi Company, was going up the Red River to establish peace and trade with the Wichita. He had gone with Nassoni Indian guides, and somewhere between the Red River and the Canadian River La Harpe and the Nassoni encountered a party of twenty Osage hunters. The Nassoni, a Caddoan tribe of the Kadohadacho group living near the Big Bend of the Red River, knew of the Osage and were afraid of them. The Osage greeted La Harpe and threatened to kill the Nassoni. La Harpe gave the Osage presents and finally convinced them to allow his party to go unmolested.[31] In both DuTisné's and La Harpe's encounters, the Osage were peaceful and willing to trade with the Europeans, but they were uneasy about the French presence among the Wichita and Caddo. The Osage wanted trade, but they did not want the French to trade

31. Margry, *Exploration des affluents,* 284–85; Wedel, "J.-B. Bénard, Sieur de la Harpe"; Ralph A. Smith, ed. and trans., "Account of the Journey of Bénard de la Harpe: Discovery Made by Him of Several Nations Situated in the West," 371.

with neighboring western tribes. In 1719, their trade connections were not strong enough, and they could not afford to anger the French. Therefore DuTisné was allowed to go to the Wichita, and La Harpe and his guides were not harmed. This all would change when more traders came into the region.

The Mississippi Company provided an expanded market for the Osage. The colony needed livestock and labor, and the Osage wanted guns and trade goods; thus an economic relationship developed. The Osage, armed by the French, raided in the west. They captured Wichita and Caddoan peoples and sold them to the French. They stole horses from the western tribes and brought them to Illinois. Furs, deerskins, bear oil, buffalo meat, and tallow were collected by the Osage and sold to the French.[32]

In 1720, Law's Mississippi Company collapsed, but the Company of the Indies, with new directors, survived and continued to administer Louisiana. Investments in Louisiana declined drastically with the collapse, and most Louisiana projects were abandoned as the Company of the Indies concentrated on the few that were profitable. That same year, an expedition of Spanish soldiers and Indians from New Mexico crossed the plains, investigating rumors of French traders in the region. This expedition, led by Lieutenant General Don Pedro de Villasur, made it as far as Nebraska, where it was destroyed by the Pawnee. Villasur's expedition convinced the French to protect their borders.[33]

In 1723, the Company of the West dispatched Etienne Véniard, sieur de Bourgmont and forty men to the Missouri River to construct a trading post and fort. The fort would defend Louisiana from the Spanish, and the trading post would service Indian allies and provide enough profits to offset the cost of the fort. After constructing his post, Bourgmont went west to meet the plains Indians, particularly the Plains Apache, and make peace

32. Surrey, *Commerce of Louisiana*, 157, 173, 257–62.
33. A. B. Thomas, "The Massacre of the Villasur Expedition at the Forks of the Platte River, August 12, 1720."

with them. The French wanted a plains Indian alliance that could defend Louisiana in wartime and eventually provide in times of peace a safe passage to New Mexico, where it was hoped the Spanish would establish trade ties with the French.

Bourgmont constructed Fort Orleans on the north bank of the Missouri River near the mouth of the Grand River across from the Missouri and Little Osage villages. With the company trading post near the Little Osage and less than one hundred miles from the Big Osage, both Osage groups increased their trade with the French. The proximity of the trading post stimulated the Osage economy, for it was closer and more convenient than the post at Fort de Chartres in Illinois. Despite their enthusiasm for Fort Orleans, the Osage did not support Bourgmont's plains peace movement. The Osage did not relish French commerce with their western neighbors, but there was little they could do to stop it. Any attack on Fort Orleans or Bourgmont's party would have brought an immediate end to trade and would provoke revenge attacks by French-armed Indian allies. The Osage consented to Bourgmont's treaties among the Missouri and Kansa but did not participate in the plains' treaties with the Plains Apache, Pawnee, and others. After starting out with Bourgmont, they soon returned to their villages before meeting with the western plains tribes.[34]

Although the Osage could not prevent the French from crossing the central plains, they could stop them in the south, where small groups went into the west seeking trade with the Wichita. The Osage were involved in serious struggles with the Wichita on the Arkansas River for control of prairie hunting grounds. The Osage, who had better access to French trade, were even-

34. Bourgmont to Directors of the Company of the Indies, January 2, 1794, Archives des Colonies, C13A, C4, fols. 117-25; ibid., C13A, A8, fols. 210-19; Frank Norall, *Bourgmont, Explorer of the Missouri, 1698-1725*, 42, 47, 133; Folmer, "Etienne Veniard de Bourgmond"; Garraghan, "Fort Orleans of the Missoury"; Stipes, "Fort Orleans, The First French Post"; Villiers, *Découverte du Missouri*, 41-69; Margry, *Exploration des affluents*, 389-448; Hill, "Has Fort Orleans Been Discovered?"; Folmer, "French Expansion," 100-199.

tually able to drive the Wichita from the Arkansas Valley. Because their success depended on their arms superiority, the Osage established a blockade on the Arkansas River and stopped hunters and traders from going to the Wichita.

The French had had a trading post near the mouth of the Arkansas River. Established initially in the late seventeenth century by Henry Tonty, the Arkansas Post was later abandoned. Law's Mississippi Company had attempted to revive it and had sent forty families there, but with the collapse of the company in 1720, most of the French departed. The revived Company of the West concentrated their efforts in the north, and the Arkansas returned to isolation.[35]

Small trading and hunting parties continued to ascend the Arkansas, but they were stopped by the Osage. In 1720, the Osage stopped a group of Frenchmen on their way to the Mento. In May 1733, the Osage were accused of attacking two pirogues carrying French traders on the Arkansas and burning eleven Frenchmen.[36] The Osage, however, went down to the Arkansas Post after that attack and claimed "that they had no thought of killing Frenchmen, and that they would submit to all satisfaction required of them."[37] Later it was discovered that the Osage had not killed and burned eleven Frenchmen but only killed one unlicensed trader and his slave. In September 1737, the Osage were once again accused of attacking Frenchmen on the Arkansas River, but in the spring they went *en calumet* (in peace) to the Arkansas Post to make amends and reestablish peace.[38]

Any peace in the Arkansas Valley would be short-lived if the French attempted to reach the Wichita. In July 1740, the commandant at Kaskaskia, Benoit de Saint Clair, wrote, "I learned from an Illinois who arrived the fifteenth of this month that the

35. John, *Storms Brewed,* 218.
36. Wedel, "J.-B. Bénard, Sieur de la Harpe," 55; Margry, *Exploration des affluents,* 303; Dunbar Rowland and A. G. Sanders, eds., comps., and trans., *Mississippi Provincial Archives, French Dominion, 1701–1743,* 3:221.
37. Nasatir, *Before Lewis and Clark,* 1:25–26.
38. Ibid., 25–27.

Osages had killed some Frenchmen of the Arkansas district and that they had brought the head of one to their villages."[39] In September 1741, the governor of Louisiana sent a party of fifteen Frenchmen to New Mexico. Led by Fabry de la Bruyère, the expedition was to establish a regular trade convoy with Spanish New Mexico. Bruyère was further ordered to find the Osage who had been attacking Spanish settlements and to convince them to stop their raids. Osage raids were a threat to any French-Spanish peace and to the proposed convoys.[40]

Bruyère went up the Arkansas to the mouth of the Canadian River and ascended it until the water became too shallow to float his pirogues. He remained on the banks of the Canadian waiting for the river to rise so he could complete his journey to New Mexico. As Bruyère waited, a party of thirty-five Osage warriors appeared. The Osage, on their way to attack the Mento in the south, asked for guns and ammunition and told Bruyère that there were six French traders back in their villages. Bruyère refused to give them guns, but he did provide them with some powder, balls, and knives. The Osage promised to return and bring Mento slaves to trade with the French.

Bruyère, fearing the Osage's return, constructed a wooden breastwork. Only seventeen Osage warriors returned, but they did bring seven horses and a mule. Suspicious of Bruyère's fortifications, the Osage became convinced that Bruyère and his men were on their way to arm the Wichita and Padouca.[41] Bruyère tried to convince the Osage that they were on their way to the

39. St. Clair to Salmon, July 28, 1740, Archives des Colonies, C13A, 26, fols. 190–91.

40. *Extrait des lettres du sieur Fabry, à l'occasion du voyage projeté à Santa-Fé,* ibid., F24, fols. 377–86, 392–406; Margry, *Exploration des affluents,* 468–70.

41. "S'imaginant qu'il cherchoit les Panis et les Padokas pour faire alliance avec eux et leur traiter des fusils" (Archives des Colonies, C13A, F24, fol. 394); Margry, *Exploration des affluents,* 475. There is a great deal of confusion and controversy concerning the identity of the Padouca. It seems clear to this author that prior to 1750 the Padouca were Plains Apache. See Frank R. Secoy, "The Identity of the 'Paduca': An Ethnohistorical Analysis"; and George E. Hyde, *The Pawnee Indians,* 350–53.

Spanish, but the Osage were not entirely convinced and refused to trade any of their horses to the stranded French. They told Bruyère they could not spare them and that the French could not reach the Spanish by way of the Canadian because it was too shallow upstream to use canoes. The Osage received some additional ammunition from the French and left for their villages. Bruyère was fortunate that he had fourteen armed men and that he had constructed the breastwork, for otherwise the Osage, discovering the French in Wichita-Osage country, would have attacked and robbed them.

This uneasy standoff on the Canadian River is symbolic of French-Osage relations. The Osage certainly wanted guns and ammunition, and just as certainly they did not want the French to trade with their Indian competitors. Both powers, the French and Osage, operated from strength. South of the Ozark Plateau along the Arkansas Valley, there were few Frenchmen. There were also no strong Indian tribes to challenge the Osage. The Quapaw were too small to be a threat, and the Caddo bands were too small and poorly armed to challenge the Osage. The Osage, a large nation without serious Indian rivals in the area, controlled the lower Arkansas Valley. They robbed and killed French traders attempting to reach their rivals.

But in the north, where the French presence was more pronounced and where large, well-armed Indian tribes were allied with the French, the Osage could not exert as much control. French soldiers and traders at Fort Orleans, Fort Cavanough, and the Illinois settlements of Kaskaskia and Fort de Chartres, and more importantly their Illinois, Iowa, Miami, Ottawa, and Potawatomi allies, forced the Osage to avoid violence and confrontation and make amends to the French when the young Osage men attacked. The Osage did not welcome the French trade and arming of the Pawnee, but there was little they could do to stop it short of attacking the French. An attack on the Missouri or Mississippi of the scale necessary to stop the French would have been foolhardy. The Osage did not want to fight the French or their allies; they did not want to lose their access to firearms and trade. Thus, the Osage cooperated with the French on the Missouri and in the Illinois districts.

The conditions were exemplified by the circumstances surrounding several murders in 1749. The Little Osage killed a Frenchman and his slave, and the French demanded the guilty ones. Reported Pierre Jacques de Jonquiere: "The said Sieur Benoit [commander at Kaskaskia] informs me also that the person called Giguiere and his slave were killed on the Des Moines River by a party of the Little Osages, but that he has had the guilty man killed by his own tribe and that Sieur de Portneuf has sent him his scalp."[42]

The Little Osage, living near the French and their Indian allies, found it expedient to acquiesce to French demands. This was not the case with the Big Osage living on the upper Osage River, away from the French settlements. The Big Osage attacked the French on the Arkansas and got away with it. The only tribe in the south that could pose a real threat to the Osage in the eighteenth century were the Chickasaw, and they were at war with the French for much of the time and would never fight the Osage for the French. Without Frenchmen and Indian allies in the south, the French were forced to accept Osage autonomy there. Pierre Jacques de Taffarel, Marquis de la Jonquiere described the situation succinctly in 1751 in a letter: "The Grand Ossages who are as haughty as the petits Ossages are submissive. . . ."[43] The Little Osage had to submit to the French, for they lived near the trading posts and forts where the French and their allies were strong. The Big Osage, when near the French or confronted with their power, reluctantly submitted to them, but in the interior away from the posts the Osage ruled the prairies.

The French were acutely aware of the situation. Outnumbered by Native Americans and fearful of Spanish and British influence, the French were forced to accept the occasional rob-

42. Pease and Jenison, *Illinois on the Eve*, 240–41.
43. Ibid., 357–58.

bery or killing; they could do little else but accept them. Louisiana Governor Pierre Vaudreuil revealed the French position in a letter written in August 1749. Two French coureurs de bois had been killed by the Osage. The Osage had gone to Kaskaskia and apologized for the killing. Vaudreuil advised,

> As it is not best to increase the number of our enemies for slight causes, and on the other hand, if the case would seem to require it, we should not be in a position to make war, especially on the Osages, who are more than two hundred leagues from our establishment in the vicinity of the Spaniards, I wrote Sieur Benoît to profit by the good disposition of both of those tribes [Osage and Iowa], assuring them that I would forget the past, but I would like very much to take them again into our friendship.[44]

The Osage and the French maintained their control where they could and compromised where they could not. The Osage reluctantly accepted French influence on the Missouri and Mississippi and exerted their influence in the interior.

The Osage had first come to the prairies in the late sixteenth century. Driven there from the eastern forests, the Osage settled along the forest edge seeking a secure life for their people. Security was short-lived, for the European presence caused great changes in Native American affairs. Driven by economic and political ambitions of their own and spurred on by European designs, American Indians expanded and seized territory from other tribes. In the eighteenth century the Osage became victims of attacks by tribes living north and east of them.

In order to resist the attacks of eastern tribes, the Osage sought powerful European firearms from French traders. To secure the weapons the Osage had to provide furs, skins, horses, and food to trade with the French. They secured furs and food from the forests and nearby prairies, but horses could only be acquired in the west. The Osage took manufactured European goods to the

---

44. Nasatir, *Before Lewis and Clark,* 1:43.

west and traded with the Wichita and Caddo groups for horses and mules.

After the War of the Spanish Succession, with the increased economic and political interest of the French in the west, more French traders came into the area. The increased presence of the French contributed to increased violence, and the Osage became active traders. By the late 1720s, trade alone with the western tribes was insufficient to meet growing Osage demands, so the Osage abandoned trade and began raiding the western villages for horses, furs, and captives to exchange with the French.

By the 1730s, the Osage had established a fairly consistent pattern. They worked to maintain peace in the east, for the eastern tribes were better armed and allied with the French. It was essential that the Osage maintain trade with the French in order to acquire the necessary weapons. While they worked for peace and trade in the east, they fought in the west. The Osage sought furs, slaves, and livestock in the west to obtain guns and ammunition to protect their homes, and those same guns allowed them to go to the prairie-plains to raid the Wichita, Pawnee, and Caddo for captives and horses. This pattern of war in the west and peace in the east allowed the Osage not only to survive, but also, in time, to prosper.

5.

OSAGE HEGEMONY

The Osages, living on the river of the same name, which empties into the Missuris [sic], have from time immemorial been hostile to the Indians of this jurisdiction; but on account of the immeasurable distance which intervenes between their establishments and that of the Comanchez, Taouaiazes, Yscanis, Tuacanas, Tancaoüeys, and Quitseys, they formerly inflicted on these tribes only slight injuries or damages. . . . But that river of the Akansa having become infested by the concourse of malefactors of which I have spoken, they soon came to know the Osages, and incited them with powder, balls, fusils, and other munitions. . . . Thus, all at once this district has become a pitiful theater of outrageous robberies and bloody encounters.

—Athanase de Mézières, 1770[1]

While the French remained along the Mississippi Valley, the Osage continued to provide military service, horses, furs, deerskins, food, and slaves in exchange for guns, ammunition, and other manufactured goods. The French presence prompted Osage expansion, and to insure their continued expansion in the 1750s the Osage maintained their peaceful ties with northeastern tribes. The Illinois were a particularly important tribe to the Osage, both politically and economically. The Osage did not want another hostile tribe on their eastern border, and French

1. Bolton, *Athanase de Mézières*, 1:167.

guns came from the east through the Illinois country. The Osage could not afford to have the trade disrupted, so they worked for peace. The French frequently noted the close ties between the Illinois and the Osage. At one time the Illinois, fearing an attack by the Piankashaw, planned to send their families to the Osage for safety.[2] The Osage protected their avenues of trade and maintained their friendships with the Illinois and any of the other eastern tribes they could, and this quality became a hallmark of their diplomacy during their period of greatest expansion.

While maintaining peace in the east, the Osage continued their aggressive activity in the west. They had begun raiding in the 1730s in the region just west of them, and by the 1740s the entire prairie-plains between the Arkansas and the Red Rivers was dominated by them. The large Wichita villages that la Harpe had visited in 1720 were no longer along the Canadian River. The six thousand people who had been there to meet with la Harpe were gone, driven away by the Osage. Only a few Wichita remained in the area, and they lived in heavily fortified villages surrounded by large earthen walls. The Wichita wanted trade and welcomed any French traders that could make it past the Osage. As late as 1749, however, the Wichita were still poorly armed, for the Osage blockade of the Arkansas was largely successful. Wichita conditions temporarily improved somewhat after 1747, for about that time they established an alliance with the Comanche.[3]

2. Pease and Jenison, *Illinois on the Eve,* 687. The Illinois tribe was made up of several groups. The Peoria, Kaskaskia, Tamaroa, Coiracoentanon, Chinko, Cahokia, Chepoussa, Moingwena, Tapouaro, Espeminikia, Michigamea, and Michibousa made up the tribe after 1673. Other tribes such as the Miami, which included the subtribes Wea and Piankashaw, once belonged to the Illinois but left the tribe by 1673. The French sometimes made the tribal distinctions among the Illinois when they discussed them, and other times they merely called them all Illinois. The author will distinguish between the various groups when possible, but when unable to will use the term Illinois to refer to all those tribes mentioned except the Miami, Wea, and Piankashaw. See Hauser, "The Illinois Indian Tribe," 127–38.
3. Mildred Mott Wedel, "The Deer Creek Site, Oklahoma: A Wichita Village sometimes called Ferdinandina, An Ethnohistorian's View," 168, 172; Elizabeth

The Comanche were newcomers to the southern plains. They had entered the central-southern plains fringes around 1700, and as they pushed south, they fought most of the central and southern plains inhabitants. They also raided the Pueblo and Spanish in New Mexico. The western raids were so troublesome that in 1746 the Spanish in New Mexico refused to allow the Comanche to come to their settlements to trade.[4] Denied access to New Mexico trade, the Comanche sought trade with the French. Some French traders avoided the Osage blockade on the Arkansas and came up the Red River to the Wichita villages located there. The Comanche made peace with the Wichita in 1747 in order to trade horses and mules with the French for guns, powder, and shot. At about the same time, they made peace with the Pawnee in the north. The Pawnee had better access to French guns than the Wichita, for the Osage were unable to stop French traders from going up the Missouri and out along the Platte and Republican Rivers. Armed and allied, the Comanche, Pawnee, and Wichita began to challenge Osage expansion on the short-grass plains in the early 1750s.

Armed with French muskets, the Comanche and Wichita launched a series of attacks on the Osage in the summer of 1751. They surprised the Osage during their summer hunt and killed twenty-two prominent Osage. Soon after the attack, a group of Osage visited their Illinois allies and asked them to help fight the Comanche and the Wichita. The Osage also visited the French at Fort de Chartres and asked them for help against the plains tribes. The French refused and reminded the Osage they had killed twenty-seven of their attackers, and that since they had been attacking the Wichita for so long it was understandable the Wichita had finally sought revenge. Instead of helping, the French suggested that if the Osage wanted to fight, they

Ann Harper, "The Taovayas Indians in Frontier Trade and Diplomacy, 1719–1768," 271; Charles W. Hackett, ed., *Pichardo's Treaties on the Limits of Louisiana and Texas,* 3:303–8.

4. John, *Storms Brewed,* 316–17.

should go fight the Chickasaw.[5] Although Chickasaw hunters occasionally intruded into the Ozarks, in 1751 they were not an important enough threat to the Osage to warrant joining a French attack on them, so the Osage returned to their prairie villages.

In 1752, the Osage returned to the plains for their summer hunt, and once again the Comanche and Wichita attacked them. Although the Osage lost twenty, they killed thirty Wichita and Comanche. After the hunt, the Osage returned to the French and Illinois and asked for help. The Illinois, under pressure from tribes east of them, were still unable to assist the Osage, and the French were still unwilling to offer little more than a few guns, some ammunition, and promises of help in the future.[6]

Despite the attacks of the Comanche and Wichita in the summers of 1751 and 1752, the Osage pressed their expansion. If the Comanche and Wichita summer attacks had continued, the Osage would have faced a dangerous challenge in the west, but the Comanche-Wichita threat faded with the outbreak of the Seven Years' War in 1754. British attacks on French shipping severely limited the amount of supplies that made it to the French posts in the west. Once the war began, fewer and fewer French traders went onto the plains.[7] The Comanche, Wichita, and Pawnee were unable to replenish their supplies of arms and ammunition, and without French weapons, they no longer posed a serious problem to the Osage.

The Osage also suffered from the economic slowdown brought about by the war. They, however, lived closer to the French outposts than the western tribes. Any trade goods that made it to the French trading posts were taken by nearby tribes. There was little available during the war, but because the Osage got what there was, very little made it out west. The Osage also had covert ties with British traders who provided additional sup-

---

5. Pease and Jenison, *Illinois on the Eve*, 357–58.
6. Ibid., 678.
7. Wedel, "Deer Creek Site," 173; John, *Storms Brewed,* 338.

plies for them. So while Comanche and Wichita raiders ran out of ammunition, the Osage used their slight arms advantage to pound any Comanche, Wichita, or Pawnee who ventured into the area between the Smoky Hill and the Red Rivers. The Comanche, living in small kin-group bands, were constantly on the move, so they escaped most of the Osage attacks. The Wichita, who lived in their large villages, were easy to find. Their fortified villages were filled with horses, mules, and potential Osage slaves, so they became magnets for Osage attackers. The Osage raids were so blistering that by 1757 the Wichita abandoned their last remaining village on the Arkansas and fled south to the Red River.[8] By 1758, the Osage thoroughly dominated the prairie-plains between the Red and Arkansas Rivers.

Not content with their domination in the west, the Osage sought control elsewhere. In August 1751, the French accused the Osage of attacking the Caddo and Quapaw near the Arkansas Post. The attacks on the Caddo were just another episode in the ongoing conflict between the invading Osage and opposing Caddo. The attack on the Quapaw, however, was unusual, and apparently not very serious, for within a year a group of Quapaw went with the Osage to attack the Wichita.[9]

The attack on the Quapaw was probably the work of overly aggressive and protective young warriors. Certainly if the Quapaw ventured into Osage hunting country without Osage consent or, more seriously, were discovered with Frenchmen on their way to the Wichita, they would indeed have been attacked. Still, sporadic, unexplainable attacks occurred among the Osage and their allies. In December 1751, a group of Missouri Indians killed an Osage they found alone with some horses. The Missouri quickly made amends with the Osage and sent presents to the family of the deceased. According to traditional Osage ways,

8. John, *Storms Brewed,* 338; Wedel, "Deer Creek Site," 174; Mildred Mott Wedel, "The Wichita Indians in the Arkansas River Basin."
9. Pease and Jenison, *Illinois on the Eve,* 313–14, 656.

payment was a legitimate way to atone for murder, and the long standing Missouri-Osage alliance remained intact.[10]

The Down Below People, the Osage northern band more commonly known as the Little Osage, had moved to the Missouri River around 1700 to take advantage of French trade. They were not content to remain along the Missouri, however, and in the late 1740s they moved north of the Missouri River along the Grand and Chariton Rivers. By 1749, they were hunting as far north as the Des Moines River. As they moved north they confronted northern tribes and fought with them in the 1740s and 1750s. The Little Osage continued to protect and expand their northern frontier. In 1751, they were secure enough to establish their winter lodges north of the Missouri River.[11]

Despite the shortages of the war, the Osage had expanded their territorial control. With the end of the war, however, the French left the region. Defeated by the British, the French left North America, leaving Canada and French Louisiana to the British. They ceded Louisiana to the Spanish as compensation for Spain's losses in the war. The Osage regretted the departure of the French after the Seven Years' War, and they made their displeasure known when a group of them went to Fort de Chartres to meet the British:

> It is well that the English do not come here, for we shall always aid our brothers in preserving their lands; besides we know only the Frenchmen for our father. Never have we heard our ancestors speak of another nation. They have always told us that it was the French who gave us life and supplied our needs. They advised us never to loose [sic] their hand. . . . Why do you, Englishman, not remain on your lands, while the red nations remain on theirs. These belong to us. We inherit them from our ancestors. They found them by dint of wandering. . . . Leave, depart, depart, depart, and tell your chief that all the red men do not want any

10. LaFlesche, "Rite of the Chiefs," 67–68.
11. Pease and Jenison, *Illinois on the Eve*, 241, 443.

English here. Pay good attention to what we tell you. . . . Leave
and do not come back anymore. We only want to have the French
among us.[12]

Despite the Osage leaders' rhetoric, there were few immediate changes for the Osage. The French commander at Saint
Louis, Captain Louis St. Ange de Bellerive, remained in charge
until the spring of 1770.[13] Governor Antonio de Ulloa instructed
the first Spanish commander to the Spanish Illinois (French
Louisiana), Don Francisco Ríu, that he should distribute Spanish
medals to loyal tribes and emphasize that little change had taken
place, "in order that they might understand that no innovation is
being made in anything."[14] Despite Ulloa's orders, there were
to be policy changes. Unlike the French, Spanish colonial policy
in North America was closely supervised by the state. Economic
exploitation was important to Spanish Louisiana, but it was not
directed by private investment companies. Indian trade was
supervised by colonial officials and conducted within the Spanish mercantile framework. Indians and their resources were to
be exploited by the Spanish and not by the British or the Americans. Legal trade was restricted to Spanish subjects, and traders
were licensed and assigned to specific tribes.

Spain licensed her traders and expected them to behave according to colonial and imperial law. The free French traders
were to be replaced by licensed Spanish traders. While many of
the new trade policies of Spanish Louisiana were ignored by
independent traders, in time these new policies did affect the
Osage economy. In December 1769, the Spanish governor of
Louisiana, Alejandro O'Reilly, issued several proclamations
that had some impact. O'Reilly outlawed the trade in Indian
slaves. Licensed traders could no longer deal in slaves, and all
Indians enslaved were to be released. Further, licensed traders

---

12. Clarence Walworth Alvord and Clarence E. Carter, eds., *The Critical
Period, 1763–1765,* 480.
13. William E. Foley, *A History of Missouri: Volume I, 1673 to 1820,* 20–23.
14. John C. Ewers, "Symbols of Chiefly Authority in Spanish Louisiana," 273.

were forbidden to trade for livestock with Native Americans, for now that Louisiana was the possession of Spain, any livestock acquired in Spanish Louisiana probably had been stolen from Spanish New Mexico and Texas. The Spanish also imposed restrictions on the trade in firearms with Native Americans. The firearms trade, although not halted entirely, was reduced to prevent wars. Indians were allowed only enough firearms and ammunition to hunt, not to wage war.[15]

Osage and Spanish goals were not compatible. The Spanish wanted peace, stability, and prosperity for the Spanish, while the Osage wanted peace, stability, and prosperity for the Osage. This trade ban, although beneficial for the Spanish, was harmful to the Osage. The Osage had been trading livestock and slaves for over sixty years. Although slaves made up only a small portion of their trade, the trade in horses and mules was a large portion of their trading economy. Without trade, the Osage could not secure weapons to defend their villages and hunting territory. Stability for the Spanish was a political and economic catastrophe for the Osage.

Accordingly, the Osage ignored the Spanish restrictions and refused to obey any external controls on their economy. The Osage were able to disregard the Spanish trade restrictions because of their large population, strategic location, and the size of their trade. Living near the British frontier and major western rivers, the Osage could trade with French traders operating out of British Canada or with British traders operating out of the Illinois country or the Ohio Valley. Eighteenth-century Osage trade was always lucrative enough to lure traders to their villages.

British traders operating out of Canada were eager to trade with the Osage to gain their furs, skins, and tallow. British traders from the Carolinas had been operating in the area for years.

---

15. Elizabeth Ann Harper, "The Taovayas Indians in Frontier Trade and Diplomacy, 1769–1779," 181–85.

As early as 1701, a French Jesuit priest, Father Jacques Gravier, wrote of the Quapaw armed with English guns. In 1719, when la Harpe visited the Wichita villages along the Canadian River, a Chickasaw trader arrived at the village with British trade goods. Throughout the French occupation, British traders and their agents visited tribes in the west. Once they acquired the region along the east bank of the Mississippi, more British traders moved west. In the 1770s, British traders frequently crossed the Mississippi to trade along the lower Arkansas River. In 1776, the leading merchant of Pensacola, Jean Blommart, established a trading camp known as the British Ozark, just across the Mississippi from the White River. The next year he sent word to the Osage to come trade with him, and he promised good prices for their furs. That same year, a Kadohadacho leader went to Natchitoches and complained that the British had established a trading post up the Arkansas River at El Cadron.[16] British traders and trappers moved into Osage country, despite Spanish efforts to stop them. French traders, who had operated among the Osage during the French regime, continued to visit the Osage after the British occupied Canada. In addition to outlaw traders, legitimate licensed traders were willing to violate the law to obtain Osage horses and furs. The Osage were thus largely able to ignore Spanish demands.

The British occupation of Canada and the Illinois country along with the Spanish occupation of Louisiana did create new political, economic, and military conditions which challenged the old balance of power in the area. The Osage, confronted

16. "Relation or Journal of the voyage of Father Gravier, of the Society of Jesus, in 1700, from the country of the Illinois to the Mouth of the Mississippi River," "Written to Father de Lamberville and Sent from Fort Mississippi, 17 Leagues from its discharge into the Mexican Gulf or sea, on The 16th of February, 1701," in Reuben Gold Thwaites, ed., *Lower Canada, Mississippi Valley, 1696–1702,* 117; Smith, "Journey of de la Harpe," 535; Margry, *Exploration des affluents,* 297; Stanley Faye, "The Arkansas Post of Louisiana: Spanish Domination," 631, 647–48; John, *Storms Brewed,* 497; Bolton, *Athanase de Mézières,* 2:141.

with new circumstances, had to adjust their diplomatic patterns to deal with the new realities. British movement into the area had an important impact on the Osage, for the British introduced new policies among the Indians east of the Mississippi. Although the British continued the French practice of trading guns for furs, their frontier was different than the French. British settlers, despite colonial efforts to stop them, moved west across the coastal ranges and began moving into the Ohio Valley. Their presence placed greater pressures on those Native Americans living east of the Mississippi as more and more people competed for decreasing supplies of game.

The Osage initially maintained their old alliances with the eastern Indians, particularly the Illinois and Miami. Indeed, even when their old enemies, the Ottawa, suggested an alliance against the Europeans, the Osage agreed. In the 1760s, the British posed little threat to the Osage, but the opportunity to make peace with the Ottawa and other northeastern tribes was too good to miss. The Osage supported Ottawa leader Pontiac's movement to resist the British occupation, but the confrontation between the Osage and the British at Fort de Chartres was probably the extent of their support.[17]

Although the Osage sought to maintain their old alliances with the eastern Native American groups, they still resisted any intrusion onto their lands, even by old allies. When eastern tribes began hunting west of the Mississippi, the Osage attacked them and drove them from the region. The Osage traded along the Mississippi on both the east and west bank settlements and wanted to continue to do so in peace, but when Kaskaskia, Miami, or Peoria hunters were seen in the Ozarks, the Osage attacked them. Consequently, when Osage hunters crossed the river to hunt or steal horses, the eastern tribes resented it. A typical incident occurred in April 1775. A group of Osage crossed into Illinois country and stole several horses. They were

17. Alvord and Carter, *Critical Period,* 481–82.

pursued by the Illinois, who eventually recovered their horses and killed two Osage in the struggle.[18]

With the British occupation of Canada and the Illinois country, Mesquakie, Sac, Potawatomi, Kickapoo, Shawnee, Delaware, and other eastern tribes increased their access to arms and ammunition. The eastern tribes were eager to exploit the rich hunting grounds of the Osage in the Ozark and Ouachita forests, and they attacked Osage villages to steal horses, mules, and women and children. The Osage, challenged by these well-armed northern rivals, increased their hunting and raiding on the prairie-plains. In order to resist the northern challenges, the Osage had to acquire weapons. Thus they took furs, skins, livestock, and slaves from their southwestern neighbors.

The Osage maintained their lucrative trade with the Europeans. Fortunately for the Osage, Spanish trade restrictions were not uniformly or strictly enforced, and the market for Osage captives and livestock remained viable. In the north, they traded with Spanish-licensed traders and with unlicensed Canadian traders. In the south, they met with Spanish, French, and British traders. The Spanish post near the mouth of the Arkansas became a gathering point for those traders who refused to obey the new regulations. Forced to obey the Spanish trade laws at Saint Louis, Sainte Geneviève, and Natchitoches, the outlawed traders had moved to areas where there was less Spanish control. One such place was the old Arkansas Post near the mouth of the Arkansas River. The post was poorly manned by the Spanish, and it was isolated. British traders crossed the Mississippi and ascended the Arkansas to trade with the Osage. Therefore, the Osage continued their southwestern raids and took their goods to the lower Arkansas.[19]

At Natchitoches, the other Spanish post in eastern Louisiana, Spanish trade laws were strictly enforced by Spanish commander

18. Orieta to Amezaga, May 1, 1775, Nasatir Papers, 3:230–31.
19. John, *Storms Brewed*, 388–89, 458–60; Bolton, *Athanase de Mézières*, 1: 166–68, 2:83–100.

Athanase de Mézières. Consequently, those traders operating out of Natchitoches were not allowed to trade for slaves or livestock, and their trade in firearms was limited. The inconsistent enforcement of Spanish trade policy benefitted the Osage, for the lack of enforcement at the Arkansas Post and the strict enforcement at Natchitoches gave the Osage a distinct advantage over the southern tribes. The Arkansas River gained new economic importance for the Osage, because they could go there and trade skins, furs, slaves, and livestock and acquire needed firearms, ammunition, or whatever else they desired. De Mézières's enforcement of Spanish policy deprived the Caddoan tribes on the Red River of trade, for most of their trading had also involved horses, weapons, mules, and slaves. The Osage continued to acquire guns while the Caddoans, under De Mézières's thumb, became virtually unarmed.

The Osage looked to the south and west and exploited the territory. Red River Caddoans and Wichita people fled from Osage raids. The economic opportunities were so lucrative in the south that in the 1760s a band of Osage left the Osage River villages and moved to the Arkansas River Valley. So many left the old villages that in 1767 an Osage leader went to Saint Louis to protest that the traders were drawing the Osage away from the prairie villages. He complained that the illicit trade took in "one-half of the nation, in bands."[20] During the latter part of the eighteenth century, the Osage River bands continually complained that members were deserting their traditional homes and moving south to the Arkansas Valley.

The Osage continued to attack the Wichita and Caddo and drive them south and west as Osage raiders sought more trade goods. De Mézières described conditions in the spring of 1770:

But that river of the Akansa [Arkansas] having become infested by the concourse of malefactors of which I have spoken, they soon came to know the Osages, and incited them with powder, balls,

20. Ríu to Ulloa, November 12, 1767, Nasatir Papers, 1:20.

fusils, and other munitions (which are furnished them by the merchants who go annually with passports to visit them) to attack those of this district, for the purpose of stealing women, whom they would buy to satisfy their brutal appetites; Indian children, to aid them in their hunting; horses, on which to hunt wild cattle; and mules, on which to carry the fat and the flesh. Thus, all at once this district has become a pitiful theater of outrageous robberies and bloody encounters, and it has come to pass that in despair the Tuacanas, Yscanis, Tancaoüeys, and Quitseys have retreated toward the south until they are now in the neighborhood of the presidios of San Saba, Bexar, and Espíritu Santo.[21]

These conditions persisted for many years. The Osage attacked their neighbors and drove them from their homes. These people, largely unarmed and living in an area rich in natural resources, became victims of this Mississippi and Missouri Valley destabilization. Native Americans living north and east of the Osage were well armed by British traders, and the Osage, responding to northeastern pressure and southwestern opportunities, moved south.

The Osage incorporated the increased hunting, raiding, and trading into their society. They enjoyed secure homes and a new prosperity as a result of their economic growth. Their families were better fed and clothed, and European trade goods came into frequent use in the village. Metal tools replaced stone and bone implements, and brass pots were used in place of Osage pottery. Wool blankets kept the Osage warm, and European paints colored their skins. Osage hunters, equipped with muskets and bows, provided abundant game and kept Osage enemies far from the villages.

Living in close proximity to Spanish settlements in Missouri gave the Osage a distinct advantage. They could easily trade with the licensed traders from the French-Spanish communities of New Madrid, Sainte Geneviève, Saint Charles, and Saint Louis. They could also trade with any Spanish or French inhabitants

21. Bolton, *Athanase de Mézières*, 1:167–68.

living away from the frontier towns. Europeans could easily meet with the Osage and conduct legal or illegal trade with them. Missouri residents could easily ignore Spanish livestock trade regulations. They could meet with the Osage and purchase horses and mules any time they needed them. The continued presence of outlaw traders along the Arkansas also provided the Osage with a lucrative market.

Osage trade grew. Osage trade in skins, furs, and other animal products increased tremendously. Having driven competing Indian groups from the region, the Osage acquired a vast territory to exploit. They hunted bear and beaver along the water of the Gasconade, Saint Francis, White, Verdigris, and Neosho Rivers, and they traveled west along the Cimarron, Canadian, and upper Arkansas Rivers to kill buffalo, capture horses, and steal livestock. Because of the nature of the illicit trade, there were no records kept of the amount of Osage trade in contraband slaves and livestock, although there is evidence that both continued. Unfortunately, most of the evidence of the legal trade no longer exists, but enough survives to demonstrate the growth of the Osage economy. In 1757, the Osage produced only 80 packs of deer and bearskin, or roughly 8,000 pounds of skins, and by 1775 the Osage were producing 22,200 pounds of pelts, which amounted to 46 percent of the Indian trade in Spanish Illinois.[22] The Osage were bringing in the same kinds of skins, but the amounts increased significantly with an active European presence, and the energy and effort of the Osage was such that they were described in the spring of 1776 as frequenting "the post which produces more than all the Missouri."[23]

While only records for legally traded furs survive, it is clear that by the 1770s the Osage dominated the fur trade of Saint Louis and Spanish Illinois. In 1777, the Osage brought in hundreds of skins and pelts. Again, the predominant pelt was deer,

22. Harper, "Frontier Trade and Diplomacy, 1769–1779," 191; Notice of the Nations, May 19, 1775, Nasatir Papers, 2:124.
23. Cruzat to Amezaga, May 26, 1776, Nasatir Papers, 2:131.

for Little and Big Osage bands supplied 64 percent of the total market in deerskins (462 packs), 98 percent of the untanned deerskins (122 packs), and 39 percent of the prepared buckskins (22 packs). In addition to the deerskin, the Osage brought in 44 packs of bearskin (88 percent), 9 packs of wildcat skin (39 percent), 16 packs of beaver skins (44 percent), and 1 pack of other skins (14 percent).[24] With such production of skins, it is not surprising that the Osage fur trade was enviously described by Balthazar de Villiers, Commandant of the Arkansas Post, in April 1778 as "the most lucrative and the most interesting of the Illinois."[25]

Because the Osage enjoyed security and prosperity from the fur trade, they constantly protected their hunting lands and continued to expand their power and influence. Throughout the 1770s and 1780s, the Spanish reported Osage attacks on various Indian groups. The Osage undeniably participated in many attacks on others in the latter part of the eighteenth century as they adjusted to the new conditions before them. Some attacks were the result of young men seeking status and profit, but most were conducted to protect the growing Osage economy. The Osage had a large Spanish market for pelts and horses, and to meet the growing market the Osage exploited more and more territory and raided further and further from their prairie villages.[26]

The growing market influenced Osage relations with the Quapaw. The Osage and Quapaw had generally enjoyed peaceful relations. Distantly related and sharing a common language, Osage and Quapaw hunters used the common resources of the Ozarks and the Arkansas River Valley. There was an abundance of game in the region, and the two groups lived far enough apart to hunt without being a threat to one another. However, both Osage and Quapaw hunters engaged in the fur trade, and more

---

24. Report of the Fur Trade, November 28, 1777, Nasatir Papers, 2:178–79.
25. De Villiers to Gálvez, April 25, 1778, ibid., 2:202.
26. Bolton, *Athanase de Mézières*, 1:167, 202, 210.

pressure was placed on the game reserves of the area. Despite the increased pressure, it seems clear that left alone, the Osage and the Quapaw would have continued to share game. Instead, the new British occupation of the territory east of the Mississippi and the increased number of French and métis trappers and traders from Spanish Illinois and the lower Ohio Valley who left the British country and moved to the lower Arkansas Valley complicated the Osage-Quapaw friendship.

The increased population and trading made for greater demands on the game, forcing the Quapaw to hunt further upstream and deeper into the Ozark forests. Along with the Quapaw penetration into Osage country came French, Spanish, and British hunters and trappers. This new intrusion occurred at the same time Osage hunters were intent on exploiting more of their territory, and they too were hunting further south. The increased hunting brought the two tribes' hunters closer together and created competition and violence as Quapaw and Osage hunters competed for the same game.

Despite the increased competition and accompanying violence, the Osage and Quapaw at first remained officially at peace, largely it seems because the Osage and the Quapaw wanted and needed peace. Violence occurred when Quapaw hunters penetrated Osage hunting territory. Osage hunters would typically beat and rob the Quapaw and drive them away. The Osage, however, needed access to the traders living at the Arkansas Post located amid the Quapaw villages, so their attacks on the Quapaw hunters were usually followed by an Osage appearance at the Quapaw villages with the calumet asking for peace.

The Quapaw, their population drastically reduced by European diseases, were in no condition to fight the Osage, so they accepted the Osage peace gestures. Both the Quapaw and Osage shared a cultural practice that allowed for payment or gift-giving as compensation for injury or death. Although both tribes would occasionally seek blood revenge for tribal killings, they generally accepted compensatory gifts in place of retaliatory killings. The Osage were willing to "cover the dead" with gifts, for they needed the trade which they found at the Quapaw villages, and they needed the Quapaw as a buffer to blunt the attacks of the Choctaw and the Chickasaw who sometimes crossed the Mississippi River. By the middle of the eighteenth century, the Osage could have easily destroyed the Quapaw. They outnumbered them and had the firepower to do so, but without the Quapaw, there would be no tribe to stand between the Osage to absorb the blows of the Chickasaw, Choctaw, and other southeastern tribes that had begun to show up in the region. The Quapaw's presence along the lower Arkansas also prevented other more threatening tribes from occupying the lower Arkansas, so the Osage continued to maintain peaceful relations with them.

The Quapaw, a small tribe, with much of their economy and indeed their survival tied to the Spanish post, were often compelled to cooperate with the Spanish commanders there. When the Spanish decided to punish the Osage for their attacks, they sent the Quapaw to fight them. Although the Quapaw went upriver and hunted for the Osage, it seems clear that they did so reluctantly. On several occasions, the Quapaw merely used Spanish animosity against the Osage to arm their hunters. On three occasions in the late summer of 1789, the Quapaw appeared at the Arkansas Post and requested ammunition to attack the Osage. They received ammunition on August 18 to go to war against the Osage, but they returned in a few days without any contact with their northern neighbors. They did, however, assure the Spanish commander that if they were supplied again they would indeed kill some Osage. On August 25 the Spanish rearmed the Quapaw, and they again went upriver. They returned shortly thereafter without fighting the Osage, but on September 2 they once again volunteered to go into the interior to fight the Osage. The Quapaw knew that in August and September the Osage were busy at their prairie villages harvesting their crops and preparing for their fall hunt. It was extremely unlikely that many Osage would be in the Ozarks, so it was possible for the Quapaw to go into the interior without actually confronting the Osage. After three "failed" Quapaw expedi-

tions, the Spanish commander refused to supply them with any
more ammunition.[27] The Quapaw may have searched for the
Osage, but what seems more likely is that they simply took advantage of Spanish opposition to the Osage to acquire needed
ammunition.

While the Quapaw were usually successful in dealing with
the Spanish, they had a much more difficult time when confronted by Indian rivals. Located on the Arkansas and near the
Mississippi, the Quapaw were caught in the middle of the per-
ilous rivalry between the Osage and other southeastern tribes.
The Quapaw were in an awkward and dangerous position. When
enemies of the Osage appeared at the Arkansas Post and insisted
the Quapaw accompany them upriver, the Quapaw could ill
afford to refuse. With the added security of Choctaw and Chickasaw hunters, the Quapaw could hunt safely in Osage country,
so they frequently accompanied the eastern tribes. In March
1778, the Chickasaw appeared at the Arkansas Post, and a few
Quapaw joined them as they went into the interior. They returned shortly after killing and scalping a twelve-year-old Osage
boy.[28] The Quapaw occasionally met with these southeastern
Indians and discussed war with the Osage. De Villiers commented on one such meeting: "These two nations appeared
resolved to continue to make war on the Osages; but I always
remain of the opinion that the Arkansas [Quapaw] will do nothing."[29] He noted that the Quapaw were dwindling, many were
drinking, and their trade had almost disappeared. De Villiers
also observed that it was unlikely that the Quapaw, in such a
diminished state, wanted to fight the Osage, "having, in my
opinion, the same origin as the Osages, since their language is
the same, there being only a little difference according to all that
I have seen and heard, there is no appearance that they would
go to war against them; that if three or four have recently joined

---

27. Vallières to Miró, October 1, 1789, Nasatir Papers, 3:246–47.
28. De Villiers to Gálvez, April 13, 1778, ibid., 2:199–200.
29. De Villiers to Gálvez, June 11, 1778, ibid., 205–8.

the Chickasaws, it is again a testimony of their weakness in that they have not dared to disoblige them."[30] The Quapaw attempted to remain at peace, and when the Spanish urged them to war against the Osage in 1786–1787, they were reluctant. Wrote Esteban Rodriguez Miró: "The Arkansas [Quapaw] have not conducted themselves on this occasion with the activity and zeal that I expected of them, after their fine words and promises to be ready whenever we might need them."[31]

For the remaining years of the eighteenth century, the pattern continued. The Quapaw avoided conflict if possible and entertained the Osage when they came to trade; the Quapaw were never a threat to the Osage and were not an effective buffer after being attacked once again by smallpox in May 1801.

While tolerating the Quapaw and using them as a protective barrier, the Osage seldom treated other southern tribes so benignly. The effectiveness of the general Spanish policies of banning livestock and slave trade and placing restrictions on firearms trade gave the Osage a distinct advantage over their southern neighbors. The restrictions on livestock and slaves deprived the Wichita and Red River Caddoans of a major part of their trade, and the restrictions on firearms trade made them vulnerable to attacks from the better-armed Osage. In time, the Osage would drive the Wichita from the upper Red River south to the headwaters of the Trinity and the Brazos Rivers and force other Caddo groups south along the Red below the Great Bend. This pattern of Osage southern expansion continued well into the nineteenth century.

The Osage took advantage of the Caddo weakness and continually raided their villages along the Red River and hunting camps in the Ouachita Mountains. Spanish records from Natchitoches were filled with reports of Osage attacks: "Thus, all at once this district has become a pitiful theatre of outrageous robberies and

30. Ibid., 207–8.
31. Miró to Dubreuil, January 25, 1787, ibid., 3:147.

bloody encounters."[32] By the mid-1760s, some of the Osage had moved south to the Arkansas Valley to live. They established their farming villages along the middle stretches of the Arkansas River, and from these southern villages they launched their southern raids. Osage raiders would head south, sometimes detouring through the Ouachitas to clear the region of outside hunters. They would skirt the western edge of the mountains until they reached the Red, where they would strike east and west against the Caddoan villages all along the river. Caddo and Wichita horses were particularly attractive to the Osage; in one month alone the Osage stole over 750 horses. Attacks during 1771 and 1772 were so severe that most of the Caddo left the Red River and moved south.[33]

The Spanish in Texas were concerned about Osage raids along the Red River. Attacks by the Osage in the northeast and the struggle among the Comanche, Plains Apache, and Wichita to the northwest kept the Texas frontier in a state of war. Athanase de Mézières, in the summer of 1772, traveled to the Kichai, Iscanis, Tawakonis, Taovayas, Wichita, and Comanche. De Mézières brought tribal representatives back to San Antonio to make peace with the Spanish and arrange for their mutual protection from the Osage.

De Mézières planned to create an alliance among the Comanche, Wichita, and Caddoan tribes to form a protective barrier for Spanish Texas. He was convinced that only by defeating the Osage would the Red River Wichita and Caddo survive. After the Osage raids in the winter of 1772–1773, he planned a large-scale attack on the Osage for the following February. The attack never occurred, for De Mézières left for France in the spring and his successor failed to carry out the planned attack.[34]

Caddo destruction seemed imminent. The Osage continued

---

32. Bolton, *Athanase de Mézières,* 1:167.
33. Mathews, *The Osages,* 236; Vaugine, April 12, 1783, Nasatir Papers, 3:48; John, *Storms Brewed,* 409, 411.
34. John, *Storms Brewed,* 429–30.

their devastating raids. A report from Natchitoches in January 1774 discussed the Osage attacks and their impact: "They throw themselves by force on this district. They have tried to pillage the *Quitseys* [Kichais]; have dispersed them, as it were, by obliging them to take refuge in places hidden and unknown to their enemies. Every day they have parties among the Big and Little Caddos which, being continually tormented, will perhaps also decide to disperse."[35]

Then, epidemic disease struck the Red River Caddo in 1777 and weakened an already weak people. More groups abandoned the Red River and moved south to the Sulfur and Trinity Rivers.[36] Those few who remained on the Red were constantly afraid of the Osage attacks. De Mézières, upon his return, recognized the Osage threat. With the Caddo at Natchitoches, he planned another expedition to punish the Osage and stop their incessant raids. His plans called for the Spanish of the Arkansas Post and Saint Louis to close trade to the Osage, thereby weakening them. De Mézières then proposed that the Spanish arm the Caddoan, Wichita, and Comanche tribes. The warriors of the allied tribes would gather at the Wichita village on the Red River and march secretly to the Osage villages in late August or early September. De Mézières wanted to deliver a fatal blow to the Osage, and a fall attack was ideal for such a blow. Destroying Osage villages in the autumn would destroy winter food supplies. Without their stored food, few Osage would survive the winter. Fortunately for the Osage and unfortunately for the Caddo, the governor of Texas, Bernardo de Galvez, never authorized the campaign, and the plan was never carried out.[37]

The Osage disrupted the Caddo winter hunt of 1780–1781 and stole horses again in 1782–1783. In November 1783, the Kichais left the Red River and moved south to escape the attacks, while the Big Caddo remained. By the 1790s, the Spanish

35. De Villiers to Monsieur (Unzaga), January 26, 1774, Nasatir Papers, 2:111.
36. John, *Storms Brewed*, 523.
37. Bolton, *Athanase de Mézières*, 2:145; John, *Storms Brewed*, 498–99.

enmity for the Osage was so great that they were willing to reverse their long-standing policy and supply guns and ammunition to the Caddo to fight the Osage.[38] The Spanish never supplied enough munitions to pose a serious threat to the Osage,
but this dramatic reversal of Spanish policy was further evidence of Osage strength. The newly armed tribes were unable
to take full advantage of their new weapons, for the Spanish
also armed their western rivals, the Lipan Apache. So the Wichita and Caddo had to contend with new Apache raids as well as
with the destructive Osage raids. Only when stronger, better-
armed tribes moved into the region from the east were the Caddo
to receive any relief from the constant pounding of the Osage.

The Wichita, living upriver from the Caddoan tribes, also
continued to suffer from Osage attacks. Driven from the Arkansas in 1757, they had moved to two fortified villages on the Red
River commonly, although mistakenly, called Spanish Fort.
Until the Spanish took over in 1769, the Wichita had participated in a lucrative trade with both European traders and the
Comanche. Traders, unable to venture up the Arkansas, came
up the Red River to the twin villages of the Wichita. The Wichita
acted as commercial middlemen. They exchanged Comanche
horses, mules, slaves, and buffalo robes for European guns, ammunition, metal tools, and textiles. The Spanish trade regulations halted the Wichita's lucrative commerce. Although trade
continued to go on, it was severely limited. Trade after 1769 left
the Wichita with inadequate arms and supplies with which to
resist the Osage. For a brief period in 1770, the Wichita went
north into the region between the Arkansas and Red Rivers to
contact the outlaw Arkansas traders, but Osage attackers forced
them back to the Red River.[39] The Osage, with their trade along
the Missouri, Mississippi, and Arkansas Rivers, continued to

38. Elizabeth A. Harper, "The Taovayas in Frontier Trade and Diplomacy,
1779–1835," 14.
39. John, *Storms Brewed*, 305, 388; Harper, "Frontier Trade and Diplomacy,
1719–1768," 279.

attack the Wichita villages at will. By 1772, their attacks had forced the Wichita to temporarily abandon their villages. Many of the Wichita fled south to the Brazos while others moved up to the headwaters of the Red.

In the fall of 1773, a Wichita leader appeared among the Caddo and complained of European traders supplying the Osage, and the Wichita were to participate in De Mézières's Osage campaign. In 1777, a group of Pawnee moved south to live with the Wichita kin and help fight the Osage. Despite the Pawnee presence, the Osage raids continued unabated. In December 1785, the Osage struck two large Wichita villages on the Red River. The attack was so destructive that again the Wichita abandoned their villages and fled two hundred and fifty miles south to the Perdenales River.[40] They later recovered and returned to their Red River forts where they remained vulnerable to Osage raiders. Even the Comanche-Wichita alliance that had successfully resisted Osage expansion in the 1750s proved unable to cope with this new crisis for the Wichita.

Relations between the Comanche and Osage remained violent as Osage raiders tried to drive the Comanche away from prime Osage buffalo country. The country between the upper Red River and the Arkansas along the Washita, Canadian, and Cimarron Rivers was extremely important to the Osage. The western plains and river valleys provided essential food, clothing, and valuable trade goods for the Osage. The wooded valleys sheltered deer, elk, fox, wolf, and other animals valuable for their food, furs, and skins. Groups of wild horses roamed the region. Most important were the great buffalo herds feeding on the short grasses in the area. The buffalo supplied essential food for the Osage, and buffalo tongues and robes were valuable trade items. Just as the Ozarks and Ouachitas were valuable in the east, so too were the western plains to Osage survival.

The Comanche tried to protect their livestock and hunting

40. John, *Storms Brewed,* 458, 495, 702–3.

grounds, but for most of the eighteenth century they were more concerned with the Apache. The Comanche had been fighting the Apache since they entered the region in 1700. As they slowly displaced the Apache during the eighteenth century, the Comanche constantly looked south and west. While they would challenge the Osage if they came in contact with them, they were more concerned with the Apache. The Osage were a large and powerful tribe, armed with French weapons. The Apache, particularly after the Spanish abandoned them, were never well armed and lived between the Comanche and the Spanish settlements of northern Mexico and south Texas.

Since the Comanche had to pass through the Apacheria to raid or trade in the south, the Comanche preferred to fight the Apache rather than the Osage. The Osage and Comanche were involved in only brief, occasional conflicts. The Comanche seldom met up with Osage hunters traveling north and east of them. When the Osage did go out on the western plains, they established their large band camps near the Arkansas River. From these camps they sent hunting and raiding parties to the west along the Canadian, Cimarron, Washita, and Red Rivers.

The territory along the headwaters of the Cimarron, North Canadian, and Canadian marked a neutral zone between the Osage and Comanche. Occasionally the Comanche hunted to the northeast. When they were allied with the Wichita they probably hunted between the Canadian and Red Rivers, but generally they stayed west and south of Osage country. The land they did share was vast and empty, and only when hunting or raiding parties encountered one another was there violence. Although rare, stories of attacks occasionally filtered out. One such description was recorded in 1792 by Louis DeBlanc, the commander of Natchitoches: "I have just received the news that the Comanches or Laytans had a fierce combat with the Osages in the autumn of last year."[41]

---

41. DeBlanc to Carondelet, July 6, 1792, Nasatir Papers, 4:89.

The Comanche preferred to attack less well-armed Apache or Pueblo Indians of New Mexico, and the Osage preferred to fight those people who posed a more direct threat to their territory to the east. The relationship of mutual respect and nonalliance between the Osage and the Comanche remained essentially unchanged until the 1830s, when they made peace with one another, and the Osage began supplying the Comanche with guns and other trade goods in exchange for Comanche horses and mules.

The Osage's other powerful western neighbor, the Pawnee, remained hostile toward the Osage throughout the eighteenth and nineteenth centuries. The Pawnee, forced from the upper Arkansas by the Osage, constantly challenged them for control of the area. That region south of the Smoky Hill River and the Arkansas was controlled by the Osage, yet the Pawnee frequently dropped down and hunted buffalo and wild horses. The Osage, better armed than the Pawnee and allied with the Kansa, were generally able to keep the Pawnee north. The Pawnee retained ties with the Wichita, and in the 1770s a group of Pawnee moved south to live with the Wichita and challenge the Osage. Unable to acquire enough trade or to defeat the Osage, they later rejoined their northern kin.[42]

The Pawnee hunted in small bands, and when the Osage discovered them south of the Smoky Hill River they attacked them. Osage-Pawnee hostility was long-standing, as the Pawnee constantly sought to regain lost southern territory, and the Osage continued to keep them north. This struggle over the buffalo country continued for years. The Osage were never able to end Pawnee hostility or keep them completely out of the region, but the Pawnee only hunted in that region with extreme caution.

The Pawnee were kept out of the region because of a combined Osage and Kansa effort. The Osage and Kansa people generally enjoyed peaceful relations, sharing a language and old kinship ties. In the eighteenth century, the two groups com-

42. John, *Storms Brewed*, 495.

peted for buffalo in the west and occasionally fought one another. The Osage, however, were willing to maintain nonviolent
relations with the Kansa, for in the early eighteenth century the
Osage were unable to defeat them. The Kansa, living along the
Kansas and Missouri Rivers, had access to French and British
guns and could easily challenge the Osage. Living along the
rivers, the major pathways for European traders, however, ex-
posed them to European diseases that eventually killed many of
them and weakened their political and military power. After
smallpox struck in the 1750s, the Kansa were no longer a threat
to the Osage. Just as with the Quapaw, the Osage used the Kansa
to buffer any attacks from northern tribes, particularly the Pawnee. The Kansa hunted west along the Kansas and Smoky Hill
Rivers, between the Pawnee and Osage buffalo country. Although the Osage were better armed and outnumbered their
Kansa neighbors, the Kansa were more valuable to the Osage as
northern allies. The Osage had little need to fight with them, so
they maintained peace with their Kansa kin.

By the 1770s, the Osage also had to contend with many non-
Indian rivals. Osage country was rich in animal resources. The
game of the Ozarks and the Ouachitas attracted hundreds of
Spanish, Canadian, and British hunters who wanted to take
deer, bear, and other fur-bearing animals. The Spanish viewed
the increased trapping as economic growth, while the Osage
saw it as deadly competition. Fur trading was a critical element
of the Osage economy, and the Ozarks and Ouachitas were the
prime hunting grounds. Commercial hunting in the region by
non-Osage, Native American, and European alike, was a threat
to Osage well-being. Therefore, the Osage drove foreign hunters
from their land. They robbed, beat, and sometimes killed to
keep competitors out. "Osages make themselves masters of all
the hunting country," wrote the Spanish commander at the Arkansas Post after the Osage had driven hunters from the Ozarks.[43]

---

43. Rousseau, February 9, 1793, Log of Galiot *La Flèche*, Nasatir Papers, 4:119.

Thus, the Osage correctly saw the movement of Indians and Europeans into the area as a threat to their very survival, and woe be to any non-Osage hunter who encountered the Osage in Osage country.

Attacks were concentrated along the Arkansas Valley and in the Ozarks, where the Osage hunted and traders attempted to reach interior tribes. Spanish reports are filled with accounts of Osage attacks. Lieutenant Governor of Illinois Fernando de Leyba reported, "The Osage Indians, after their many promises, not only continue robbing as before but with more excesses. . . . All [traders] are returning to this post, some entirely stripped, others partly so." At the Arkansas Post, Lieutenant Joseph Orieta recorded, "Last September there arrived four parties of hunters despoiled and robbed by the said Osage Indians, and on the second of this month there arrived three parties also despoiled by the said Osages without any more clothing than the shirts on their backs." In July 1779, De Leyba again wrote the governor of Louisiana, Bernardo de Galvez: "The insult of the Big Osages on the hunters of the river of the Arkansas is a very old matter." The Osage continued throughout the 1780s to disrupt their competitors' hunting. On November 22, 1782, the commander at Natchitoches, Etienne Vaugine, wrote Governor Esteban Rodriguez Miró complaining of Osage attacks: "Ascending upstream in the direction of the Arkansas River one reaches the prairies and the passage way of this enemy nation which does a great deal of harm to the two provinces, the whites and savages not being able to make their hunt without danger."[44]

The Osage sometimes only robbed the intruders, as Miró described: "You inform me of the return to your post of four hunters whom the Osages had robbed to their shoes." At other times, the Osage destroyed their rivals' goods. In April 1786, the Osage were reported as "destroying the entire hunt by cutting

---

44. De Leyba to Amezaga, September 11, 1771, ibid., 2:35–36; Orieta to Unzaga, October 17, 1774, ibid., 118; De Leyba to Gálvez, July 13, 1779, ibid., 222; Vaugine to Miró, November 22, 1782, ibid., 3:42.

the deerskins and bison tongues, and dumping out the bear fat and tallow." The Osage occasionally killed hunters, as noted by the commander at the Arkansas Post, Ignacio Delinó, in August 1791:

> The ones named Bayonne Duchassin and Migel Bonne both hunters from this post have just informed me of their having found on the banks of the White River from when they came, four cadavers from which they recognized those of Carlos Dauteulle and Pedro Picar, both hunters of this district. The other two they could not recognize because of their heads having been cut off and of their being stark naked. They informed me that it was the Osages who committed this crime.[45]

Spanish records are replete with such reports. It is clear that these attacks were not the work of a brutal, sadistic people, but of a people under pressure struggling to survive. The attacks were intended to keep commercial hunters out of the region. Robbery supplied the Osage with extra European goods, but more importantly, it served to drive people out. The killings and decapitations were brutal, but they were an effective means of intimidation. The majority of these attacks occurred in the Ozarks, Arkansas Valley, and south in the Ouachitas. Clearly they were used to stem the flood of competing hunters, for at the same time hunters were being robbed and killed in the south, traders were peacefully conducting business in the Osage villages.

In January 1778, when the commandant at the Arkansas Post reported still more Osage robbery and murder along the Arkansas, traders were doing a brisk business in the northern villages. While Osage hunters were killing in the south, traders returned from the northern Osage villages "entirely contented and with some great profits in the commerce which they have made with

---

45. Miró to Vallière, May 27, 1789, ibid., 2:239; DeBlanc to Miró, April 10, 1786, ibid., 3:119; Delinó to Miró, August 8, 1791, ibid., 4:55–56.

them."[46] This pattern reoccurred throughout the period. The Osage attacked in the south to protect their resources while maintaining peace in their villages where they conducted trade.[47] European hunters, not traders, were a threat to the Osage, unless of course the Europeans attempted to trade with Osage enemies. In the Osage villages, the traditional leadership, eager to facilitate trade, could enforce the peace required. Away from the villages, Osage hunting parties were free from the control of the *Ga-hi-ge, A-ki-da,* and *Non-hon-zhin-ga.* So while peace was maintained in the north, violence continued in the south.

The Spanish showed no understanding of the Osage attacks. When hunters were killed or mistreated, the Spanish demanded that the Osage surrender the culprits and compensate for the damages. They also demanded hostages to insure peace. The Osage tried to comply but were seldom able to produce any of the accused attackers or hostages. Occasionally they tried to provide compensatory gifts to assuage the Spanish. Despite Spanish efforts and intrusions, the Osage continued to work contrary to Spanish goals. Therefore, the Spanish sometimes resorted to direct economic interference to control them. Realizing how important trade was to the Osage, the Spanish curtailed trade with them. Generally, however, the economic blockades were simply annoyances to the Osage and did little other than make them mad. "The Big Osages are extraordinarily outraged because we did not send traders to them last year," reported Zenon Trudeau.[48] The Spanish could never entirely stop trade with the Osage, for it was too lucrative for both the Osage and Europeans.

Ironically, the trade embargoes, rather than stopping violence, created more violence. Deprived of needed weapons and

46. De Villiers to Gálvez, January 26, 1778, ibid., 2:187–88; Cruzat to Gálvez, February 22, 1778, ibid., 195–96.
47. Cruzat to Gálvez, March 30, 1778, ibid., 199; Cruzat to Miró, June 23, 1784, ibid., 3:80–81; Dubreuil to Miró, May 21, 1786, ibid., 121.
48. Trudeau to Carondelet, April 11, 1794, ibid., 4:207.

ammunition, the Osage attacked anyone in the area. They had to have ammunition and guns if they were to protect their villages. If the Spanish would not voluntarily trade, then the Osage would take what they needed. Gayoso de Lemos observed, "It is the general opinion that the Osages have no other object than that of trade; that if they have trade they would be peaceful."[49]

The Spanish were not content merely to trade, for Osage challenges in the interior were a threat to the Spanish trade policy and international diplomacy. Thus, for the duration of Spanish occupation of the region, the Spanish attempted continually to control the Osage. The Osage were large enough to challenge the Spanish militarily. They were strategically located to take advantage of the Spanish and British traders, and they were possessors of a profitable trade. Until these conditions changed, the Osage were able to resist any outside control and maintain hegemony over the prairie-plains. In time, however, conditions and situations did change, and so too did the Osage.

49. De Lemos to Carondelet, February 20, 1797, ibid., 5:141–42.

6.

DISHARMONY AND INSTABILITY

*. . . it is some fools over whom I am not master. Do you not have
fools among your young men?*

—Jean Lafond, 1787[1]

The eighteenth century was a time of dramatic change for the
Osage. The increased raiding, hunting, and trading created new
opportunities for wealth and prestige which were not always
recognized by Osage society. Increased wealth and status challenged Osage social, political, and economic systems, and in
time the Osage changed to meet the new challenges. The changes
were never uniform or consistent, but they were always shaped
according to the familiar patterns of Osage culture. In the course
of the eighteenth century, the Osage would move apart, leaving
the core village group along the Osage River and forming several autonomous bands. Within the bands, clan prerogatives
were abandoned, and in some the dual leadership positions
withered away, replaced by single band leaders. The hereditary
nature of Osage political leadership was also challenged as successful hunters and raiders, often denied status and power within
the old system, sought power and position. These internal demands were aggravated by the interference of outsiders.

Europeans, attracted to the Osage because of their strategic
location and valuable trade, intruded into Osage society and at-

---

1. Cruzat to Miró, November 12, 1787, Nasatir Papers, 3:209.

154

tempted to alter Osage polity to their advantage. The combination of increased opportunity and outside interference changed the way the Osage lived. With more emphasis on hunting, raiding, and trade than on agriculture, the Osage moved away from their prairie villages. Some moved north to hunt and trade along the Missouri River, while others moved south to hunt and trade along the Arkansas.

The Osage semisedentary existence was altered by this eighteenth-century economic and geopolitical expansion. The entire tribe no longer had to hunt as one. With horses and guns, smaller groups could hunt as successfully as larger groups had in earlier times. The success of these smaller hunts contributed to the division of the tribe into several independent bands. European traders visiting Osage villages rewarded those Osage who produced pelts by providing guns, ammunition, and other attractive trade goods, such as blankets, metal tools, and utensils. Osage hunters within the older traditional framework had always provided food and clothing for their families, but with the European presence Osage hunted not only for subsistence but also to acquire needed firearms and important European trade goods.

Trade goods not only insured the survival of the Osage and created a more comfortable life for them, but they also affected the tribal social structure. Osage elite maintained their positions by giving. Giving was a valued and respected trait among the Osage. One acquired and maintained status and social standing by feeding friends and kin and giving them gifts. Jean François Buisson de St. Cosme, a French Jesuit visiting one of the Illinois tribes in 1699, described a female leader who maintained power by such giving: "As she has many sons and sons-in-law who are good hunters, she often gives feasts, which is the way to acquire the esteem of the savages and of all their nations in a short time."[2] Osage leaders did much the same to acquire sta-

2. Kellogg, ed., *Early Narratives*, 353.

tus. Successful Osage hunters who secured extra food and pelts gained prestige by inviting people to their lodges and feeding and entertaining them. Ambitious Osage also distributed trade goods to gain support and to influence potential followers. In 1773, a Missouri hunter sought to usurp his village chief's authority: "He forced the traders to contribute a small present which he divided among those of his faction in order to prove his noble birth."[3]

The presence of the traders in the village also upset the traditional political system. In a society where material possessions were meager yet influential in determining power and social position, anyone who possessed wealth could radically affect the village structure by favoring particular individuals or families. Since it was the responsibility of the *Tsi-zhu Ga-hi-ge* to entertain friendly visitors to the Osage village (the *Hon-ga Ga-hi-ge's* responsibilities focused solely on hostile visits), the European traders always stayed in the lodge of the *Tsi-zhu Ga-hi-ge*. The continued presence of European traders in his lodge contributed to the growing influence of the *Tsi-zhu Ga-hi-ge*.[4]

While the mere presence of European intruders indirectly affected the traditional political structure of the Osage, these newcomers also became directly involved in shaping Osage politics to their advantage. European powers in North America wanted to establish good relations with the Osage because these Indians had over one thousand warriors and could control entry into the west by sealing off the Missouri or Arkansas Rivers. Because the Osage were located between the French and Spanish frontiers and later the British and the Spanish frontiers, they assumed further importance, particularly when these competing powers attempted to expand their influence in the region. The French, Spanish, and British all attempted to establish and maintain an alliance with the Osage. One means of achieving

3. Piernas to Unzaga, December 12, 1773, Nasatir Papers, 2:107.
4. Bailey, "Osage Social Organization, 1673–1906," 44.

such an alliance was by providing trade goods and gifts for prominent tribal members.

Europeans also gave tribal leaders special symbolic gifts to distinguish them as leaders. Typically, tribal leaders were given European flags, medals, gorgets, hats, coats, and uniforms to symbolize their importance and their alliance with the particular European power. In 1719, when Claude-Charles DuTisné visited the Wichita village and made an alliance with them, he left a French flag as a symbol of that alliance. When an Osage chief went to Paris in 1725, the director of the Indian Company gave him a complete French outfit that included a blue dress coat, silver ornaments, and a plumed hat trimmed in silver. The King of France gave him a royal medallion on a gold chain, a rifle, a sword, and a watch. These symbolic items provided outside recognition which in turn contributed to additional internal tribal status. The medals, gorgets, and other symbols, which initially were merely symbolic recognition of already existing conditions, in time became instrumental in creating authority. These goods tended to elevate men to power.[5]

Europeans did not have a complete understanding of the Osage system, and what they did know they tried to destabilize. The system of dual *Ga-hi-ge* and *Non-hon-zhin-ga* was not recognized by Europeans, for it was not consistent with a European political framework. The Osage system entailed a number of tribal leaders behaving within prescribed roles. There was a sharing of power within the tribe. The council of tribal elders, the *Non-hon-zhin-ga,* dealt with outside problems confronting the group. The *Non-hon-zhin-ga* met and discussed opinions and options, and all major tribal decisions were arrived at by all of the clan *Non-hon-zhin-ga.* The responsibilities of the two *Ga-hi-ge* were also limited by tradition and only involved internal village is-

5. "Le sieur DuTisné y planta le pavillon blanc le 27 Septembre 1719 au milieu de leurs villages, qu'ils recurent avec plaisir" (Margry, *Exploration des affluents,* 312); Ellis and Steen, eds., "An Indian Delegation," 394, 402; Ewers, "Symbols of Chiefly Authority," 278–82.

sues. Assisted by their *A-ki-da,* the *Ga-hi-ge* worked for village harmony and stability.

The Europeans went into Osage communities and looked for a polity that was consistent with their culture. They witnessed activity and individual behavior and generally misunderstood everything they observed. When Europeans established relations with the Osage, they attempted to create a political system consistent with their conceptualizations. Europeans sought out prominent Osage men and bestowed symbolic gifts on them and in so doing created their own hierarchy of Indian leadership.

This interference created new political positions and undermined traditional polity functions. Europeans recognized only a few positions within each tribe and made distinctions between first, second, and third chiefs. This was particularly true during active Spanish-Osage relations, a period from about 1767 to 1803. The French had introduced the policy of "creating chiefs" by granting symbolic items. Etienne Véniard, sieur de Bourgmont's account of his peace mission onto the plains in 1724 mentioned the presentation of a French flag and a variety of other gifts for the Padouca (Plains Apache) and others. Spanish records dealing with the Osage in particular contain frequent references to "medal chiefs" and requests for various political medals.[6]

The imposition of European political conceptualizations caused considerable trouble among the Osage. Europeans were conditioned because of their political experience to assign supremacy to a single leader, creating the concept of one tribal leader. The sharing of leadership responsibility was weakened by the European recognition of only one leader. Traditionally, an Osage *Tsi-zhu Ga-hi-ge,* because he was the representative of the peace element of the tribe, would have greeted any visitors to the village.

---

6. Folmer, "French Expansion," 167, 173, 179; Norall, *Bourgmont,* 68–80; Nasatir, *Before Lewis and Clark,* 1:98, 101, 144, 284, 327–38.

Europeans, looking for a single leader, would naturally, within their political conceptualization, assume that the *Tsi-zhu Ga-hi-ge* was the supreme Osage leader, which was not the case. The shared decision making and responsibility was lost on or ignored by Europeans. This outside recognition elevated certain tribal members, and at times it created "internal" jealousy and eventually helped break up the old traditional system.

The combination of horse, gun, and new trade placed a new, greater dependence on the hunt. The Osage, encouraged to hunt by the newcomers, would in time abandon much of their horticultural traditions and rely almost totally on the hunt. The new emphasis on mounted, armed hunting and raiding also had an impact on the traditional Osage political system. As raiding increased, the *Non-hon-zhin-ga* authorized smaller raiding parties. The increased hunting and raiding may have contributed to new marriage locations and an emphasis on polygyny. Pelt preparation, which assumed a new importance with increased trading, was performed by Osage women. Increased emphasis on the pelt trade would have given increased economic importance to women's roles in the individual household. The increased raiding may also have decreased the number of available marriageable males and reinforced polygyny.[7]

Just as Osage society was altered by the new economic focus, so were village sites and political customs. By the mid–eighteenth century, however, some of the Osage who were hunting and raiding in the south and west refused to go back to the north and remained in the Arkansas Valley. They established villages along the Arkansas River and began challenging the traditional leadership for control of the southern group. In December 1767, the commander at Saint Louis, Francisco Ríu, wrote to Governor Antonio de Ulloa: "The principal chief of the *Grandes Aguas* [Osage] nation, named Clermont, having come to speak with

7. LaFlesche, "Rite of the Chiefs," 66; Mathews, *The Osages,* 76; Bailey, "Osage Social Organization, 1673–1906," 44.

me, he heartily asked me to prohibit entirely commerce in said district, in as much as to continue it will be the ruin of his nation, since it takes in one-half of the nation, in bands."[8]

This letter is especially significant. It reveals that the Spanish had distinguished one chief among the Big Osage, contrary to Osage tradition. This chief, called Clermont by the Spanish, was *Gra moie* (Moving Hawk) or *Gra-to-moh-se* (Iron Hawk), a *Tsi-zhu Ga-hi-ge*.[9] As peace chief, it was only natural that Clermont would deal with any non-Osage. The Spanish, unaware of the real nature of Osage political leadership and conditioned by their own experience, assumed that Clermont was a single principal chief. It was to their advantage to maintain good relations with the Osage leader, whose good graces would insure healthy trade and good behavior of his people, so throughout the late eighteenth century the Spanish accorded Clermont a great deal of respect and importance. Unfortunately, they incorrectly regarded him as the only leader of the Osage.

The letter also reveals that the peace chief Clermont could not restrain large numbers of his people from hunting, raiding, and trading along the Arkansas. This is consistent with the nature of Osage political power, which did not permit much direct control of individual tribal members. The *Ga-hi-ge*'s power was extremely limited outside the village.

Clermont clearly wanted to use the Spanish to strengthen his power and influence. He requested that the Spanish stop trade

8. Ríu to Ulloa, November 12, 1767, Nasatir Papers, 1:20.
9. LaFlesche, "Rite of the Chiefs," 59–71; Burns, *Osage Bands and Clans,* 4, 13, 44; Mathews, *The Osages,* 237, 299. Burns insists that *Gra moie* was a member of the *Tsi-zhu* Peace Maker clan, which is the proper clan for the *Tsi-zhu Ga-hi-ge*, while Mathews claims that his name was *Gra Mo'n*, meaning Arrow Going Home, and that he was in the *Hon-ga* moiety. Yet Mathews also contends that Clermont had claim to the *Tsi-zhu Ga-hi-ge* position, an impossibility if he were *Hon-ga*. It is certain that *Gra moie* was the *Tsi-zhu Ga-hi-ge*, and Mathews, who does not always agree with what the leader's name means, confirms that Clermont was indeed the proper *Tsi-zhu Ga-hi-ge*. One of Clermont's names meant Passing or Moving Hawk, and Arrow Going Home was probably a special honor name.

on the Arkansas. This forced both his people and the Europeans to trade at his village, where he had nominal control. As Clermont was willing to cooperate with the Spanish and traders from Saint Louis, it was to the traders' advantage to strengthen his influence both economically and diplomatically. Saint Louis traders were eager to secure all the profits of the Osage trade, and Spanish colonial officials were eager to maintain their alliance with Clermont.

Despite Clermont's appeal to stop the southern trade, the Osage continued to separate. By the 1770s, the Little Osage remained in the north along the Missouri. The main group of the Big Osage, led by Clermont, were anchored along the Osage River, and a growing third group moved to the Arkansas Valley. Throughout the period of Spanish rule, there were frequent reports of three major groups of Osage.

The Osage along the Arkansas, however, were not content, and they challenged the traditional polity. The Osage attracted to the south were ambitious ones who often did not have a place in the older social system. They refused to give up their southern trade, and they often challenged village leaders when they did return home from the south. A letter written by a French trader in the village of the Osage along the Osage River in June 1772 reveals both the nature of Osage control and the challenge posed by the new conditions. Osage raiders had killed three Frenchmen, one near Natchitoches and two on the Arkansas River. Two other Frenchmen had survived, and an Osage warrior had brought them back as prisoners to the northern village. When the captives arrived in the village, the French trader in the village appealed to the *Ga-hi-ge* and the *Non-hon-zhin-ga* to free the French prisoners. The *Ga-hi-ge* and the council members took the captives from the raider and placed them in a headman's lodge, probably the *Tsi-zhu Ga-hi-ge* lodge, for the lodge of the *Tsi-zhu Ga-hi-ge* was traditionally a place of refuge. During the night, the Osage warrior lured one of the captives out of the chief's lodge. He took the captive back to his own lodge and refused to release him. "The head man that same night reported to the chiefs and in the morning a 150 of them met. They obtained the prisoner by demanding him and they put him back with his friend."[10] Later it was discovered that the warrior was planning to take at least one of his captives to sell at the Arkansas Post. The *Non-hon-zhin-ga* released the captives, but the warrior, who had captured the Frenchmen and killed their companions in the south, had challenged the traditional leadership and twice had to be confronted and controlled. It was this type of individual who was drawn to the Arkansas and away from the old village.

The Spanish had helped create an Osage hierarchy and insured its cooperation by permitting trade via Saint Louis. It was to the newly recognized political leaders' advantage to maintain the status quo which would guarantee their position and keep trade open with the Spanish. At the same time, the ambitious and aggressive Osage were frustrated by tribal leadership. Access to power was extremely limited within the traditional village and limited further by Spanish sanctions. Both social and economic opportunity lured the Osage to the Arkansas Valley, and their movement gradually weakened the traditional systems.

The internal dissension among the Osage intensified as the Spanish continued the French policy of awarding medals to chieftains. This external recognition by the Spanish created jealousy, resentment, and an artificial system not consistent with the traditional system. In the spring of 1776, two chiefs of the Little Osage went to Saint Louis and requested medals. The Saint Louis commander refused to recognize the dual nature of the *Ga-hi-ge,* and he refused to give them both a medal. He wrote the Governor in New Orleans, explaining that

> although the two chiefs have their personal merit, the second is the most listened to in the nation and the traders assure [me] that his band excels that of the former. . . . By contenting both, results in the inconvenience that the second chiefs of the other nations will

10. Rouquière to Piernas, June 14, 1772, Nasatir Papers, 2:53.

have a basis for claiming the same [treatment]. By signifying the deprivation of the second chief, giving it only to the first, I have had the effects of his displeasure, reproach and envy, as stealing horses from the residents of these *pueblos,* insulting the hunters and traders. . . . [11]

The Spanish also noted two chiefs of the Big Osage, but assigned them different ranks. They recognized Clermont as the first chief and Jean Lafond as the second chief, apparently referring to the *Tsi-zhu Ga-hi-ge* Clermont and the *Hon-ga Ga-hi-ge* Lafond. In 1777, the Spanish representatives met with them both in Saint Louis. The Spanish commander in Saint Louis, Francisco Cruzat, and the "two principal chiefs" agreed to prevent the Osage from going to the Arkansas.[12] Clermont and Lafond were eager to stop the movement south, because the migration to the Arkansas weakened their villages, and the Arkansas Osage challenged their authority. They were willing to use Spanish influence to keep their people off of the Arkansas. The Spanish, because the Osage in the south were attacking Caddoan tribes and killing or robbing French and Spanish hunters, also wanted the Osage to remain in the north. Soon after this agreement was made between the Osage leaders and Cruzat, word arrived at Saint Louis that the Spanish officer in charge of the Arkansas Post had sent flags and calumets to the Big Osage village and urged that one of the principal chiefs, either Clermont or Lafond, descend to the post to make peace with the Quapaw. Clermont, having just met with the Spanish in Saint Louis to limit southern movement, was not about to go to the Arkansas Post, so although he agreed to the peace proposal with the Quapaw, he declined to descend to the Arkansas.

When the Spanish messengers left the village, however, several Osage went back to the Arkansas Post with them. There they met with the Arkansas commander, who gave them each a

11. Cruzat to Unzaga, March 18, 1776, ibid., 128–29.
12. De Villiers to Gálvez, April 7, 1777, ibid., 141; Cruzat to Gálvez, July 6, 1777, ibid., 152–55.

flag and urged them to return in the spring to trade.[13] The two who received flags promised to return to the Arkansas the next spring with one hundred men. This act on the part of Balthazar De Villiers, the Arkansas commander, angered Cruzat in Saint Louis and the Osage chiefs. De Villiers's behavior in the south undermined the authority of the two chiefs and aggravated internal tribal strife. Both the Osage in the north and the Spanish in Saint Louis agreed that it was to their mutual advantage to stop the Arkansas drift, yet at the same time another Spanish official was encouraging further tribal division.

This divisive activity continued and worsened in time. Groups of Osage moved to the south and traveled to the Arkansas Post and demanded traders. The Arkansas commander apparently was unwilling or unable to stop them and continued to trade with them. The Arkansas Post was a low-paying and isolated one. Opportunities existed for an officer to increase his meager salary by trading with the Indians. The legal trade with the Quapaw was less lucrative than the illegal Osage trade, and thus Osage trade continued, further exacerbating political strife within the Osage nation.[14]

This was especially true in 1783 and 1784. In December 1783, an Osage warrior arrived at the Arkansas Post with a band of followers. The warrior and his band had come upon another Osage group along the upper Arkansas who were about to kill some hunters. He stopped the killing and saved the lives of two European hunters. The warrior, named Cuchechire by the Spanish, requested a small medal. The Spanish officer awarded him a medal, "in order to give him more authority and encourage him to maintain tranquility in the districts."[15] By awarding him a medal, even a small one, the Spanish had granted him considerable political status. The governor at Saint Louis later heard from traders among the Osage that

13. Cruzat to Gálvez, July 6, 1777, ibid., 152–55.
14. Stanley Faye, "Spanish Domination," 632, 634–36, 638, 641–50.
15. Dubreuil to Miró, December 21, 1783, Nasatir Papers, 3:61.

such has been the displeasure of the two principal chiefs and the entire nation, generally, upon seeing a youth who did not merit any consideration elevated to the character of chief by a commandant upon whom they did not depend, that various debates were held among the said Big Osages, from which it originated that all the aforesaid nation was divided in three parties, one of them—which was that of the two said principal chiefs—remained to trade with the traders who were sent to them; the second, at the head of which was referred to new chief Cuchechiré, went to winter on the Arkansas river about one hundred and seventy leagues from the indicated Fort Charles III (Arkansas Post), on a site called *El Campamento de Gascon,* and traded until this spring with the traders which he had promised them, and whom in fact, the said commandant sent them; and the third party penetrated further into the prairies to be able more opportunely to make war on the Pani Piques [Wichita] of the dependency of Natchitoches and other nations.[16]

The internal problems persisted as more Osage went south to trade and were encouraged to trade by the Arkansas officials. In Saint Louis, the Spanish commander working with Saint Louis–based traders and Spanish-recognized Osage leadership expressed continued dismay over the situation and tried to stop it. In February of 1785, a group of fifty Osage from Cuchechire's band arrived at the Arkansas Post. The leader of the group was an Osage named Bru Caiguais, who already had a big medal of his father's. Bru Caiguais must have been a son of one of the earlier Osage leaders sanctioned by the French or Spanish but without a position in 1785. Jacobo Dubreuil, the Arkansas commander, sent Bru Caiguais and another unnamed prominent Osage to New Orleans to receive a small medal of his own and "a large flag, a dress coat, and a hat" for Cuchechire.[17] Upon arrival in New Orleans, Governor Esteban Rodriguez Miró granted them Spanish medals, and since a Caddo group was present in the city, Miró urged the two groups to make peace. The Caddo were

16. Cruzat to Miró, June 23, 1784, ibid., 81–82.
17. Dubreuil to Miró, March 18, 1785, ibid., 86.

reluctant, for they "declared the people who are in your post [Arkansas] to be of no value, and, therefore, the peace, towards which you tell me the said Chief was only little inclined, is of no value." Despite these remarks, Governor Miró convinced the Caddo to make peace with the Osage and sent both groups home, the Osage with a coat and hat for "Chief" Cuchechire. In addition to the gifts, Miró promised to send a trader from the Arkansas Post upriver to trade with the Osage if they kept the peace.[18]

Later in the year, when Miró prepared a description of Louisiana and Illinois Indians, he described the Osage along the Arkansas, but he identified them as the Little Osage. This is confusing, for nowhere else are the Little Osage mentioned on the Arkansas, yet Miró had met with these people just months before this report was prepared. Miró, in the same report, placed the Big Osage on this river and another group of the Little Osage on the Missouri. It is not clear who the dissidents along the Arkansas were, but clearly they were a splinter band of one of the major Osage groups and may indeed have been members of the Down Below People Band. Earlier, in 1773, a larger group of Little Osage fled the Missouri River Valley and temporarily sought refuge among the Big Osage when they were attacked by tribes north of the Missouri.[19] They could have easily gone south to the Arkansas Valley.

Despite the promise of peace made to Dubreuil and Miró, the southern Osage continued to raid in 1786. The economic opportunities were too great, and the peacemakers were of doubtful political authority. The opportunities for trade were excellent and the Osage neighbors owned horses and occupied prime hunting grounds. The Caddo were unarmed and were unable to resist Osage advances. The Osage were unwilling to allow non-

18. Miró to Dubreuil, May 25, 1785, ibid., 88; Miró to Dubreuil, April 28, 1785, ibid., 94.
19. Miró to Rengle, December 12, 1785, ibid., 98, 101, 104; Piernas to Unzaga, July 6, 1773, ibid., 2:98.

Osage trappers to invade their hunting grounds or arm their enemies, so they continued to rob and kill to discourage the European intruders.

The ongoing violence between the Osage and the Caddo angered Governor Miró. Miró wrote Dubreuil at the Arkansas and told him to withdraw the traders from the Arkansas Osage and compel them to stop their trading. Miró was particularly angered because the chief he had met with and awarded the medal to, Bru Caiguais, had led the raid on the Caddo. Miró demanded that Bru Caiguais surrender himself as a hostage against further outbreaks along the Arkansas.[20]

Dubreuil was unable to secure Bru Caiguais as a hostage, but surprisingly he did secure his medal, flag, and commission, in one of the few instances where an uncooperative leader was stripped of his symbols.[21] Later, the Spanish discovered that Bru Caiguais had instigated the attack on the Caddo because he feared that Cogisiguede (Cuchechire) would go to New Orleans. Bru Caiguais feared that he "could not uphold his reputation as the greater personage if his companion carried out his purpose [going to New Orleans]," so he had attacked the Caddo to prevent any possible trip to New Orleans.[22] Once again the Spanish contributed to the confusion and violence they had sought to eliminate.

The Osage political system was in turmoil, for the parent group of Big Osage, led by Clermont and Lafond, were angry that Dubreuil had created Cuchechire as a chief, and the splinter group also suffered from internal dissension as Cuchechire and

20. Miró to Cruzat, March 24, 1786, ibid., 3:115–17; Dubreuil to Miró, May 21, 1786, ibid., 122.

21. Dubreuil to Miró, December 13, 1786, ibid., 137; Kinnaird, ed., *Spain in the Mississippi Valley,* 2:171–72, 182–84, 196–97, 253–56; Ewers, "Symbols of Chiefly Authority," 280–81.

22. Miró to Sonora, February 1, 1787, Nasatir Papers, 3:152–58. *Cuchechire* is written *Cogisiguede* in Miró's letter. It is clear, however, that Cogisiguede, Couzichequeday, and Kuchechire are all attempts to write the Osage *Ko-zhi-ci-gthe* or *Ka-zhi-ci-grah,* which means Makes Tracks Far Away.

Bru Caiguais struggled for power and Spanish recognition. How-ever, the struggle among the splintered Arkansas Band retained essential Osage traditions. Cuchechire was from the *Hon-ga* moiety, a member of the Panther People clan.[23] Panther clan members were among the leaders of the Osage, as the *A-ki-da Ton-ga* (Great Soldier) was chosen from the Panther People. Cuchechire, while not a member of the proper *Ga-hi-ge* clan, did have a legitimate tie to Osage political power. Bru Caiguais, as a member of the Osage elite, also had a claim to political power. His possession of his father's big medal is evidence that he was a member of the *Tsi-zhu Wa-shta-ge* clan from which the *Tsi-zhu Ga-hi-ge* were selected. He had obviously not been chosen to replace his father as *Tsi-zhu Ga-hi-ge,* but he sought to create a new political base along the Arkansas River with Cuchechire, the *Hon-ga* leader.

These two men, representing *Hon-ga* and *Tsi-zhu* moieties, continued traditional Osage chieftainship patterns, but Cuche-chire's claim to power was tenuous. Not a member of the *Pon-ka Wa-shta-ge,* he was only eligible for an *A-ki-da* position, and ini-tially he only requested a small medal from the Spanish, consis-tent with his rank. In time, however, either because of his grow-ing influence or because the Spanish wanted him to have more power, he was granted a big medal.

Cuchechire's growing influence also explained Bru Caiguais's resentment. Bru Caiguais was a *Tsi-zhu* from the proper *Ga-hi-ge* clan and was forced to share power with upstart Cuchechire. Bru Caiguais was willing to share power with Cuchechire, yet Cuchechire was gaining influence and prestige while Bru Cai-guais seemed stuck in a subordinate position. Bru Caiguais had made the effort to go to New Orleans, which was consistent with the role of a peace chief. He negotiated a treaty with the Spanish and Caddo, and when he left for home he still received only a secondary medal. Bru Caiguais was behaving in the Osage

---

23. Mathews, *The Osages,* 299; Burns, *Osage Bands and Clans,* 4.

way. A peace chief, albeit a newly created one among the splinter group, he had treatied with outsiders, yet they ignored him and rewarded the *Hon-ga* chief Cuchechire. This, in part, explains his attack on the Caddo to demonstrate his power and weaken that of Cuchechire.

When the raiding continued along the Arkansas and among the Caddo along the Red River, the Spanish demanded that the Osage stop. They threatened to cut off trade with the Osage and called on the leadership to send hostages to New Orleans. The Spanish maintained that until hostages were sent and raiding stopped, the Osage would be viewed as enemies, trade would cease, and they would be attacked by Indians armed by the Spanish. In 1787, Miró ordered trade halted, again demanded hostages, and declared that "it will also be useful to move and excite the Arkansas [Quapaw] so that they may fall upon the Osages."[24]

The Spanish were forced to use economic blockades and rely upon their Native American allies to deal with the Osage, for their military presence was extremely limited in Spanish Louisiana. Throughout the late eighteenth century, there were fewer than 150 Spanish soldiers in the area, forcing the Spanish to rely on locally recruited militia. Yet the combined Spanish army and militia made up only about 350 men. Thus, the Spanish had to employ friendly Indian tribes to conduct their campaigns, and most of the Indians were reluctant to fight the Osage, who could field over one thousand armed men.[25]

The Osage were in an excellent position, for they had a sizable military force that was armed and intimately familiar with the terrain. The Spanish economic boycott was perhaps the only Spanish strength, yet it could be undermined by going north to the Des Moines River and trading with Canadian traders or by

24. Miró to Vallière, May 15, 1787, Nasatir Papers, 3:167.
25. Filhiol to Miró, May 20, 1784, ibid., 79; Kinnaird, ed., *Spain in the Mississippi Valley*, 3:xxi, 104; Nasatir, *Before Lewis and Clark*, 1:51–52; Foley, *History of Missouri*, 28.

traveling south and getting supplies from the outlaw traders along the Arkansas River who always ignored Spanish trade regulations. Despite their strong position, the Osage clearly did not desire war, and they attempted to keep the peace and negotiate with the Spanish.

The Osage sent two hostages to the Spanish, "since it was better that they should suffer rather than the whole nation in general," but upon arriving at the Arkansas Post the hostages escaped and returned to the Big Osage village on the Osage River.[26] In October 1787, the principal chiefs, Lafond and Clermont, again went to Saint Louis to deal with the Spanish. They argued that their people had not attacked any Spanish outpost and had only killed "a few men scattered in the woods." They explained they had done that because indeed they had been at war with other Indian groups, and "when we go to war or when we are returning from it, we are obliged to strike against those who present themselves." They continued to explain that the trouble on the Arkansas was not their fault. Lafond noted, "It is not I, or the young men who are here, who have killed; it is some fools over who I am not master. Do you not have some fools among your young men?" Continuing, Lafond advised, "One should be angry at the Arkansas [Post]. If they did not ask for us, we would not go there." Lafond concluded with a comment on his own internal political problems: "The chiefs are not obeyed as among you. . . . But we have not been masters of the fools; there are some everywhere."[27]

Despite this and other meetings with the Spanish, the Osage living along the Arkansas continued to raid Caddo groups to the south and west and pillage hunters between the Missouri and Arkansas Rivers. They raided because it insured tribal security, and it provided status and wealth for the participants. The Osage leadership, unable to stop them, tried to explain to the Spanish

26. Testimony of Luis Darrac, June 23, 1787, Nasatir Papers, 3:199.
27. Cruzat to Miró, November 12, 1787, ibid., 208–10.

their predicament, but the Spanish refused to accept the Osage explanation and continued to demand hostages and reparation for raids (head for head, in the words of one Spanish writer). When the Spanish did not receive compensation, they eventually decided to impose a trade embargo and go to war against the Osage.

The war was brief, for the Lieutenant Governor in Saint Louis, Manuel Pérez, was reluctant to attack the Osage. Pérez feared the expense of a war and potential loss of men. The proposed boycott was unsuccessful, for the Osage simply stopped traders going up the Missouri to other tribes or traveled north to the Des Moines River and traded with Canadian-based merchants.[28] Pérez finally proposed in October 1791 that it would be cheaper to construct a fort near the Osage village than it would be to fight them:

> I believe the matter will be so easy that it will have on its side two-thirds of the nation with the principal chiefs and warriors who always (at least in appearance) have disapproved of the raids of the others, without having sufficient authority of themselves to repress them; but seeing near them a fort, I am more than persuaded that these chiefs and warriors will make themselves powerful enough to arrest and hand over the murderer or the robber with the stolen goods.[29]

Despite Pérez's suggestion, the fort was not constructed, and the Osage continued to steal horses and kill several non-Indians in the area. The Spanish tried to halt trade with the Osage and encouraged other Indians to attack them. Then, on December 22, 1792, Governor General Francisco Luis Hector, Baron de Carondelet, ordered Saint Louis commander Lieutenant Governor Zenon Trudeau, who replaced Pérez, "to prohibit all and any trade with the Big and Little Osages." He further demanded that Trudeau issue a proclamation encouraging others to kill the

---

28. Nasatir, "Ducharme's Invasion of Missouri," 3–25.
29. Pérez to Miró, October 5, 1791, Nasatir Papers, 4:60.

Osage: "It is extremely important to humiliate or destroy those barbarians, which can only be done by using severity."[30]

The campaign against the Osage was an utter failure. The Osage continued to receive weapons, and the tribes that had been urged to attack the Osage either refused to attack or only skirmished with small raiding parties. The major campaign contemplated never came about. In January, a group of Little Osage leaders journeyed to Saint Louis and offered to return their medals and explained that they could not prevent the raiding nor return the stolen property. The Spanish refused to accept the Osage response and continued to demand hostages and reimbursement. In August, the Big and Little Osage once again came to Saint Louis and asked to negotiate, yet nothing came of the meeting, for they continued to refuse to send hostages or pay for losses.[31]

The war against the Osage ended in the spring of 1794. Local settlers, suffering from repeated Osage raids and thefts during the "war," complained loudly about the failure of the campaigns, and Governor Carondelet became more concerned with a new threat to the Spanish in upper Louisiana. Edmond Genet, a representative of the new revolutionary government in France, was traveling in the United States and marshalling support for his country in its war against Spain and England. Genet was planning an invasion of Spanish Louisiana to be led by George Rogers Clark. Carondelet, alarmed by Clark's call for volunteers, sought to end the war with the Osage. The unrealistic Genet-Clark threat was considered a more serious matter to Louisiana than the Osage threat, and Carondelet feared that alienated Osage might join Genet and Clark and attack the Spanish.[32]

Therefore, when Auguste Chouteau, a prominent French

---

30. Carondelet to Trudeau, December 22, 1792, ibid., 115–16.
31. Trudeau to Peyroux, August 20, 1793, ibid., 167–68; Trudeau to Vallé, August 20, 1793, ibid., 168.
32. Trudeau to Carondelet, January 15, 1794, ibid., 198–99.

trader in Saint Louis, proposed a solution to end the war with the Osage and provide peace in the south, the Spanish agreed. Auguste and his younger half-brother Pierre Chouteau had been in the Missouri region for many years. As a teenage boy, Auguste had founded Saint Louis in 1763, and almost immediately thereafter, he and Pierre began trading with the Osage. Auguste lived in Saint Louis, while Pierre spent much of his time with the Big Osage. Although he probably did not travel to the plains with them, Pierre clearly spent a great deal of time with them in the fall and winter at their villages. Pierre apparently could speak the Osage language, and it is likely that he took an Osage wife, as did many other French and métis traders.[33] The Chouteaus, with their close economic and kin ties to the Big Osage, sought to continue their profitable trade that had been hampered by the violence between the Spanish and Osage.

Auguste Chouteau took six Osage leaders to New Orleans to meet with the Spanish governor of Louisiana and to negotiate a peaceful settlement of their mutual problems and bring an end to the violence in Osage country. Chouteau took with him one of the Big Osage moiety leaders, Lafond. The other *Ga-hi-ge,* Clermont, refused to go to New Orleans with Chouteau and remained at the Osage River village. Three other prominent members of the Big Osage Band, probably *A-ki-da* or prominent *Non-hon-zhin-ga,* accompanied Chouteau: Cheveux Blanc (White Hair, or Pawhuska), Roble Tolle, and Petit Oiseau (Little Bird). Two Little Osage also went along with Chouteau: one was a *Ga-hi-ge* named La Vent (The Wind), and the other was a prominent Osage called Soldat du Chene.[34] Chouteau and the six Osage left

33. Delassus to Carondelet, April 26, 1794, ibid., 5:4. "He has an absolute power over this entire nation, which he has known from infancy. His brother [Pierre] is, perhaps, the only man who has made himself feared and respected by all those who compose it" (Trudeau to Carondelet, April 27, 1794, ibid., 6); William E. Foley and C. David Rice, *The First Chouteaus: River Barons of Early St. Louis,* 20–21, 45; Tanis Chapman Thorne, "The Chouteau Family and the Osage Trade: A Generational Study," 109–19; Mathews, *The Osages,* 285, 297.
34. Trudeau to Carondelet, April 24, 1794, Nasatir Papers, 5:1–4. The name

for New Orleans in the spring of 1794. This was a significant trip, for several events occurred that were to radically shape the Osage political system.

While in New Orleans, Governor Carondelet negotiated with the Osage to end the attacks on traders and Caddo. In hopes of bringing peace to the area, Carondelet agreed to continue trade with the Osage, and to that end he granted Auguste Chouteau permission to erect a fort and trading post at the Osage villages on the Osage River. Chouteau was to use the fort to control the Osage. In return for stopping Osage aggressions, Carondelet granted Auguste and his brother a six-year monopoly of the Osage trade.[35] Chouteau promised to "strengthen the authority of the chiefs for restraining the young warriors, preventing them from making raids, and punishing with death those who commit murders in our districts, at the same time endeavoring to secure restitution for the robberies which they might commit."[36]

Carondelet awarded a big medal to *Ga-hi-ge* Lafond, a small medal to Cheveux Blanc, and two Spanish captain's commissions to Roble Tolle and Petit Oiseau. He granted another large medal to La Vent, *Ga-hi-ge* of the Little Osage, and a small medal to Soldat du Chene. Carondelet had by these acts recognized Lafond and La Vent as principal chiefs of the Big and Little Osage. He had also recognized the positions of Cheveux Blanc and Soldat du Chene as secondary leaders above captains Roble Tolle and Petit Oiseau.

---

is unclear. It may have been Soldat du Chene, which would have been Oak Soldier, or Soldat du Chiene, Dog Soldier. In 1804, a Little Osage chief named Dog Soldier went to Washington, D.C., to meet President Jefferson. See Donald Jackson, ed., *Letters of the Lewis and Clark Expedition with Related Documents, 1783–1854*, 1:304. There was also a prominent nineteenth-century Osage soldier called Soldier of the Oak. Although one cannot be completely sure of who went to New Orleans with Chouteau, it seems that the Soldat du Chene was probably Dog Soldier, either the *Hon-ga Ga-hi-ge* for the Little Osage or the leading *A-ki-da* for La Vent. See Trudeau to Carondelet, April 24, 1794, Nasatir Papers, 5:1–4.

35. Trudeau to Carondelet, April 27, 1794, Nasatir Papers, 5:5–7; Petition of Auguste Chouteau, May 18, 1794, ibid., 7–10.

36. Document of Carondelet, May 21, 1794, ibid., 14–15.

In all of this there exists a great deal of tragic irony. The Spanish, ready for peace and eager to control these powerful Indians, attempted to establish an alliance with them by recognizing Osage political leadership. Unfortunately for both the Spanish and Osage, the officials in New Orleans did not have a real understanding of Osage political power. Blinded by their own political conceptualization, the Spanish imposed another new arrangement that was consistent with Spanish experience but inconsistent with Osage political reality.

Carondelet created single Osage chiefs, ignoring the dual chieftainship tradition. In the case of the Big Osage, he erred further by awarding the big medal to the *Hon-ga* leader, Lafond. Lafond, the *Hon-ga Ga-hi-ge* and a prominent Big Osage leader, was not the man the Spanish should have been impressing. *Tsi-zhu Ga-hi-ge* Clermont would have been the proper leader for outsiders to deal with, for that was the culturally defined role of the peace chief. Clermont had refused to go with Chouteau, Lafond had agreed; thus, the Spanish conferred the big medal on Lafond.

The Spanish were unknowingly creating a new political pattern which undermined the traditional system they were trying to use to implement their imperial policies. Carondelet clearly was unaware of any such problem, and the one man who did understand, Auguste Chouteau, apparently believed that he and his brother could manipulate the Osage and control them despite the confusion created by the Spanish officials at New Orleans.[37] Thus, the Spanish were weakening the very system they believed they were strengthening. This inconsistency would create further problems for both the Osage and the Spanish.

Unfortunately for the Osage, less than one hundred miles from New Orleans the Osage were attacked by a band of Chickasaw. The Chickasaw, seeking revenge for an earlier Osage attack, killed Lafond, La Vent, and Soldat du Chene. The Euro-

---

37. Auguste Chouteau to Carondelet, November 10, 1793, ibid., 1; Trudeau to Carondelet, April 24, 1794, ibid., 1–4; Delassus to Carondelet, April 26, 1794, ibid., 4; Trudeau to Carondelet, April 27, 1794, ibid., 5–7.

peans were not attacked, so Chouteau and the others escaped. Fearing another attack upriver, the Osage survivors left the river and traveled home overland.[38] Chouteau, who was not the intended victim of the Chickasaw attack, continued on up the Mississippi to Saint Louis. Despite a dangerous journey through hostile Caddo country, the three Osage survivors arrived safely back in the Big Osage villages in the fall. With the death of Lafond, La Vent, and Soldat du Chene, the traditional leadership of both the Big and Little Osage had been severely decimated. Chouteau quickly went to the Osage: "I was obliged to cover the dead in order to conform to their customs which obliges all partisans returning from any expedition whatsoever and who have lost one of them who has followed him to cover *au grés* the dead of the family."[39]

Chouteau, clearly familiar with Osage traditions, paid compensation for the dead. He was operating within the Osage cultural context, and he correctly assumed the position and the responsibilities of a *Do-don-hon-ga,* an Osage party leader.[40] Both Auguste and his brother Pierre were highly knowledgeable about Osage culture and used this knowledge to their advantage in the future. Pierre Chouteau also assumed the role of Spanish agent among the Osage. He passed the Spanish medals of Lafond, La Vent, and Soldat du Chene on to their sons. "As these nations are accustomed always to pass medals and *patentes* from fathers to sons or closest relatives, it has seemed to me essential to deliver those of the dead men to their sons."[41]

The three sons of the dead leaders were all about twenty years old and were considered too young to assume the chieftain role. Therefore, Chouteau appointed "regents" for them. He selected

38. Auguste Chouteau to Carondelet, June 1, 1794, ibid., 21–22; Carondelet to Lemos, June 3, 1794, ibid., 22–24; Auguste Chouteau to Carondelet, June 12, 1794, ibid., 28–29.

39. Auguste Chouteau to Carondelet, September 17, 1794, ibid., 45.

40. McDermott, *Tixier's Travels,* 174; Bailey, "Osage Social Organization, 1673–1906," 22.

41. Trudeau to Carondelet, September 15, 1794, Nasatir Papers, 5:43.

the uncle of the principal chief Clermont as regent for Lafond's son, and he named two uncles of La Vent and Soldat du Chene's sons as their regents. Chouteau also asked the Spanish in New Orleans to send another big medal for the principal chief of the Osage who had refused to make the trip with Chouteau, Clermont.[42]

Again the Spanish were caught up in their lack of understanding of Osage politics. They correctly attempted to assuage Clermont by sending another big medal, yet at the same time they blundered again by appointing Clermont's uncle (who was also Pawhuska's brother) as a regent for Lafond's son. This was a mistake, for Lafond and his son were *Hon-ga,* or members of the Earth moiety. Lafond's son was to be a *Hon-ga Ga-hi-ge,* but Chouteau, who clearly knew better, appointed a *Tsi-zhu* member as his regent. A *Tsi-zhu* regent could not, according to Osage traditions, act as a *Hon-ga Ga-hi-ge.*

The Spanish in New Orleans were relying on the advice of the Chouteau brothers. Both possessed a keen understanding of Osage culture and polity and knew what they were doing. Pierre had lived among the Osage for years and had established close ties with prominent Osage families. As a wealthy trader, he also possessed considerable economic power. The Chouteaus clearly believed that Pierre's influence was powerful enough to impose this abnormal pattern upon the Osage. It is not clear, however, why they would want to do such a thing. Many of the Osage resented Pierre's influence among the northern bands. Perhaps Pierre did not want to give power to an individual who was the culturally appropriate guardian but who threatened his influence. Pierre may have intentionally created such an awkward and foreign system to weaken the authority of the *Hon-ga* moiety leadership. While their motives remain hidden, their actions are clear. The Chouteaus would soon take advantage of the political instability they had helped to create. This unnatural imposition caused resentment and confusion, and once again the Spanish

42. Ibid.

had created a political system that would only cause disorder and trouble in the future.[43]

During most of the eighteenth century, the Osage were able to go south and west and take slaves, horses, pelts, and food. This was encouraged because they could trade these products for the European goods they desired. The goods they acquired, horses and guns, only fueled Osage territorial expansion, which in turn increased their economic growth. The Osage were in an interesting, lucrative position, but this same position placed pressure on the traditional political structure.

The successful young hunters and warriors gained possessions and status within the tribe that could not be reconciled with the traditional social and political framework. The pressure was such that the tribe splintered, breaking into separate independent bands. In 1700, and again in 1785, two bands left the parent group and formed new Osage groups. The first split involved the group known as the Little Osage, and not much is known about their departure. The second split probably occurred for the same reasons, yet was aggravated by outsiders. Intruders came and lived among the Osage and created a political system with new offices and functions. The French and Spanish sought to shape an Osage government along lines familiar to them. They refused to recognize the dual chieftain system and virtually ignored the *Non-hon-zhin-ga.* Traders also became involved within the traditional political system and contributed to its eventual collapse.

The increased warfare and the ever-present economic opportunity forever altered the traditional leadership. The disgruntled, ambitious Osage who had no power within the old system broke away and formed small, independent bands. Ironically and tragically, the Osage were losing their tribal unity at a time when unity was needed to confront the growing pressures from the east and west.

43. This unusual regent was clearly a *Tsi-zhu* for the Spanish stated that he was a brother to Pawhuska, a *Tsi-zhu,* and an uncle to Clermont, the *Tsi-zhu Ga-hi-ge.*

7.

CHALLENGES TO HEGEMONY

We want no War, there are the Chickasaws, Chocktaws, [sic]
Cherokees, Delawars [sic] and Arkansas are all at War with us,
we dont [sic] want to be at War with them, we want to hunt and
Kill our Game in Peace.

—Cashesegra, 1806[1]

In the second half of the eighteenth century, the Osage expanded and prospered. Buoyed by their successful exploitation of the resources of the forests, prairies, and plains, the Osage enjoyed remarkable economic and military success. Having escaped most of the eighteenth-century epidemics, they remained numerically strong. Living between the Missouri and the Arkansas Rivers, the Osage were in a strategic location that allowed them to control access to the west, while occupying the middle ground between competing European colonial frontiers.

Their military and economic gains, however, placed increasing pressures on traditional Osage society and polity. Initially, the new demands for power and prestige were defused by the resilient Osage culture. The Osage accommodated the growing demands by creating new social and political institutions that provided additional opportunities for status. With the continued success of Osage hunters, traders, and soldiers, single bands were unable to integrate all of the demands for position,

---

1. Bright Relative to Osage, *Letters Received Secretary of War, Main Series.*

so the Osage separated and created new bands. The creation of new bands produced an entire array of new positions to provide status, power, and prestige for the ambitious. Before band mitosis, the Osage lived in three distinct bands. In the 1760s, the Big Osage Band remained along the headwaters of the Osage River, the Arkansas Band occupied the Three Forks region of the Arkansas River, and the Little Osage Band lived along the Missouri River.

Osage expansion did not go unchallenged. Neighboring tribes continued to encroach on Osage lands. By the 1780s, neighboring tribes began aggressively challenging the Osage for land and resources. The Potawatomi, Kickapoo, Sac, Mesquakie (Fox), and other tribes living northeast of the Osage continued their intrusions into Osage territory. At the same time, old allies among the Illinois Confederacy and new rivals such as the Delaware and Shawnee, pushed westward by Anglo-American settlement, began crossing the Mississippi and establishing villages on the fringes of Osage territory. Aggressive southeastern tribes, such as the Chickasaw, Choctaw, and Cherokee, also began crossing the Mississippi and traveling up the Arkansas to hunt and raid in the Ozark and Ouachita forests. Although the Osage had successfully driven the Caddo south of the Ouachitas and the Wichita out of the Arkansas Valley, they had to remain alert to retain control of the southwest, as these tribes continually sought to return to their former homelands. Although the Comanche were a growing threat in the west, they were occupied with the Spanish, Apache, and Ute in the west and south and only occasionally confronted the Osage. This uneasy standoff with the Comanche allowed the Osage to focus on their greatest challenge on the plains, the Pawnee. The southern bands of the Pawnee were a constant threat in the west, always challenging the Osage for the great buffalo herds found along the Arkansas and the Smoky Hill Rivers. The Osage alliance with the Kansa insured that the Pawnee would be kept out of the region, but their presence in the west was a continuing risk to summer buffalo hunts. Surrounded by aggressive and dangerous rivals, the Osage continued to confront their enemies with success and maintain their domination of the southern prairie-plains.

This success, however, created important internal problems. Prominent warriors and hunters demanded prestige and power, and the Osage were hard-pressed to satisfy those demands. Outsiders who understood Osage lifeways took advantage of the rapid social and political changes taking place among the Osage and of the thwarted ambitions of Osage individuals to promote, to their own advantage, the interests of those who could be manipulated. The Chouteau family of Saint Louis was particularly guilty of such behavior. The Chouteaus continually used their knowledge of Osage traditions and their position as long-time traders and wealthy friends of the Osage to manipulate them. They created new *A-ki-da* sympathetic to the Chouteaus' interests and placed Pawhuska, a cooperative but traditionally unqualified individual, in place as a single leader of all the Osage. Their interference accelerated tribal factionalism and deeply divided the Osage people. The combination of powerful outside challenges and ongoing internal disputes would over time weaken the Osage and prevent them from maintaining their hegemony of the southern prairie-plains.

Despite their economic and military success and their skillful accommodation of internal social and political stress, the Osage still had to contend with threats to their hegemony from neighboring Indian groups as the eighteenth century came to a close. Much of the pressure came from the east, as Native American nations attempted to move away from the Anglo-American frontier. Sac, Mesquakie, Potawatomi, Miami, Shawnee, Delaware, Choctaw, Chickasaw, and Cherokee hunters increased their intrusions into the Ozark and Ouachita forests, seeking game and a refuge from the Anglo-Americans. The Osage struggled to protect the animal base of their economy, but in the 1790s the intrusions increased despite Osage opposition.

The Iowa, Sac, and Mesquakie frequently hunted and raided in Osage country. The Mesquakie and Sac had originally lived well to the north of Osage country, but the Mesquakie, devastated by wars with the French in the early eighteenth century, sought the protection of the Sac, and in the 1780s both had moved to the Mississippi Valley. The Sac remained on the east bank while the Mesquakie crossed the Mississippi and occupied the land between the Des Moines and Mississippi Rivers. Both the Mesquakie and the Sac had access to Canadian traders who came among them or traded with the Indians at Prairie du Chien. The Sac were particularly aggressive. When they hunted along the Des Moines River, they occasionally went south into Osage country. The Osage hunted north of the Missouri along the Grand and Chariton Rivers, but they generally hunted south of the Des Moines Valley. The territory between the Des Moines watershed and that of the Grand and Chariton Rivers marked the uneasy border between the Osage hunting ground and that of the Iowa, Sac, and Mesquakie. The boundary was never exact; instead, it was a vaguely defined region between the tribes. This neutral zone was shared by the peoples, but one group occasionally challenged the other's control of the area.[2] When Iowa, Sac, or Mesquakie hunters ventured down the Grand or Chariton Rivers, the Osage would attack them and drive them north, and if the other groups discovered Osage hunters in their territory, they would drive them south. Osage, Sac, Mesquakie, and Iowa were equally matched, for all were well armed and supplied with trade goods and guns. For most of the late eighteenth and early nineteenth centuries, these peoples maintained a tense peace, interrupted by outbreaks of violence when hunters encountered rival hunting parties.

In 1788, British traders, eager to secure Osage trade and loyalty, urged the Sac to bring the Osage north to trade on the Des Moines River. The Spanish, who were gravely concerned about any British influence among Indians in Spanish territory, wanted to prevent any British-Osage contact. In 1790, when the Spanish

2. Michael D. Green, " 'We Dance in Opposite Directions': Mesquakie (Fox) Separatism from the Sac and Fox Tribe"; White, "Winning of the West," 334.

learned of possible British-Osage trade, they urged the Sac to attack the Osage. Despite Spanish efforts to encourage warfare between the Sac and the Osage, the two tribes made peace and hunted together in the fall of 1791. The peace was short-lived, however, and by the spring of 1792 they were fighting once again. In 1793, the Spanish, hoping to control the Osage, halted trade with them. In order to maintain the essential flow of arms and ammunition, the Osage went north and made peace with the Mesquakie and the Sac and traded with Canadian traders along the Des Moines River.[3]

The temporary peace among the Osage, Mesquakie, and Sac survived until 1795, when the British evacuated their northwestern forts. Once the British left, the United States occupied the territory up to the Mississippi. With the United States occupation came aggressive frontier settlement in the northwest, which pushed the Sac and Mesquakie further west.

Despite the British evacuation of the northwestern forts, Canadian traders continued to come south to trade with the Osage. The Spanish, still concerned by the continued British influence among the Osage, once again encouraged the Sac to attack them. The lieutenant governor of Spanish Illinois, Zenon Trudeau, wrote, "The Sacs, who are very numerous, hunting on the Missouri killed ten or twelve Osages after having shaken hands with them and promised peace. I believe that it is very important that these two nations are continually in discord in order to stop the communications of the Osages upon [with] the upper Mississippi. They are doing little damage to each other and never go away to wage warfare the one against the other."[4] The struggle continued between the two peoples with little change for years. Even an 1801–1802 smallpox epidemic among the Osage, which weakened the northern bands, did not prevent

---

3. Pérez to Miró, November 19, 1788, Nasatir Papers, 3:230–31; Pérez to Miró, August 6, 1790, ibid., 4:16–17; Trudeau to Carondelet, October 21, 1793, ibid., 186–87.
4. Trudeau to Mon Général (Carondelet), March 12, 1795, ibid., 5:59–60.

the Osage from keeping the Sac and Mesquakie north of the Missouri River.[5]

Other groups living north and east of the Osage, such as the Kickapoo and Potawatomi, had occasionally crossed the Mississippi to hunt and raid in Osage country for most of the eighteenth century. Their raids continued, for Osage horses and captives remained attractive to the Potawatomi and Kickapoo. Osage hunting camps in northeast Missouri were usually small and poorly protected, yet they contained horses and other valuables. The Potawatomi and Kickapoo lived far enough away from the Osage to prevent any serious retaliation, and the distances between the groups and the size of the raiding parties kept the hostilities on a small scale, but by the early nineteenth century the region along the Missouri River had become a more dangerous place for the Osage.[6]

Early in the spring of 1799, a group of Kickapoo surprised an Osage bear-hunting camp while most of the men were away. The Kickapoo killed forty-five Osage, mostly women and children. In May 1804, a Sac war party led by Paunblanche ambushed a group of Osage on their way to Saint Louis. They killed several Osage and took some prisoners. In October 1805, the Osage met with the Sac and Mesquakie and agreed to peace, but this détente had little effect as long as these tribes were competing for economic control. Less than two months after the treaty, a band of Potawatomi raiders led by Main Poche attacked an undefended Osage village south of the Missouri. Most of the Osage men, engaged in the winter's hunt, were away from the village, so the Potawatomi were able to kill thirty-four women and children and take sixty prisoners.[7]

5. Map prepared according to Auguste Chouteau's notes, 1816, in "Glimpse of the Past Notes of Auguste Chouteau on Boundaries of Various Indian Nations," *Missouri Historical Society Bulletin* 7 (October–December 1940): 12; Fred W. Voget, *Osage Research Report,* 25–30; Clemson, et al., to Eustis, July 16, 1812, Carter, *Territorial Papers,* 14:587–90.

6. Clifton, *Prairie People,* 143, 190.

7. Delassus to Casa Calvo, April 24, 1800, Nasatir Papers, 6:7–8; Jackson,

As Kickapoo, Sac, Mesquakie, and Potawatomi attacks increased, the Osage had to contend with a new threat from those tribes living south of the Potawatomi and Kickapoo, the Illinois. The Osage sought to maintain their peaceful relations with the various Illinois tribes, but as other eastern Indians and Anglo-American settlers pushed into their country and killed their game, the Illinois nations began hunting more frequently across the Mississippi in Osage territory. As hunts increased, so did Osage opposition to their onetime allies. As with other neighboring eastern tribes, however, Osage relations with the Illinois fluctuated. The Osage sometimes traded peacefully with the Illinois in their settlements along the Mississippi Valley, but when the Kaskaskia, Miami, or Peoria hunted in the Ozarks, the Osage attacked them.

The Ozark forests were particularly important to the Osage. Fur-bearing animals, especially the important bear and beaver, which supplied fur and fat for the Osage, thrived in the forests. This important natural resource was vital to their trade economy, and any threat to it was a serious threat to Osage survival. The Ozarks were also strategically important to the Osage. The rugged mountain country served as a buffer from eastern tribes. It was important for the Osage to keep rival nations out of the Ozarks and far away from their prairie villages. The Ozarks protected the Osage from the south and east, and the Osage constantly struggled to drive the outsiders from the Ozarks.

In an attempt to insulate their settlements from the Osage, the Spanish in the 1780s encouraged several Illinois tribes to cross the Mississippi and settle into the eastern edge of the Ozarks along the White and Saint Francis Rivers. In addition to the Illinois, other eastern tribes, such as the Delaware and Shawnee, feeling the pressure of the Anglo settlement, began accepting Spanish inducements. In the spring of 1787, a group of Dela-

---

Letters of Lewis and Clark, 1:196–97, 200; Pierre Chouteau to Dearborn, December 1, 1805, Pierre Chouteau Letterbook; Clifton, *Prairie People,* 190; Jackson, *Journals of Pike,* 2:32.

ware arrived at the Arkansas Post and requested permission to move to the White River.[8] In December 1788, a group of Miami came to the Arkansas Post and complained that Americans were abusing them and requested to settle in Spanish territory. The commandant there, Joseph Vallière, reported that

> the said party presented itself and explained to me that they came to take refuge under our flag on account of the Americans' not allowing them to be peaceful, and that within a few days another great party of them, as well as of the Chabank Indian nation, friends of theirs and also at war with the said Americans, were to arrive [here]. The said Miami Indians have asked me for permission to establish themselves on this river [Arkansas].[9]

The Spanish agreed to the Miami move, yet worried that they might ally themselves with their old friends, the Osage, and together threaten the Spanish. A little later, another group of Miami moved southeast along the Ouachita River, where they lived with Caddoan Indians in the area.[10] The Osage of course did not ally themselves with the Miami living in the Ozarks; instead, they tried to drive them out. The Osage considered protection of their important Ozark hunting grounds a higher priority than maintaining old friendships. The Indian resettlement program, whether encouraged by the Spanish or sought by other Native Americans, was thus vigorously resisted by the Osage. Trudeau observed that "they [the immigrating tribes] had been scarcely encamped when they were harassed by the Osages and

8. "By order of January 30, last, Your Excellency orders me that whenever any Indian tribe or nation presents itself with the intention of transmigrating themselves from [*sic*—to] this side that they be permitted to do so" (Trudeau to Carondelet, May 16, 1793, Nasatir Papers, 4:154); Vallière to Miró, June 3, 1787, ibid., 3:174–75.

9. Vallière to Miró, December 22, 1788, ibid., 3:234. It is not clear who the Chabank Indians were. They may have been the Shawnee, who are sometimes written as Cha8anons with the 8 copied as a B, or they may have been an Illinois subtribe.

10. Vallière to Filhiol, September 10, 1789, ibid., 244–45.

they immediately retired to the American district to pass the winter."[11]

Despite continued Osage resistance, eastern groups continued to push across the Mississippi into Osage country. Encouraged by the Spanish, two small groups of Shawnee and Delaware settled just south of Sainte Geneviève. Shortly thereafter, Louis Lorimier, a French Canadian, established a trading post for them at nearby Cape Girardeau.[12] Because of the Shawnee and Delaware's close ties with the Spanish and Lorimier, the Osage were never able to drive them back across the river, but the Osage managed to keep them east of the Saint Francis River. In the fall of 1792 Osage raids on the various eastern tribes increased, and a group of Delaware, Miami, Ottawa, Potawatomi, Peoria, and Shawnee asked Trudeau for help against the Osage. They complained that Americans forced them to leave their old homelands east of the river and move to the Spanish country, but as soon as they settled, "We were attacked on every side by the Osages who killed us and stole our horses. . . . We appeal to you, my father, to make him keep them and prevent them from killing us and stealing our horses."[13] The Osage continued to attack them until well after the American occupation in 1804.

As American settlers moved into the Old Southwest and took game and land from the Indian people living there, these Indians began moving further west. The Chickasaw, Choctaw, and Cherokee were reported along the Arkansas and Red Rivers in the late eighteenth century. As they intruded into Osage country, they were met with violence by the Osage. As early as 1775, Chickasaw hunters had been reported at the Arkansas Post. Joseph Orieta observed, "The 14th of March, last, thirty Chick-

11. Trudeau to Carondelet, May 16, 1793, ibid., 4:154. In the same letter Trudeau explains that the eastern Indians would rather stay east of the Mississippi, "although always living in fear of the Americans," than confront the Osage.

12. Foley, *History of Missouri,* 38; Nicolas de Finiels, *An Account of Upper Louisiana,* 34–35, 39, 119.

13. Loups (Delaware), Miamis, Outaouas (Ottawa), Poutouamis (Potawatomi), Peoria, and Chouesons (Shawnee) to Trudeau, 1792, Nasatir Papers, 4:104–7.

asas [sic] Indians arrived at the Arkansas villages. The following day, the 15th, the latter assembled and in common agreement both nations went out to charge upon the said Osages."[14]

Chickasaw raids were particularly violent. The Chickasaw, living far from any Osage settlements, and well armed by British and American traders, launched successful strikes against the Osage. Chickasaw raiding parties traveled into Osage country to take advantage of rich forest hunting. The Osage hunted in small groups in the winter and spring in the Ozarks, and those hunting in the eastern fringes were frequently the victims of the Chickasaw. The Chickasaw villages, located east of the Mississippi, far from the Osage villages, were secure from any Osage retaliatory attacks.

Chickasaw and Osage animosity was heightened in the summer of 1794. The two groups attacked each other, maintaining that retaliation was necessary for past losses. Chickasaw attacks insured continuing violence between the two peoples. Chickasaw raids also threatened Caddoan tribes living south of the Osage. The Spanish attempted in 1795 to create an Osage-Quapaw-Caddo alliance to resist the increasing Chickasaw invasions, but the proposed alliance never materialized. The Caddoan tribes, who had suffered from years of Osage abuse, were leery of any Osage truce and refused to make peace with them.[15] The Chickasaw continued to hunt and raid in the southeast Osage country, and the Osage continued to try to keep them out of the region.

Although the Osage were challenged by eastern tribes in the late eighteenth and early nineteenth centuries, they faced little

14. Orieta to Amezaga, May 1, 1775, ibid., 2:123.
15. The Chickasaw attack was made on the Osage leaders returning from their meeting with Carondelet in New Orleans. Although the Chickasaw maintained that the attack was only in retaliation for the Osage murder of one of their leader's sons that had happened in the previous winter, the Osage were angered by the attack. See incomplete document in Carondelet's handwriting, June 4, 1794, ibid., 5:24–25; Carondelet to Trudeau, June 10, 1794, ibid., 26–27; Villemont to Carondelet, February 1, 1796, ibid., 82–83.

danger from the south and west. The Osage maintained their trade and arms superiority over the western tribes, and they continued to hunt in the west and raid at will the Caddo villages in the south and the Wichita villages in the west. The two large Wichita villages on the Red River remained vulnerable to Osage raids until well into the nineteenth century. Even after the American occupation of Louisiana and the accompanying increased trade, the Osage continued to assault the Wichita. Two such attacks were described by an American trader who was staying with the Wichita in their Red River villages. The trader, Anthony Glass, described the brazenness of Osage attacks and provided an account of two Osage raids:

> A party of Ozages made their appearance on Horseback advancing directly to the village as though it was their intention to enter it, but it was soon discovered that their only object was to get between the Village and some of the Panie (Wichita) Horses, which they effected and drove off a number. The Panies (Wichita) sallied out upon them and killed one of them and the Ozages wounded a Pani so that he died the next day. . . . About a month ago they [the Osages] came and hoisted two flags between the Villages in the day about 12 o'clock, one red and the other white, and drove off five hundred horses. They appeared so strong that the Pawnees (Wichita) did not think proper to sally out and attack them.[16]

The Comanche-Wichita alliance that had resisted the Osage expansion in the 1750s fell apart. Never again would either the Wichita or Comanche enjoy sustained military successes against the Osage. The Osage dominated the Wichita, while relations between the Comanche and Osage remained occasionally violent. Osage raiders in small parties sometimes sought Comanche horses, mules, and slaves, and they fought to keep them from the prime Osage buffalo country, causing friction. But the Comanche generally hunted and raided west and south of Osage

16. Dan L. Flores, ed., *Journal of an Indian Trader: Anthony Glass and the Texas Trading Frontier, 1790–1810,* 52–53, 64–65; Elizabeth A. H. John, "Portrait of a Wichita Village, 1808," 420, 424, 431.

country. For much of the eighteenth and early nineteenth centuries, the Comanche were more intent on fighting Apache in the south and raiding the Pueblos and Ute to the west. Thus, the headwaters of the Cimarron, North Canadian, and the Canadian became a neutral zone between the Osage and Comanche in the late eighteenth century. The Comanche and Osage preferred to fight those people who posed a more direct threat to their territory and interests. Their relationship of mutual respect, nervous peace, and nonalliance remained essentially unchanged until the 1830s, when they made peace with one another.

The Pawnee, however, remained hostile toward the Osage throughout the late eighteenth and early nineteenth centuries. The Pawnee, who outnumbered the Osage, were never as well armed, and they constantly challenged the Osage for the prime buffalo territory south of the Smoky Hill River. The area was so important to both groups that they fought for control of the region throughout the eighteenth and nineteenth centuries. While the Osage eventually made peace with the Wichita, Comanche, Kansa, and Kiowa later in the nineteenth century, they never made peace with the Pawnee. The buffalo country was too important to the Osage. It was too critical for any compromise.[17]

The Pawnee were kept out of the region because of a combined Osage and Kansa effort. The Kansa were valuable to the Osage, for they acted as a buffer for attacks from both the Pawnee and Iowa to the north, yet their smaller population insured that they were never a serious military or economic threat to the Osage. The Osage maintained their alliance with the Kansa into the nineteenth century, and together, they kept the Pawnee north of the Smoky Hill River.

Because of the constant pressure from the northern and eastern tribes and the opportunities in the southwest, the Osage

17. Brooks, "Sibley's Journal," 180, 185, 198, 205; McDermott, *Tixier's Travels,* 220–25; Voget, *Osage Research Report,* 270–315.

Nation continued to expand in that direction. The Osage carried on a process that had begun in the seventeenth century when the Little Osage (Down Below People) had moved to the Missouri River to trade with the Europeans. With the increased presence of both Indian challengers and Euro-American traders, the process continued, and more Osage left the two northern bands to live in separate bands. Toward the end of the eighteenth century, the division was accelerated by the interference of Pierre and Auguste Chouteau.

The Chouteaus completed their fort and trading post near the forks of the Osage River by August 1795. They graciously named their fort after the governor who gave them the lucrative Osage monopoly, Baron de Carondelet. By securing the Osage monopoly, the Chouteaus had acquired approximately 42 percent of the entire Upper Louisiana Indian trade.[18] The Chouteaus clearly got a bargain, for they apparently spent little on the construction of Fort Carondelet. Although their contract called for a large, two-story structure with high brick or stone walls and tile roofs, two years after it was abandoned there was no sign of it along the river. Apparently, it was little more than a wood-frame trading post. The twenty-man militia, paid for by the Spanish government to occupy the post, was apparently nothing more than Chouteau trappers and traders.[19]

Governor Carondelet granted the Chouteaus the Osage monopoly in exchange for controlling the aggressive behavior of the Osage. In order to exert control, Auguste and his brother Pierre established their own power base among the Osage River group by creating an Osage clique loyal to Pierre, who resided at the Big Osage village. While Pierre Chouteau was building the fort, Auguste was busy soliciting additional Spanish medals

18. Petition of the Syndic of Trade, May 1, 1794, Nasatir Papers, 4:211–12.
19. Jackson, *Journals of Pike*, 1:306; "I have heard, the twenty militia men are just that many servants whom he [Auguste Chouteau] employes [*sic*] in the labors of his traffic" (Morales to Gardoquí, December 1, 1796, Nasatir Papers, 5:126–27).

for his brother's followers. Auguste Chouteau explained to the governor that the Osage chief had four captains at his sides to enforce his orders. Therefore, Pierre Chouteau "needs six of these captains at his side in order to lend him aid and a strong hand for his authority."[20] Pierre Chouteau, keenly aware of the Osage political arrangement, was using traditional forms to acquire power. It is unknown whether Pierre had established kin ties with the proper Osage clans through marriage, but it is clear that he was trying to set himself up as an Osage *Ga-hi-ge* with his own Osage *A-ki-da* to exercise control in the Osage River villages. The Chouteaus secured the necessary commissions and gorgets for Pierre's six *A-ki-da,* and by 1798 Pierre Chouteau was influencing Osage behavior "by means of the accredited ascendency [*sic*] which he has among both tribes."[21]

This intrusion into the Osage political organization maintained some of the trappings of the traditional form and allowed Pierre to exert influence to his family's economic advantage. The monopoly of Osage trade was a valuable possession. Throughout the last years of Spanish occupation of Osage country, the Osage provided a great many furs. In 1798, they traded 24,000 pesos worth of pelts; in 1800, 950 packs; and in 1802, 1,240 packs of skins. With Pierre living among the Osage at the fort, the Chouteau brothers were able to somewhat limit northern Osage aggression and were persuasive enough to demand and receive reimbursement for some of the Osage thefts in Missouri.[22]

Yet they were not completely "in control" of the Osage people, and attacks, particularly south along the Red River and west along the upper Arkansas River, continued. Despite Pierre Chouteau's "accredited ascendency," he was unable to stop these strikes, for there were significant social and economic rea-

---

20. Trudeau to Carondelet, November 26, 1794, Nasatir Papers, 5:54.
21. Trudeau Report, January 15, 1798, ibid., 187.
22. Ibid., 186–88. Copy of the estimate of annual consumption of merchandise for Indian Trade of this district. Memorandum in packet to Dearborn, October 7, no year, Pierre Chouteau Letterbook, found between letters of November 1804 and January 1805.

sons for the Osage to continue raiding. In July 1795, a party of Osage departed the Osage River villages and headed for the Arkansas. Later that summer, the principal leader of the Osage River Band, Clermont, led a party of Osage warriors south after a group of Natchitoches of the Caddo Confederacy had attacked Clermont's lodge and killed his father-in-law.

This raid took place in August, just after the Osage returned to their prairie villages. Clermont's father-in-law probably was one of those left behind during the summer hunt, because it was unlikely in 1795 for the Natchitoches to venture north and confront an entire Osage village. This particular attack gained a great deal of historical significance, because many scholars claimed that this retaliatory raiding party remained in the south to form the Arkansas Band. This is incorrect, however, for the Arkansas group had been in existence for years before the 1795 raid, and equally important, Clermont did not remain in the south but returned from the attack in September.[23]

Throughout the Chouteaus' tenure at Fort Carondelet, they continually intruded and manipulated Osage polity to their advantage. They repeatedly requested medals for political positions among the Osage. In April 1795, the Chouteaus regarded additional commissions of utmost importance, and in the next month Auguste traveled to New Orleans and returned to Saint Louis with twenty new medals for the Osage. The Chouteaus vigorously created chiefs of various grades and *A-ki-da* in hopes of controlling the Osage tribe and protecting their valuable trade monopoly.

The Chouteau monopoly expired in 1799, but it was renewed twice, in 1799 for one year and in 1800 for four years before ending abruptly in the summer of 1802. Many Saint Louis traders sought the lucrative Osage monopoly, and in June of 1802 Manuel Lisa went to New Orleans to negotiate with the new

23. Trudeau to Carondelet, August 30, 1795, Nasatir Papers, 5:72; Trudeau to Carondelet, September 26, 1795, ibid., 73; Carl H. Chapman, "The Indomitable Osage in Spanish Illinois (Upper Louisiana), 1763–1804."

governor in hopes of securing the Osage trade. Lisa offered to pay the salaries of the fort's militia and to build a gristmill at his expense. Lisa also argued that the Chouteau monopoly unfairly limited the wealthy trade to a single family, and since his company was owned by several families the lucrative Osage trade would be spread more equitably among the community. Governor Salcedo accepted Lisa's argument, and despite the Chouteaus' contract, Salcedo canceled their monopoly of Osage trade and awarded it to Lisa's company. Lisa arrived in Saint Louis in August 1802 and presented his license and monopoly to Lieutenant Governor Charles Dehault Delassus in the presence of Auguste Chouteau. By October 1802, Lisa had assumed control of Fort Carondelet.[24]

Much has been made of the Chouteaus' loss of the Osage monopoly in 1802. Most scholars claim that with the loss of the Osage trade monopoly, the Chouteaus used their influence among the Osage to convince a leader named Big Track to break away from the Big Osage along the Osage River and move to the Arkansas Valley where the Chouteaus could continue to trade with them. Thus, the Chouteaus have also been given the distinction of creating the Arkansas Band. Although the Chouteaus did indeed have remarkable influence among the Osage, they did not create the Arkansas Band of the Osage.

By the time the Chouteaus lost their monopoly, there were already three distinct bands of Osage Indians. In 1802, two groups, the Big Osage and Little Osage, lived near one another in villages along the upper Osage River. The Big Osage lived where they had been for over a hundred years. In 1785, the Little Osage, who had lived along the Missouri River for about one hundred years, were still listed as inhabiting their villages on

---

24. Petition of Auguste Chouteau, May 18, 1794, Nasatir Papers, 5:7–10; Casa Calvo to Delassus, December 30, 1800, ibid., 6:36–37; Petition of Lisa, et al., June 4, 1802, ibid., 60–64; Decree of Salcedo, June 12, 1802, ibid., 66–68; Delassus to Salcedo, August 28, 1802, ibid., 76–77; Lisa to Moro, n.d., ibid., 115–16; Din and Nasatir, *Imperial Osages,* 335–37.

the Missouri, and since the Mississippi tribes (Sac and Mesquakie) were hunting peacefully with the Little Osage in 1791, the Little Osage were still living along the Missouri at that time.[25] In 1793, the Little Osage temporarily moved near the Big Osage, but later that year they were reported back on the Missouri. In 1794, Jean Baptist Truteau, a French trader, wrote that attacks by Mississippi tribes had driven the Little Osage from the Missouri River and forced them to take refuge with the Big Osage along the upper Osage River. This time they moved permanently back to the Osage River. It is likely that when the Chouteaus erected their trading post along the Osage River in 1794, the Little Osage set up their villages near the fort to secure trade and protection.

The third group of Osage lived to the south along the lower Verdigris River, just above the Three Forks where the Verdigris and Neosho join the Arkansas River. This group was made up of Big Hill and Upland Forest Bands who were at various times called the Chenier Osage (Osage of the Oak), Shainers, Arkansas Osage, Big Track's Band, and Clermont's Band. These southern-dwelling Osage had been living in the Three Forks area since the 1760s.[26] Having driven the Wichita from the Arkansas Valley area in the 1750s, Osage hunters, rather than return to the northern prairie villages, remained in the region to take advantage of both the illegal traders ascending the Arkansas and the proximity of the horses, furs, and slaves among the Wichita and Caddo. This band originally was made up of young peo-

---

25. "Journal of Jean Baptiste Truteau on the Upper Missouri, 'Premier Partei,' June 7, 1794–March 26, 1795," 303. Little is known about the split of the Big and Little Osage, as it occurred before there were any European outposts near either group. The few Europeans who were in the area at the beginning of the eighteenth century failed to record any facts about the breach. For more information about the Little–Big Osage division, see Mathews, *The Osages,* 143–53; Nasatir, *Before Lewis and Clark,* 1:150. Sometime after 1791, the Little Osage left the Missouri River and moved back among their Big Osage relatives, but they later returned to the Missouri River.

26. Bolton, *Athanase de Mézières,* 2:110; Ríu to Ulloa, November 12, 1767, Nasatir Papers, 1:20.

ple who wanted to take advantage of the southwestern opportunities for hunting and raiding and to avoid the trouble in the northeast. They often defied the controls of the traditional Osage leadership.

The Arkansas Band's existence was not the result of the Chouteau intrigue. This band did, however, demonstrate clear examples of blatant European interference in Native American political organization and an attempt by a native people experiencing transition to adjust to new situations with old political forms. Those who have argued that the Chouteaus were responsible for the Osage split have relied almost solely on the accounts of Zebulon Pike and James B. Wilkinson, two American military men who briefly visited the Osage in the fall of 1806. Both Pike and Wilkinson credited Pierre Chouteau for initiating the division. They claimed that the Chouteaus, angry over the loss of the Osage monopoly to Lisa in 1802, convinced an Osage leader named Cashesegra to lead his band of Osage to the Arkansas Valley where the Chouteaus still had legal control of Osage trade.[27]

While both Pike and Wilkinson did blame the Chouteaus for the creation of the Arkansas Band, a closer examination shows the situation to be much more complicated. Pike and Wilkinson were both relative newcomers to Osage country, and they were ignorant of a great many things about the Osage. They were also suspicious of the Chouteaus, Lisa, and other French and Spanish traders in the west. The two Americans believed that the Chouteaus and others were involved in some sort of ill-defined

27. Wilkinson wrote, "About 58 or 60 miles up the Verdigrise, is situate[d] the Osage village. This band some four or five years since, were led by chief Cashesegra, to the waters of the Arkansaw, at the request of Pierre Chouteau, for the purpose of securing their trade. The *exclusive trade* of the *Osage river,* having at that time been purchased from the Spanish governor, by Manuel Lisa, of St. Louis" (Jackson, *Journals of Pike,* 2:16). Pike wrote, "The Arkansaw schism was effected by Mr. Pierre Chouteau, 10 or 12 years ago, as a revenge on Mr. Manuel De Sezei [Lisa], who had obtained from the Spanish government the exclusive trade of the Osage nation, by way of the Osage river, after its having been in the hands of Mr. Choteau for nearly 20 years" (ibid., 32).

plot to help the Spanish regain control of Louisiana or simply start illegal trade with the Spanish in Santa Fe. Considering that James Wilkinson had been sent by his controversial father, General James Wilkinson, who had plotted with Aaron Burr, to accompany Pike on a highly dubious enterprise, it is ironic that they were suspicious of the Chouteaus' loyalty. It was, however, an uncertain time in the border region of Missouri, and unfortunately their suspicions and uneasiness colored their accounts.[28]

Wilkinson, the general's son, left Pike on the upper Arkansas and descended the river, visiting the Arkansas Band along the way. He charged that Pierre Chouteau had caused the split four or five years before his visit, which would have made the division in 1801 or 1802, close to the time that the Chouteaus lost their monopoly. Pike claimed that the split had occurred ten or twelve years previously. Unfortunately, it is not clear whether Pike meant ten or twelve years before his visit in 1806 (1794 or 1796), or ten or twelve years before his report was published in 1810 (1798 or 1800). In any event, both of Pike's dates were wrong, because the Chouteaus had the monopoly from 1795 until the summer of 1802. Not only were Pike and Wilkinson mistaken about the cause of the split, but they also could not provide a date that was consistent with the most critical part of their argument—the date when the Chouteau monopoly ended.

The Chouteaus might have used their influence among the northern Osage to convince some of them to go south to the Ar-

---

28. Pike to James Wilkinson (the father), July 22, 1806: "I assure you Sir that I am extreamely [sic] pleased with the Idea that Messrs. Cadet and Manuel will meet with their merited reward; and I on my part am determined to shew [sic] them that it is not there sinister movements that can derange the objects of our Voyage" (ibid., 122); James Wilkinson (the father) to Dearborn, August 2, 1806: "The outline of the plan is to make a grand establishment at the towns of the Osage, or those of the Panis republique, from whence a connection is to be formed with the I,ya,tans, and under their protection, art, intrigue, and corruption, are to be employed to open a channel of intercourse with St. Affee" (ibid., 129); Wilkinson (the father) to Pike, July 18, 1806: "Manual is a Black Spaniard. . . . I shall dress Manual & Cadet aussi. I will teach them how to interrupt national movements, by their despicable Intrigues" (ibid., 118–19).

kansas in 1802 to continue trading with them, and the Chouteaus may have had some special relationship with Cashesegra. In 1795, the commander of the Arkansas Post reported that the Osage chief Cashesegra (called La Grande Piste by the Spanish) had arrived there as a messenger for one of Chouteau's traders and had urged the Arkansas hunters there to join the Osage on a hunt. This might have been a frequent occurrence, but it does not suggest that the Chouteaus were responsible for the creation of the Arkansas Osage.[29] Their real responsibility lay in creating political turmoil among all of the Osage and accelerating the breakup of the traditional Osage polity among the northern band, which they had begun long before their loss of the Osage monopoly in 1802.

Osage families lived along the Arkansas River as early as 1767. The southern group was involved with the Spanish as early as 1770. In 1784 and 1785, the Spanish reported Osage living along the Arkansas River. In 1784, an Osage named Cuchechire came to the Arkansas Post and requested a chief's medal. Throughout 1785, a "Chief" Cuchechire from the Arkansas Valley turned up in Spanish reports. In May 1795, Pierre Chouteau requested a gorget and a commission for one "Kuchechire," also known as La Grande Piste. His Osage name was *Ko-zhi-ci-gthe* or *Ka-zhi-ci-grah,* which literally means Makes Tracks Far Away. This individual, alternately called Cuchechire, Kuchechire, Couzichequeday, Cashesegra, La Grand Piste, and Big Track, was one person.[30]

For approximately twenty years, Cashesegra led a splintered faction of Big Osage along the Arkansas River. Cashesegra's group fluctuated in number, as Osage families from the other

29. Villemont to Carondelet, February 1, 1796, Nasatir Papers, 5:82–83.

30. De Mézières to Amezaga, September 4, 1774, Bolton, *Athanase de Mézières,* 2:110; Nasatir, *Before Lewis and Clark,* 1:87; Burns, *Osage Bands and Clans,* 10; Mathews, *The Osages,* 299. In the September 1818 treaty with the United States and the Osage, a "Kohesegre, or the Great Tract," signed the treaty. See Institute for the Development of Indian Law, *Treaties and Agreements of the Eastern Oklahoma Indians,* 44.

two Osage groups joined them to hunt and raid. The Osage frequently moved among the three groups as they had earlier between the Big and Little Osage Bands. Cashesegra led the southern band, but he never had the sanction of the traditional Osage. What Cashesegra lacked was the legitimacy of the traditional polity. He aspired to a chief's position, which he was obviously not entitled to within the older, orthodox framework. This was made obvious by the displeasure of the two traditional moiety leaders, Clermont and Lafond, who complained when the Arkansas Post commander gave Cashesegra a chief's medal.[31] Despite his lack of Osage sanction, Cashesegra remained in the south and led the southern hunters and raiders. He finally gained some legitimacy in the late 1790s, when a young *Tsi-zhu Ga-hi-ge,* who possessed the proper kinship title to the *Ga-hi-ge* position, moved to the Arkansas to lead the southern band alongside Cashesegra.

This young man became one of the most important leaders of the Arkansas. His name, too, was Clermont. Because the Osage often passed on to the sons of chiefs the same name, it has been difficult to identify this Arkansas Band Clermont.[32] Some have suggested that this Clermont was the same one who had been the principal chief of the Osage since the 1760s, but the nineteenth-century Clermont of the Arkansas Osage was not the eighteenth-century Clermont. From existing records it is clear that the prominent eighteenth-century Big Osage leader Clermont was not the same man who led the Arkansas Band in the nineteenth century. The eighteenth-century Clermont died sometime around 1800, and the nineteenth-century Arkansas Band leader, also known as Clermont, was probably his son.

After the ill-fated trip to New Orleans in 1793, when three Osage leaders were murdered, the Chouteau brothers erected

31. Dubreuil to Miró, March 18, 1785, Nasatir Papers, 3:85–7; [Miró] to Dubreuil, May 25, 1785, ibid., 87–88; Cruzat to Miró, June 23, 1784, ibid., 81–82.

32. Luengo to Intendant, August 28, 1802, ibid., 6:78.

their trading post and began aggressively interfering in internal Osage affairs. They continued their meddling with the Osage village polity, but all of the Chouteau maneuvering had not gone unchallenged. One particularly recalcitrant Osage was the *Tsi-zhu Ga-hi-ge* named Clermont. His Osage name was *Gra-to-moh-se* (Iron Hawk) or *Gra-moie* (Moving Hawk), but he was recorded by the French and Spanish as Gredamanse, Clarmont, and Clermont. Clermont refused to go with Auguste Chouteau on the important New Orleans' trip despite vigorous attempts to force him to go. At one point Chouteau's Osage supporters kidnapped Clermont's wife and put her aboard the Chouteau's boat in order to persuade him to go.[33]

When the survivors of the disastrous trip returned and regents were appointed, Pierre Chouteau reported that Clermont wanted a new big medal, for he was the principal chief. Chouteau dutifully requested a big medal for Clermont. At the same time, however, he began requesting a great many new medals for the Osage. It is not clear who the medals were actually intended for, however, because of confusion in the historical records. In November 1794, Pierre Chouteau requested, via Trudeau, a larger medal for Gredamanse, who he wrote had the common name of Cheveux Blanc. He requested again in May 1795 a large medal for "Gredamanse," whom he once again identified as Cheveux Blanc, a small "medal" chief of the Big Osage.[34]

This is very confusing, for Gredemanse is the Spanish version of *Gra-to-moh-se*, the name of Clermont, not of Pawhuska (Cheveux Blanc, or White Hair). Thus, it is not at all clear who the Chouteaus were getting the medals for in 1794 and 1795. The May request for a large medal for a small medal chief probably refers to Pawhuska, who was a small medal chief. Pawhuska had received such a medal in New Orleans. In 1795, Auguste

33. Trudeau to Carondelet, November 10, 1793, ibid., 5:1–4.
34. Trudeau to Carondelet, September 15, 1794, ibid., 42–43; Trudeau to Carondelet, November 26, 1794, ibid., 56; Trudeau to Carondelet, May 30, 1795, ibid., 69.

Chouteau was carrying ten large and ten small medals for the Big Osage, Little Osage, and Kansa nations.[35] While it is not clear just who the Gredemanse was who got the medal in 1794, it is clear that shortly thereafter there is no mention of Clermont in the Spanish records. Clermont's name does not appear in the existing records for the remaining years of the Spanish in Louisiana. This is peculiar for such a prominent individual among the northern band. At a time when Chouteau and Lisa were among the Osage and other leaders are frequently mentioned in the official accounts, there is no Clermont. Interestingly enough, just as Clermont disappears from the records, Chouteau's companion, formerly the small medal chief Pawhuska, is recognized not only as one of the big medal chiefs, but as the single Big Osage leader.

In April 1797, Pawhuska traveled to Saint Louis with Pierre Chouteau to surrender two Osage "culprits" to Spanish authorities, and in April 1800, Pawhuska was reportedly puzzled because a part of his people had totally abandoned him and had "withdrawn from his authority."[36] At the same time, however, Pawhuska made an extraordinary offer. He volunteered to go south and destroy those Osage parties in the Arkansas.[37] Before

---

35. Burns, *Osage Bands and Clans,* 74. There was some confusion between what Trudeau asked for and what Carondelet sent. Also, Trudeau wrote the name "Gredamanse" in both letters next to the French name "Cheveux Blanc," yet Cheveux Blanc, or White Hair, or Pawhuska was not called Gredamanse by anyone else. In November 1809, when the Arkansas band signed the 1808 treaty, the first signer was "Gresdanmanses or Clermond," and in 1815 "Gradamnsa or iron kite," signed the treaty of peace with the U.S. See Institute for the Development of Indian Law, *Treaties and Agreements,* 25, 32. When Thomas Nuttall visited the Arkansas Band of the Osage in 1819, he met Clermont, whose identity he explained thus: "The principal chief is called by the French Clarmont, although his proper name is Iron bird, a species of eagle. . . . [T]he rule was conferred on Clermont, son of the chief of White Hair's village, on the Osage river" (Nuttall, *Journal of Travels,* 194). It is not clear who was to receive the Big Medal. See Carondelet to Trudeau, 30 May 1795, Nasatir Papers, 5:68–70; Carondelet to Trudeau, May 11, 1796, ibid., 89.
36. Auguste Chouteau to Carondelet, April 18, 1797, Nasatir Papers, 5:154; Pierre Chouteau to Delassus, April 15, 1800, ibid., 6:5.
37. Delassus to Casa Calvo, April 24, 1800, ibid., 6:9–10

he could actually launch such an attack against the Arkansas Band, he was diverted in August by Pierre Chouteau, and together they went to Saint Louis to surrender an Osage murderer to the Spanish.

The August meeting was an interesting one. Although the Spanish recorded that some leaders of the Arkansas Band came to Saint Louis for the meeting, there is no mention of either Clermont or of Cashesegra. Only a chief called La Chenieres is noted attending the conference for the Arkansas Band.[38] At this fall meeting, Pawhuska was regarded by the Spanish as the single principal chief of the Osage, and Lieutenant Governor Charles Dehault Delassus threatened the Arkansas Band with war if they did not return to the fold. Delassus wrote, "If the *partido* of La Chenieres [Oak—common name for Arkansas Band] did not reunite with that of Les Cheveaux Blancs, I was to oblige the latter to destroy them and employ all possible means by summoning for that purpose all the Indian nations and whites of the other shore to attack you."[39] After these harsh words, La Chenieres promised to rejoin the Big Osage in the north if he could convince his young men to do so, and with that promise, Delassus gave the Osage a lavish amount of gifts: one hundred muskets, one hundred pounds of powder, three hundred pounds of bullets, two hundred pounds of tobacco, and an abundance of other trade goods. The gifts were so lavish and out of the ordinary that Delassus was later reprimanded by the governor for being so extravagant. The next fall, Pawhuska reported that the Arkansas Osage had once again joined him, but the number must not have been significant, for at the same time Pierre Chouteau reported that a group of Osage were raiding in the south.[40]

The Chouteaus relinquished Fort Carondelet to Lisa in

---

38. Delassus to Casa Calvo, September 25, 1800, ibid., 16–23.
39. Ibid., 19.
40. Relation of present given to the nation of Big Osage, ibid., 26–27; Casa Calvo to Delassus, March 18, 1801, ibid., 38–39; Casa Calvo to Delassus, May 13, 1802, ibid., 57–58.

October of 1802, and supposedly this was when they urged Cashesegra to move to the Arkansas to trade. Yet in late August 1802, Cashesegra was down at the Arkansas Post asking for traders. The Arkansas commander welcomed the Osage and requested a large medal for Cashesegra.[41] It is curious that at the time the Chouteaus were charged with luring Cashesegra to the south with offers of trade that the Arkansas Osage leader was already there requesting trade from the Arkansas Post. The truth is that Cashesegra had been in the south for years, and he frequently visited the Arkansas Post for trade, and if Chouteau did anything at all in 1802 it was simply to provide trade for the Osage who were already there, which he had done in the north since 1794. The creation of the Arkansas Band had nothing to do with the Chouteaus' loss of the Osage monopoly.

Lisa's monopoly lasted less than two years, for it ended with the purchase of Louisiana by the United States in 1804. After the change in Louisiana's administration, Pierre Chouteau and his brother quickly took advantage, housing and entertaining the new United States officials, such as the first territorial governor of Upper Louisiana, William Henry Harrison, Captain William Stoddard, William Clark, and Meriwether Lewis. The Chouteaus used their newly gained influence once again to reestablish their official positions with the Osage and to manipulate them. At the request of Meriwether Lewis, Pierre Chouteau took Pawhuska and other northern Osage leaders to Washington, D.C., in the summer of 1804 to meet with President Thomas Jefferson. Pierre Chouteau was made the United States agent for the Osage, and once again Chouteau power and prestige survived a transfer of national sovereignty. The Chouteaus immediately began to recapture all of the Osage River trade. They were eager to have the Osage consolidated in their northern villages along the Osage River. Those villages were more accessible for their Saint Louis–based traders, and there they

41. Luengo to Intendant, August 28, 1802, ibid., 77–80.

had kin ties, influence, and established positions and power. Pawhuska, too, wanted the southern Osage to return to his villages in the north, and he worked with Chouteau to bring that about. They used their influence with the new government to force such a move. Throughout the 1804 Osage visit to Washington, there was repeated negative reference to the Arkansas group led by Cashesegra (Great Track). President Jefferson urged the Osage to reunite and told their new agent, Pierre Chouteau, to bring them back together.[42] "I was sorry to learn that a schism has taken place in your nation, and that a part of your people had withdrawn with the Great-Track to the Arkansas river. We will send an agent to them, and will use our best offices to induce them to return."[43] Pierre Chouteau returned with the Osage, and in December 1805 he sent a group of Little Osage off to Washington, D.C. Without a hint of irony he included in his advice to Secretary of War Henry Dearborn that only a few medals should be distributed, for a "multiplicity of medals spread in a nation only excite jealousies which often become dangerous."[44] Having been deeply involved in passing out a "multiplicity of medals" for the last ten years, he knew full well the impact of such a policy.

Pierre Chouteau visited the Arkansas Osage in the fall of 1806. He went there via Pawhuska's village, and while he was there he met with Pike and Wilkinson, who were leaving for a Kansa village. Chouteau left shortly thereafter to go south. Just before he arrived, a trapper, Jacob Bright, who had spent the summer trading among the Arkansas Osage, left the Arkansas Band bearing a message for Jefferson from the Arkansas Band. Bright reported that the Arkansas Osage were led by two chiefs: Cashesegra (called Couzichequeday by Bright) and Clermont.[45] Cashesegra

42. Foley and Rice, *The First Chouteaus*, 90–92; Jefferson to Osage, July 16, 1804, Nasatir Papers, 7:10–11.
43. Jefferson to Osage, July 16, 1804, Nasatir Papers, 7:12.
44. Pierre Chouteau to Dearborn, December 1, 1805, ibid., 52.
45. Bright Relative to Osage, *Letters Received Secretary of War, Main Series;* Ryan, "Jacob Bright's Journal," 512–20; Mathews, *The Osages*, 298–300.

was old and ill, and it was obvious to Bright that Clermont was the principal chief, for he was accorded respect by the Osage and did most of the talking. Recorded Bright, "Clearmont then got up and demanded of me, if I did not understand that he was the greatest Chief of all his Nation."[46] Clermont complained to Bright that his father had died and that he was entitled to his rank, yet it had been denied him. Clermont stated "that under the Spanish Government they withheld it from him by telling him that he was too Young and at the Same time Give the Great Medal to the White hair [Pawhuska] who had no Claim to it."[47] Clermont asked Bright to tell the new government that he was loyal to the United States, and that he wanted the great medal to which he was entitled. Clermont expressed a great deal of bitterness toward Pierre Chouteau. He made it clear that he resented Chouteau's interferences, and that his father died while the Spanish were in control. Clermont asked Bright to send him a flag and a medal, but not with Chouteau: "If the Medal comes through Mr. Choteau [sic] he Cannot Consider it the Same as if it had Come through the hands of a friend."[48]

It seems clear from Bright's report that this man was not the eighteenth-century Big Osage Band *Tsi-zhu Ga-hi-ge*, but a younger man bearing the same name. Since Osage sons often took their fathers' names, it is likely that the nineteenth-century Clermont on the Arkansas (hereafter referred to as Clermont II) was the son of the eighteenth-century Clermont (Clermont I).

Cashesegra also complained about Pawhuska, explaining that he came to the Arkansas area "because the White hair [Paw-

46. Ryan, "Jacob Bright's Journal," 516; Bright Relative to Osage, *Letters Received Secretary of War, Main Series.*

47. Ryan, "Jacob Bright's Journal," 512.

48. Ibid. When Thomas Nuttall visited the Osage in 1819, he noted that the chief of the Arkansas Osage was Clermont, who was the son of a former chief of Pawhuska's village. Nuttall mistakenly believed that Clermont had usurped the chief's position in the Arkansas band from the son of the last chief among them, but Nuttall simply did not know the circumstances. See Nuttall, *Journal of Travels,* 194.

huska] would not give me Powder and lead."[49] Cashesegra went on to lament that traders would not come to the Arkansas River. Even so, his band would never rejoin Pawhuska's band in the north. Cashesegra explained that he had been to see the Spanish father who gave him "Coats and Silver Ware," and that he wanted his son to act for him as chief. Cashesegra introduced Bright to his eldest son and explained that although his son was a small chief, he would one day become a great chief.[50]

Bright unwittingly described an Osage polity among the Arkansas Osage that maintained the traditional dual chieftainship. Clermont II was the *Tsi-zhu Ga-hi-ge* and Cashesegra was acting as the *Hon-ga Ga-hi-ge*. Bright did not note any animosity between Cashesegra or Cashesegra's son with Clermont II, as there was no need. In the traditional political structure that the Arkansas Osage were practicing, Clermont II and Cashesegra were not competing for power, for they shared it. *Tsi-zhu Ga-hi-ge* Clermont II enjoyed a greater degree of influence, but that was probably because of Cashesegra's age and shaky claim to the title. His more powerful role was also consistent with traditional Osage form whereby the *Tsi-zhu Ga-hi-ge* took the initiative when entertaining outsiders. Equally consistent was Cashesegra's desire for his son to replace him as *Hon-ga Ga-hi-ge*. Cashesegra was old, and Clermont II was the apparent leader, but they had a common bond. Clermont II and Cashesegra both were angry and resentful of the northern Osage imposter, Pawhuska, and both blamed the Chouteaus for setting him up as the Osage leader and ultimately forcing them to leave the northern village.

Pierre Chouteau was to send the leaders of the Arkansas Band to Washington, D.C., and he arrived among the Arkansas Osage shortly after Bright's visit. In light of Cashesegra and Clermont II's remarks about Chouteau, it is not surprising that Chouteau

49. Ryan, "Jacob Bright's Journal," 515; Bright Relative to Osage, *Letters Received Secretary of War, Main Series.*
50. Ryan, "Jacob Bright's Journal," 515, 520.

did not take either Cashesegra or Clermont II. He declined to invite Cashesegra, because he later explained the elder leader was too ill to go to Washington. He did, however, take Cashesegra's son.[51] Clermont II declined "the repeated invitations to accompany Mr. Chouteau." If in fact Clermont II was invited, apparently Pierre Chouteau was secure enough to chance a trip with Clermont II, a trip that would undoubtedly give power and prestige to an Osage leader he could not control. Clermont II may have been so resentful of Pierre Chouteau that despite his strong desire to visit the President and establish trade, he adamantly refused to go with Chouteau.[52]

Despite the complexity and the confusion of all of this, it appears that while the Chouteaus did not create the Arkansas Band, they did interfere in Osage politics and deepened divisions among the Osage. After the disastrous New Orleans trip, the Chouteaus took advantage of the vacuum created by the deaths of the tribal leadership to set Pierre up as a *Ga-hi-ge*.

The Chouteaus, however, were challenged by Clermont, the other *Ga-hi-ge*. Clermont, suspicious of the Chouteaus, refused to give them control. Sometime between 1794 and 1806, Clermont disappeared from the records, and another Clermont did not appear until 1806, when Bright and Wilkinson met him leading the Arkansas Band. The Clermont of 1806, however, was not the eighteenth-century Clermont. In 1806, Clermont was a vigorous, mature man. If we assume that the eighteenth-century Clermont was at least twenty when he was recognized as the *Ga-hi-ge*, he would have been sixty years old by 1806, hardly the active man who entertained Bright with horse races and hunting trips. It is very unlikely that the original Clermont lived beyond 1795–1796, perhaps dying in the 1800–1801 smallpox epidemic.[53]

51. Pierre Chouteau to Dearborn, August 18, 1806, Pierre Chouteau Letterbook; Jackson, *Journals of Pike*, 2:32.

52. Treat to Dearborn, November 18, 1806, *Arkansas Trading House Letterbook, 1805–1810*.

53. Trudeau to Carondelet, August 30, 1795, Nasatir Papers, 5:72; Trudeau to

While there are hints to his identity, it is uncertain who the Arkansas Clermont was, how long he had been on the Arkansas, and how he came to be there. Careful examination of the records leads to two possible conclusions. The Arkansas Clermont may well have been the Clermont who refused to go with the Chouteaus on the trip to New Orleans. In 1794, before the Osage left on their fatal trip with Auguste Chouteau, the lieutenant governor described the Osage River Clermont as a nephew of Pawhuska, and remarked that Pawhuska "is himself already considered as the chief since he governs his nephew, who is stupid and incapable." In 1806, John Treat described the Arkansas River leader as "Clermont Nephew to the White Hair." Yet Wilkinson, who visited the Arkansas Band at the same time Treat was describing Clermont as Pawhuska's nephew, wrote that Clermont "is the greatest warrior, and most influential man. . . . He is the lawful sovereign of the Grand Osages, but his hereditary right was usurped by Pahuska, or *White Hair,* whilst Clermont was yet an infant. White Hair, in fact, is a chief of Chouteau's creating, as well as Cashesegra." A little while later, a resident of the Arkansas Post, Pearly Wallis, wrote Governor Frederick Bates that "Claremont which I believe to be a great and a good man says White Hare and Shoto [*sic*] are his mortal enemies the one because his father was the only great Cheaf [*sic*] of Ossages [*sic*] and that Dignity belonged to him [Claremont] and the other because he wished him to leave his village on the Arkansas River and move over to Missuri [*sic*]."[54]

Unless more information is discovered, the mystery of Clermont's identity will never be solved. What is clear, however, is

---

Carondelet, September 26, 1795, ibid., 73. "I believe the true motive is the mistrust which he [Clermont] has of us although he has never done us any wrong but neither has he ever done us any good" (Trudeau to Carondelet, April 24, 1794, ibid., 3); Delassus to Lorimier, May 23, 1801, ibid., 6:46.

54. Trudeau to Carondelet, April 24, 1794, ibid., 5:3; Treat to Dearborn, November 18, 1806, *Arkansas Trading House Letterbook;* Jackson, *Journals of Pike,* 2:16; Wallis to Bates, December 18, 1808, Thomas Maitland Marshall, ed., *The Life and Papers of Frederick Bates,* 1:46.

that once the Chouteaus established their trading post, the *Ga-hi-ge* Clermont was a continual threat to their power and control and, more importantly, their monopoly. As agents for the Spanish Crown, the Chouteaus might simply have refused to give Clermont the big medal and instead given it to Pawhuska, someone who was more cooperative. Clermont might have then left the northern band and moved permanently to the Arkansas Band. That would partially explain his disappearance from the official records. The Chouteaus, intent on keeping Clermont from power, would have pointedly ignored his existence and attempted to keep him from the Spanish officials. However, if Clermont was as prominent as he apparently was in 1794, it seems unlikely that the Chouteaus could have successfully removed a *Ga-hi-ge*, and if an adult Clermont was living on the Arkansas after 1795, why did he not visit the Arkansas Post at least once in eleven years? What seems more likely is that the Clermont of the 1790s died sometime after 1795, and the Chouteaus used his death to their advantage.

With the death of Clermont I, the Chouteaus chose their friend from the New Orleans trip, Pawhuska, to replace him. Pawhuska had a legitimate claim to the position. His father had been a *Ga-hi-ge*, and he was the uncle, brother, or brother-in-law of Clermont I.[55] Clermont I's son, Clermont II, might have been too young to assume the position, and the Chouteaus might have picked Pawhuska to act as his regent, although unlike other 1794 appointments, there are no records of such a decision. The Chouteaus simply could have refused to accept the son of such a troublesome Osage leader. Since the Chouteaus were the liaison between the Osage and the Spanish government, and since the only traders allowed at the trading post were Chouteau employees, no outsider would have known the difference. It is also important to note that in 1799 the veteran lieutenant governor in Saint Louis, Zenon Trudeau, who knew Clermont I, was

---

55. Trudeau to Carondelet, April 24, 1794, Nasatir Papers, 5:2.

replaced by a newcomer, Charles Dehault Delassus. The new Spanish lieutenant governor, Delassus, did not know anything about Osage polity, and he did not know any of the individual Osages involved. In a September 1800 meeting with Pawhuska and other Osage leaders, Delassus reprimanded the Osage, saying, "I thought that you had not received the words which I have sent to your great chief, Les Cheveux Blancs, since the time when I first arrived here, when I appointed him the great chief of your tribe."[56] The Chouteaus might have attempted to retain the dual structure of moiety leaders with Pierre and Pawhuska acting as *Hon-ga* and *Tsi-zhu Ga-hi-ge,* or with Clermont I out of the way they might have simply replaced the two moiety positions with one, Pawhuska. Either way, the Chouteaus were in control.

Whether the Chouteaus successfully deposed a traditional *Ga-hi-ge* and drove him south or prevented his son from rightfully assuming the position to which he was entitled, the end result was political and social turmoil and increasing factionalism among the Osage. It is clear that this outside interference caused a great many problems for the Osage. The institution of a single Osage chief was inconsistent with their traditions. Any Osage leader who tried to usurp the other *Ga-hi-ge*'s position would have had trouble, and a leader who had assumed the job under questionable circumstances would have had serious problems controlling the Osage, as Pawhuska did. In April 1800, Chief Pawhuska reported that part of his people had totally abandoned him and had "withdrawn from his authority." In September 1800, Pawhuska complained that the Osage in the south would not listen to him. On May 3, 1803, Pawhuska wrote to the Spanish in Saint Louis and complained that "one-half of my village no longer remembers the *parole* that you gave them."[57] Pawhuska's problems would only increase in time.

56. Delassus to Casa Calvo, September 25, 1800, ibid., 6:16–17; Houck, *Spanish Régime,* 2:304.

57. Auguste Chouteau to Carondelet, April 18, 1797, Nasatir Papers, 5:154;

The Chouteaus' outside interference only exaggerated the divisions among the Osage and widened the split between northern and southern bands. Pierre and Auguste Chouteau had little influence among the Arkansas Osage, and what better place for Clermont I's son to go but to the Arkansas Band, where he could assume his proper role as the *Tsi-zhu Ga-hi-ge* among the Arkansas Osage alongside *Hon-ga Ga-hi-ge* Cashesegra? The southern band would have welcomed a leader with all of the proper clan ties and a legitimate claim to political power. Pike mentioned that many young and aggressive Osage were going to the Arkansas Band, and what better place for a young man who had been denied his chieftainship?[58]

Prevented by the Chouteaus and the pretender Pawhuska from assuming his proper place with the northern band, Clermont II went to the group where he had opportunity to gain his chieftainship. Cashesegra, who had left the northern group years before to live on the Arkansas, would have accepted Clermont II's decision to join his band. By assuming the position of *Tsi-zhu Ga-hi-ge*, Clermont II would have forcefully reestablished the dual chieftainship within the Arkansas Band and strengthened Cashesegra's legitimacy as an Osage moiety leader. The Arkansas Band might have been a breakaway band, but it had at least one legitimate *Ga-hi-ge*, Clermont II.

So, along the banks of the Arkansas, with the northern bands in political turmoil and their traditional polity in tatters, young Clermont II and Cashesegra worked together to retain the old, traditional forms and ways of life for the Osage. The Chouteaus had exacerbated already existing social and political divisions within the Osage. Their repeated intrusions into Osage politics helped alter the traditional polity, and this would in time weaken

---

Pierre Chouteau to Delassus, April 15, 1800, ibid., 6:5; Delassus to Casa Calvo, September 25, 1800, ibid., 16–17; Cheveux Blanc to Delassus, received May 3, 1803, ibid., 102.

58. "Indeed the Cheveux Blanche appears to be very delicately situated, as the village on the Arkansaw serves as a place of refuge for all the young, daring, and discontented . . ." (Jackson, *Journals of Pike*, 2:146).

the Osage and help destroy their economic and military power on the southern prairie-plains. Once the United States moved into Osage territory, the Chouteaus continued their meddling in Osage society and used their influence with foreign governments to intrude further into Osage life.

8.

COMPROMISES

When we want meat for our women and Children and clothing our dependance is in the woods. If we do not get it there we must go hungry and naked . . . when he [President of the United States] sent the Cherokees on this side of the great River and gave them Land we had sold him he Certainly did not give to the Cherokee all the Beaver, Bear, Buffaloe [sic] and Deer on our Lands. . . . [W]hen the Cherokees hunt in our Land and kill our Game we will always have trouble they will steal our Horses and our young men will kill them.

—Clermont II, 1821[1]

When Amos Stoddard assumed control of Louisiana in March 1804, the Osage was the most powerful tribe in the prairie-plains region. They dominated the area between the Missouri and Red Rivers. American soldier and explorer Stephen Long described their situation: "The claim of the Osages to this country appears to have a better foundation, and can probably be more easily substantiated than that of any other tribe or nation of Indians. . . . These people had acquired by conquest from other Indians a vast extent of territory, having enlarged their possessions so as to include all the Country from Red River to the Dey Moyen."[2]

---

1. Bradford to Calhoun, October 1, 1821, Carter, *Territorial Papers*, 19:321.
2. Stephen Long to Thomas A. Smith, January 30, 1818, ibid., 5.

Clermont, the *Tsi-zhu Ga-hi-ge* of the Arkansas Band of the Osage. This is probably Clermont II, but it may be his son, Clermont III. Clermont's name was *Gra-to-moh-se* (Iron Hawk), or perhaps *Gra moie* (Moving Hawk). George Catlin painted this portrait during his 1834 visit to Fort Gibson. National Museum of American Art, Smithsonian Institution. Gift of Mrs. Joseph Harrison, Jr.

The Osage, numbering approximately 6,300 people, including about 1,500 warriors, dominated the region and lived throughout the forests, prairies, and plains.[3] Establishing and maintaining their hegemony by alliance, diplomacy, subjugation, or combat, the Osage were in control of the southern prairie-plains. "The truth is," observed Thomas Jefferson in 1804, "they are the great nation South of the Missouri, their possession extending from thence to the Red river."[4] Their location and numbers became an important element of the early Indian policy of the United States.

The Osage discovered after 1804 that the world as they knew it was rapidly disintegrating. They responded with confrontation, and after failing to stem the tide, they compromised. These compromises culminated in a series of questionable treaties and dependence on the United States.

An important element of Osage relations with non-Osage in the nineteenth century was the political situation among the Osage. Always important, political power and control was necessary to conduct and carry out effective diplomatic relations. The traditional powers of the Osage *Ga-hi-ge* and *Non-hon-zhin-ga* had been limited to certain prescribed functions, thereby allowing a great deal of freedom for individual Osage. Yet those powers were weakened as pressure drew the Osage north, south, and west.

Because of the success of Osage expansion in the eighteenth century, the tribes' five bands living in three groups began moving farther apart and more frequently. They established their spring and winter villages with greater intervening distances, making it extremely difficult for non-Osage Indians to negotiate with them. Members of the northern bands, living closer to Saint Louis and linked to the powerful Chouteau family, acted as

3. "Apercu de la population des diverses tribus du District de la Louisiane" (Nasatir, *Before Lewis and Clark*, 2:759–60); *American State Papers: Indian Affairs*, 4:707–8.

4. Jackson, *Letters of Lewis and Clark*, 1:200.

the spokesmen for the entire Osage tribe. The United States government for years would only deal politically with the northern bands, while the Arkansas Band denied northern diplomatic and political control and operated independently. This political division, combined with only limited Osage control over their own members, led to countless misunderstandings.

As a part of his Indian policy, President Thomas Jefferson wanted to move those tribes living east of the Mississippi to the west. Aware of continuing problems between Native Americans and white settlers in the east, Jefferson was convinced that removing the Indians from the region was the solution to the nagging problem.[5] Before the eastern Indians could be uprooted, however, room had to be made for them in the west. Jefferson and his administration wanted, therefore, to consolidate the Osage either in the north or the south to make room for these eastern tribes.

The Chouteau family, for reasons different than Jefferson's, also wanted to consolidate the Osage. Because of the Chouteaus' close ties with the northern Big Osage and their leaders and because of the general animosity toward Pierre Chouteau among the Arkansas Band, the Chouteaus sought to force the southern band to rejoin the northern bands.[6] The Osage River villages were closer to Saint Louis, and it was easier for the Chouteaus to conduct trade from their Saint Louis base. The desire to consolidate the Osage in the north was a constant goal of the Chouteau family, and it became an important element of United States Osage policy, for Pierre served as the United States Indian Agent for the Osage for many years, and his sons, Auguste Pierre (A. P.) Chouteau and Paul Liguest Chouteau, later served as agent and subagent to the Osage. The Chouteau family was very influential in shaping United States–Osage relations, and they con-

5. Bernard W. Sheehan, *Seeds of Extinction: Jeffersonian Philanthropy and the American Indian*, 242–75; Reginald Horsman, *Expansion and American Indian Policy, 1783–1812*, 104–14, 138–39.
6. Wilkinson to Dearborn, July 27, 1805, Carter, *Territorial Papers*, 13:170.

sistently worked to use United States–Osage policy to their advantage. The Chouteaus participated in all major United States treaties with the Osage in 1808, 1818, and 1825, and their underlying motivation to reunite the Osage was implicit in these agreements.

When Pierre Chouteau first went to Washington in 1804 to take the northern Osage to meet Jefferson, he urged Jefferson and Secretary of War Henry Dearborn to force the Arkansas Band north. Jefferson, unaware of the situation in the region and eager to establish peaceful relations with the western tribes, accepted the claims of Pierre Chouteau and his Osage ally, Pawhuska, about the illegitimacy of the southern bands. Jefferson supported the consolidation of the Osage, for the reunion of the Osage in the north would make room in the south for the southeastern tribes. When Chouteau and Pawhuska left Washington, they took messages from Jefferson to the Arkansas Band, urging them to rejoin their northern kin.

The Chouteaus also used their influence to convince Louisiana Territory Governor James Wilkinson to close trade along the lower Arkansas, Saint Francis, and White Rivers, hoping to force the Arkansas Osage back north to the legal traders.[7] The closing of the Arkansas trade occurred at a peculiar time, for just as Wilkinson was closing the fur trade of the lower Arkansas, the federal government was constructing a government trading factory at the mouth of the Arkansas River. The trading factory was established at the Arkansas Post in the fall of 1805, just after Governor Wilkinson closed the Arkansas River trade. Shortly after the factory opened, several Osage came to the Ar-

---

7. "In order to bring back the Osage chief Big Track [Cashesegra] and his Band from the Arkansaw to his Nation, it is recommended by P[.] Chouteau, that I should prohibit all Traders from passing the post of the Arkansaw" (Wilkinson to Dearborn, July 27, 1805, ibid., 170); Wilkinson to Dearborn, September 8, 1805, ibid., 197–99; "By depriving these latter [Arkansas Osage] of the necessities and comforts which commerce brings them they will be forced to return to the river of the Grand Osage and to reunite with Chief White Hair" (Pierre Chouteau to Wilkinson, July 18, 1805, Pierre Chouteau Letterbook).

kansas Post and asked to exchange Spanish flags and medals for United States symbols. They expressed concern about a short-age of supplies and asked to trade with the United States factor, John B. Treat.[8]

Treat, unable to trade with the Osage because of Wilkinson's ban, sent them home and urged them to rejoin their northern brethren. The Osage refused to consider returning to the north and went home without trading their furs. Shortly after their visit, a trader who had been upriver with them arrived at the Arkansas Post and reported that the Osage, despite any restric-tions of trade and lack of trade goods, were adamant about re-maining in the south. The Osage had told him, "As their Fathers have done they will cultivate corn, which God will cause to grow in abundance." They stated that there was an abundance of game in the south, and that they would stay where they were. The trader reported that opportunities in the south were such that many were abandoning the northern groups. "Already are they daily coming over, more than one hundred and sixty hav-ing arrived," and more were leaving the northern bands every day. Although the Osage were short of needed supplies, they continued to collect furs and tallow. "The Indians are much in want, and at this time have considerable quantities of Peltry." Another trader who had been among them prior to the ban re-turned with over three thousand "prime winter skins."[9]

In early March 1806, Jacob Bright, representing a New Or-leans trading company, Morgan and Bright, arrived at the Ar-kansas Post to trade with the Osage. The company had acquired a two-year trading license directly from Secretary of War Dear-born, and they claimed, therefore, that they were exempt from Wilkinson's ban. The other traders at the Arkansas Post were angered when Morgan and Bright were allowed to go into the interior, and they complained to Factor Treat. While Treat worked

8. Treat to Dearborn, November 15, 1805, *Arkansas Trading House Letterbook.*
9. Treat to Dearborn, December 27, 1805, ibid.

to rescind Wilkinson's trade ban, Morgan and Bright conducted a vigorous trade and shipped 267 packs of deerskin, 1,500 pounds of beaver skins, 930 bearskins, 72 other skins, and considerable amounts of tallow, all this obtained largely from the Osage as "their [Morgan and Bright's] license is a monopoly of that of the Osages."[10]

In April 1806, Secretary of War Dearborn revoked the Wilkinson trade ban, and traders flocked to the interior. Bright traveled upriver in July and erected a trading post among the Osage. Pierre Chouteau, recognizing this policy setback, hastened to join the competition and sent two boatloads of trade goods up the Arkansas. The reopening of the legal Arkansas trade was met with enthusiasm by the Osage. They traded with Chouteau, Morgan, Bright, and others, and within the year the Osage shipped $20,000 worth of furs through the Arkansas Post, a remarkable amount of furs, since traders were paying only 40 cents per pound for deerskins, $1.50 to $2.00 each for bearskins, and only 25 cents for small animal skins. The large amount of trade and low prices for skins reveal the tremendous time and energy that the Osage were devoting to hunting in the early nineteenth century. Indeed, the Osage trade was considered so important by the United States factor that he repeatedly requested permission to construct a subfactory among the Osage.[11]

As the southern Osage took thousands of animals, so did the northern groups. The northern bands, not subject to any trade restrictions, were able to hunt and deal with the traders from nearby Saint Louis. While the southern group was producing $20,000

10. Treat to Davy, February 27, 1806, ibid.; Treat to Davy, April 15, 1806, ibid.

11. Dearborn to Treat, April 29, 1806, ibid.; Treat to Dearborn, November 18, 1806, ibid.; Treat to Davy, April 15, 1806, ibid.; "They the winter past provided or sold the different traders peltry of furs to more than twenty thousand dollars value a considerable proportion of which was in Beaver and Otter—also their Deer Skins are always greatly to be prefered [sic] they being well cleansed together with the heads & shanks taken off" (Treat to Shee, December 31, 1807, ibid.); Treat to Mason, March 21, 1808, ibid.; Treat to Mason, September 20, 1808, ibid.

worth of furs, the northern Osage were producing $43,000 worth.[12] The northern Osage, although living and trading along the Osage River, were hunting and raiding in the south and west in order to acquire more fur-bearing animals and horses. This increased activity in the southwest indicated the beginning of animal shortages in the north. In August 1806, when Zebulon Pike visited the northern bands, he noted that the Arkansas bands were growing: "The village on the Arkansaw [sic] serves as a place of refuge for all the young, daring, and discontented; and added to which, they are much more regularly supplied with ammunition, . . . they are at liberty to make war without restraint, especially on the nations who are to the west, and have plenty of horses."[13] Pike also observed that many of the Osage were going south to join the southern bands because of greater opportunity.

Despite the relative prosperity of the Osage in the first decades of the nineteenth century, they had to contend with serious threats to their economy. Tribes living northeast continued to invade Osage country. The Osage also were confronted by stronger Native American rivals. Thousands of well-armed and powerful eastern Native American tribes moved into Osage country to live and hunt. American settlement and United States policy worked to remove tribes east of the Mississippi and place them in the west. The Osage were soon outnumbered by the immigrant tribes, and their animal resources were depleted by the new hunters. Osage country between the Missouri and Red Rivers became the pathway for western expansion, and the Osage were soon overwhelmed by a powerful invasion of their homeland. Ironically, the most immediate and grave threat to the Osage was Native American invaders.

Commercial Indian hunters killed the region's game and pushed the Osage west. In order to resist the Indian invasion, the Osage

---

12. Pierre Chouteau to Dearborn, October 7, no year, Pierre Chouteau Letterbook; Treat to Davy, April 15, 1806, *Arkansas Trading House Letterbook.*
13. Jackson, *Journals of Pike,* 2:146.

were forced to ally themselves with the United States. The Osage had to have access to guns and ammunition to protect their territory; their survival as a people depended upon it. In 1805, a band of Potawatomi raiders attacked an undefended Osage village and killed thirty-four women and children and took sixty prisoners.[14] This 1805 Osage River Massacre marked an important departure in Osage diplomacy. Potawatomi had attacked the Osage before to steal captives and livestock, but this brutal attack was different; it was not followed by a retaliatory attack by the Osage. The Osage had to have access to guns and ammunition and other trade goods, and they were thus forced to cooperate with the United States government. The government insisted on peace, so federal officials persuaded the Osage not to retaliate. Zebulon Pike later discussed the Osage River Massacre and reported,

> The humane policy which the United States have held forth to the Indian nations, . . . has succeeded to a miracle with the Osage of the Grand village, and the Little Osage. In short, they have become a nation of Quakers, as it respects the nations to the north and east of them; at the same time that they continue to make war on the naked and defenceless [sic] savages of the west. An instance of their forbearance was exhibited by an attack made on a hunting party of the Little Osage, . . . by a party of Potowatomies, . . . in obedience to the injunctions of their great father, they forebode to revenge the blow!![15]

The Osage were also challenged in the south. The Osage hunting grounds on the Ozark plateau were being slowly encroached upon by Chickasaw, Choctaw, Shawnee, Delaware, and Cherokee bands. At the same time Native American groups were entering their hunting grounds, the Osage had to contend with non–Native Americans moving west. The presence of new-

---

14. Pierre Chouteau to Dearborn, December 1, 1805, Pierre Chouteau Letterbook; Clifton, *Prairie People*, 190; Jackson, *Journals of Pike*, 2:32.
15. Jackson, *Journals of Pike*, 2:32–33.

comers, both Indian and non-Indian, posed a threat to the Osage economy, for as more people moved into the area more game was taken. As early as 1807, Factor Treat reported that the Osage were upset about the intruders and the resulting shortage of game, for they "seek every opportunity to Rob and destroy those of other Nations who go into their Neighbourhood."[16] Not only did the intruders destroy the game in forested and prairie regions, but they often stole Osage horses and occasionally killed Osage hunters. The Osage, hunting in the south and west, remained protective of their hunting territory. They robbed, beat, and sometimes killed the intruders to keep them out of the Osage economic domain. The Osage also continued to steal horses from Indians in the area or from nearby non-Indians. They then traded the horses for supplies.

In the spring of 1808, the Osage continued to resist intrusions by mistreating competing hunters, stealing horses, killing cattle, and pilfering things from settlers. This behavior was simply a continuation of minor robberies that had gone on for years. This time, however, the new governor of Louisiana, Meriwether Lewis, decided to act aggressively against the Osage. Lewis, who had been in Saint Louis for only a month in March, set about to control the Osage. After a series of thefts he immediately ordered a stop to all trade with the Osage. He ordered all of the hunters and traders in Osage country to return to Saint Louis and not to allow any gunpowder to remain in the hands of the Osage. The Osage were upset when the traders left the villages because they needed powder, ammunition, and other supplies for their summer hunts, but the traders, protected by Pawhuska and his followers, retreated safely.[17]

Pawhuska and leaders of the Little Osage went to Saint Louis to meet with Lewis and asked for help in controlling their people. Pawhuska claimed that his people were still leaving and re-

16. Treat to Shee, September 30, 1807, *Arkansas Trading House Letterbook.*
17. Meriwether Lewis to Dearborn, July 1, 1808, *Letters Received Secretary of War, Main Series.*

fused to stay in the north. "The White Hair informs me," wrote Meriwether Lewis, "that he cannot govern his people, and that we must therefore take such measures with rispect [*sic*] to them as we deem most proper."[18] Conditions were so lucrative in the south and so difficult in the north that Pawhuska could only stop the migration by appealing to United States power. Lewis, not content with the trade embargo, decided to move even more aggressively against the Osage.

The Secretary of War, unaware of Lewis's embargo against the Osage, had been planning to construct a trading factory and fort at the Osage River villages, hoping to use trade as an instrument of persuasion and control. Lewis decided to use the fort and trading post to coerce the Osage into cooperating with the United States. He decided against building the trading post at the Osage River villages as originally planned. Lewis claimed that the Osage River was not usable all year, and instead he ordered Captain Eli Clemson and the government trader, George Sibley, to construct the fort and trading post at Fire Prairie on the Missouri River, eighty miles north of the Osage villages. Lewis explained that the Fire Prairie site was closer to the hunting grounds of the Kansa, Iowa, and the Sac. Lewis, ignorant of the realities of the lower Missouri, claimed that by establishing the so-called Osage post on the Missouri, the Indians of the region "will find it absolutely necessary to live in peace with each other and consequently this establishment from it's [*sic*] situation would in the course of a few years be very instrumental in bringing about a permanent peace between the nations on the lower part of the Missouri."[19]

Governor Lewis ordered Pawhuska to take his followers to Fire Prairie on the Missouri River, and he met with the Kickapoo, Shawnee, Delaware, Iowa, and Dakota and encouraged them to attack any Osage not with Pawhuska.[20] Lewis then sent Captain

18. Ibid.
19. Ibid.
20. Ibid.

Eli Clemson and William Clark with a company of federal troops
and eighty mounted dragoons into Osage country. Clark began
constructing the fort at Fire Prairie and sent Nathaniel Boone
and Paul Loise to tell Pawhuska to come to the fort or face attack. Within a few days, Pawhuska and his followers arrived at
the fort asking for peace and explaining that they had sent all of
the stolen horses to Saint Louis with Pawhuska's son and Big
Soldier, one of the Little Osage *Ga-hi-ge.* Clark took advantage
of the situation and persuaded Pawhuska's people to sign a
treaty of peace with the United States.

This 1808 Treaty was significant for the Osage. Clark called
upon the Osage to establish a line separating them from the
United States to insure the peace. Unfortunately for the Osage,
when Clark drew the line it compelled the Osage to give up almost all of their lands east of their Osage River villages. The
treaty provided for a cession of over "50,000 Squar [sic] Miles
of excellent country."[21] In exchange for fifty thousand square
miles of land, the Osage agreed to remain near the Fire Prairie
fort, later named Fort Osage, where they would be supplied
with a blacksmith, grain mill, plows, two log houses, and a trading post. In addition, the Big and Little Osage people would receive twelve hundred dollars every year from the United States
if they were peaceful.[22]

There was, however, a good deal of misunderstanding about
this first treaty. When Clark returned to Saint Louis with the
treaty, he met with seventy-four Osage who had remained in
the city after returning the stolen horses. There were several
prominent Osage leaders among the group, and upon hearing
the provisions of the treaty, they objected to it. They claimed
that the Osage at Fort Osage could not give away the land without their approval. This claim was legitimate in the context of
traditional Osage political traditions, because decisions were

21. Clark to Dearborn, September 23, 1808, ibid.
22. Institute for the Development of Indian Law, *Treaties and Agreements,*
21–25.

not acceptable unless there was a consensus, and obviously with some of the principal Osage leaders absent a true consensus had not been achieved. Furthermore, a group of Osage who had been with Clark at the treaty negotiations and had returned with him to Saint Louis maintained that they had not given up any land. They had only agreed to allow the United States to hunt in the area; they had created a neutral buffer zone and had not intentionally given up control of it. Clark later admitted to Secretary of War Dearborn that he brought up the treaty by suggesting that a line be established "between them and the U: States."[23]

The idea of a shared hunting territory was familiar to the Osage. They had shared hunting territory with other friendly nations such as the Kansa and Quapaw, so it was understandable that they might agree to the creation of another such shared region with the new nation. It is doubtful, however, that the Osage "Chearfully [sic] approved" of giving up their lands and "that every individual of the Little Osage nation, and a great majority of the Great Osage were perfectly Contented and favourable to the Treaty" as Clark claimed. The Osage's objections about the treaty were more than complaints about a bad bargain. It seems clear that there were many misunderstandings because of culture and language, but there was also outright deception. Clark conceded that throughout the negotiations the Osage had insisted on retaining the hunting rights on the White River and clearly believed that they retained them, yet the final draft eliminated their legal hunting rights there.[24]

Both Clark and Lewis insisted that the Osage had been treated fairly. Despite the fact that Lewis had closed all trade to them just before their crucial summer hunt, encouraged several In-

23. Clark to Dearborn, September 23, 1808, *Letters Received Secretary of War, Main Series.*
24. Clark to Dearborn, December 2, 1808, ibid.; Kate L. Gregg, ed., *Westward with Dragoons: The Journal of William Clark on His Expedition to Establish Fort Osage, August 25 to September 22, 1808,* 37–43.

dian tribes against them, and sent soldiers into their country to force the Osage to sign the treaty, he insisted that no unfair advantage had been taken. Rather than accepting the possibility of misunderstanding or the unfairness of the treaty as cause for disagreement, the governor blamed Pierre Chouteau, who had not been present at the treaty negotiations, for encouraging Osage complaints. Lewis, however, rewrote the treaty, and despite his suspicions about Chouteau, sent him back to get the required Osage signatures at Fort Osage.[25] To insure that the Osage approved it, Lewis instructed Chouteau to inform the Osage that "if they are to be considered the friends and allies of the United States and receive their protection, they must sign the treaty, conform to it's [sic] stipulation, and establish their permanent village near the Fort." If they refused to sign, Chouteau was to stop all trade with the Osage and to inform Lewis of their refusal by special messenger, "in order that I may place the frontier in the best state of defence [sic] and make the necessary preparation for an expedition against them."[26] Lewis's suspicions about Chouteau were confirmed when Chouteau returned with a signed treaty that included a provision that granted him a large section of land near the mouth of the Osage River. Lewis accepted the treaty, but refused to accept Chouteau's land claim.[27]

It is clear that there were cultural misunderstandings involved in the treaty negotiations.[28] With the threat of another trade em-

25. Clark to Dearborn, September 23, 1808, *Letters Received Secretary of War, Main Series; American State Papers: Indian Affairs,* 1:765–67; Lewis to Dearborn, December 15, 1808, *Letters Received Secretary of War, Main Series.*

26. Letter of Instructions for Mr. Peter [Pierre] Chouteau, enclosed in Lewis to Dearborn, December 15, 1808, *Letters Received Secretary of War, Main Series.*

27. "I do not consider these reservations as binding. . . . I will venture to assert, that, if the Indians are permitted to bestow lands on such individuals as they think proper, the meanest interpreter in our employment will soon acquire a princely fortune at the expense of the United States" (ibid.); *American State Papers: Indian Affairs,* 1:767.

28. "They denied haveing [sic] given their lands in the other Treaty, they say that the interpreter did not explain to them" (Clark to Dearborn, December 2, 1808, *Letters Received Secretary of War, Main Series*); "[T]hat the Indians complained they had been deceived with respect to the stipulations of the treaty and that they intended to convey to us by that instrument no more than the privilege

bargo and an attack against their villages, the Osage did what their kinsman Pierre Chouteau urged them to do: they signed the treaty. The northern Osage had not intended to give up traditional homelands and hunting rights to the extent the treaty demanded. It is not clear exactly what the Osage understood they were signing in November at Fort Osage. A witness to the negotiations claimed that Chouteau threatened the Osage and informed them if they did not sign they would be treated as enemies of the government, and "the treaty was accordingly signed on the same day; and so much were the Osages awed by the threat of Mr. Chouteau, that a very unusual number of them touched the pen; many of whom knew no more the purpose of the act than if they had been an hundred miles off; and I here assert it to be a fact, that to this day the treaty is not fairly understood by a single Osage."[29] It is clear, however, that the Osage continued to complain about non-Osage hunters in the ceded region, and the Osage continued to hunt in the region, contrary to the treaty's provisions, for many years. In 1816, when the boundary line was finally surveyed, they were outraged when the line was within view of their Osage River villages.[30]

---

of hunting in that tract of country relinquished by the treaty . . . that they had no intention when they signed it of conveying any lands to the U'States" (Lewis to Dearborn, December 15, 1808, ibid.);

> The idea that their right in the country has passed from them in consequence of a transaction of two or three of their chiefs, unauthorized by the town, appears to them highly unreasonable and unjust. They allege also that the compensation made them was trifling and utterly disproportionate to the value of the land. On this topic their mode of reasoning is not a little ingenious and striking. After enumerating the water, the stones, the trees, the grass, the different sorts of wild fruit, and other particulars embraced in the sale, they ask who would be able to pay for all those things; and even if they could be paid for once, they observe that the next year there would be a new growth of grass, the water would still be flowing, and everything would remain unwasted; whereas goods received in payment are of a very perishable nature (Extract from Reverend William B. Montgomery's Journal, August 6, 1833, *Missionary Herald* 30 [January 1834]: 23).

29. This comes from an account of George Sibley, who was at Fort Osage during the negotiations. While it is clear that Sibley did not like the Chouteaus, the threats to cut off trade and declare the Osage to be enemies of the United States were included in Pierre Chouteau's written instructions from Lewis Edwin James. See James, comp., *Account of S. H. Long's Expedition,* 16:276.

30. Clark et al., to Crawford, December 7, 1816, William Clark Papers, Missouri Historical Society.

The Arkansas Osage did not participate in the making of the Fort Osage Treaty. While the northern Osage were meeting with Clark at Fort Osage, Clermont II and other Arkansas Osage leaders, reacting to Lewis's trade restrictions, went down to the government trading post to meet with John Treat. The Osage claimed they were starving and asked for trade. They asked Treat to establish a trading post up the river near their villages. Treat agreed that such a trading post would be a good idea, but he told them he could not build one.[31] The Osage explained that although they were hungry, they would not return to the northern villages. They ignored the demands of the United States government, because they believed the demands were those of Chouteau, not the government. They insisted that the command that they move to Fire Prairie was simply "a plan of Mr Pre Chouteau to Join their Towns that he might have the exclusive trade of all the Osages, as under the Spaniards." The Arkansas Osage blamed Pierre Chouteau, maintaining that "it was his wish for them to return that his son would have the benefit of there [*sic*] hunts."[32]

Shortly thereafter, James McFarlane, who had been sent by Governor Lewis to the Saint Francis and Arkansas Rivers to stop illegal trade, persuaded these Osage to go to Saint Louis to meet with Lewis to negotiate peace and to reestablish legal trade with the United States. In December, Clermont II and another leader, probably young Cashesegra, set out with McFarlane for Saint Louis. McFarlane, believing that his position as a government agent would protect the Osage, took them through the Cherokee towns on the White River. The Cherokee stopped

31. McFarlane to Lewis, December 11, 1808, *Letters Received Secretary of War, Main Series;* Treat to Mason, September 20, 1808, *Arkansas Trading House Letterbook;* Treat to Dearborn, September 19, 1808, *Letters Received by the Secretary of War Relating to Indian Affairs, 1800–1823;* Armstead to Bates, November 30, 1808, Marshall, *Life of Bates,* 2:45.
32. McFarlane to Clark, February 20, 1809, Carter, *Territorial Papers,* 14: 269; Armstead to Bates, November 30, 1808, Marshall, *Life of Bates,* 2:45.

McFarlane and the Osage and held them captive for several weeks; the Osage were not allowed to go to Saint Louis. After securing an Osage promise to return in the spring to make peace with the Cherokee and Delaware, the Cherokee allowed the Osage to return to their villages.[33] The next summer, Clermont II, Cashesegra, and several other prominent members of the Arkansas Osage went safely to Saint Louis to meet with the new Governor, Frederick Bates.

Finally given the opportunity to speak directly with the United States representative without Pierre Chouteau's interference, the Arkansas leaders assured the United States of their friendship and good intentions. The Arkansas Band had consistently maintained that they only wanted peaceful relations and honest trade with the United States. Trade was critical to the Arkansas Osage, as evidenced by their repeated visits to Treat's trading post. They needed guns and ammunition to protect themselves from the Choctaw, Chickasaw, Shawnee, Delaware, and Cherokee hunters and raiders who were invading their Ozark forests. By dealing directly with the United States, Clermont II and Cashesegra acquired official recognition as Osage leaders. Because Bates was willing to recognize their band's independence and tacitly acknowledged the permanence of their separation from the northern groups, the Arkansas Osage agreed to the treaty. By signing the treaty they restored peace, reopened trade, and gained some prestige in their ongoing struggle with Pawhuska. With both sides eager for peace and trade, Clermont II, Cashesegra, and thirteen other southern Osage leaders signed the 1808 Treaty, revised by

33. Wallis to Bates, December 18, 1808, Marshall, *Life of Bates,* 2:45–46; Honey to Bates, January 12, 1809, ibid., 59; "McFarlane having assured them that while he was with them no person dare lay hands upon them! They consented and left this place with him, and got as far as the Cherochee [*sic*] village on the St. Francis river where . . . the Osage Indians were detained by the Cherochees [*sic*]" (McFarlane to Clark, February 20, 1809, Carter, *Territorial Papers,* 14:268–69).

Lewis, in August 1809, whereupon Bates reopened trade with the Arkansas Osage.[34]

Although the treaty was not ratified by Congress for two years, it did have an immediate effect on the northern Big and Little Osage. They initially abided with Lewis's demand that they live near the fort on the Missouri River. All of the northern bands spent the winter of 1808–1809 there, but after the first season many returned to their traditional village sites along the upper Osage River. Soon only the Little Osage, the longtime Missouri River dwellers, remained at the fort, while most of the others returned to the old villages, where they traded with the Chouteaus and other Saint Louis traders.

Captain Eli Clemson, commander of Fort Osage, wrote, "[T]hey [Osage] made Corn in the vicinity of the Fort, but at that time it was visible in their every movement, that they began to grow tired of their new residence, a great number of them returned to their old Towns, the fall & winter of 1809-10."[35] Living along

---

34. Pierre Chouteau, Jr., wrote to Dearborn on September 1, 1809:

Last spring, the Governor thought proper to ingratiate himself with the Band of Osages established on the River *Arkansas*, but still without communicating his projects to my Father: he sent to them Mr McFarlane, second Agent to the Osage Nations. Neither my Father nor myself have any knowledge of the Instructions that were given him. Mr McFarlane, in the name of the Governor, made immense promises to the Osages, and arrived at St Louis with the Chiefs of that Band: it was immediately proposed to them to proceed to Washington City with Mr McFarlane; but the Savages refused to accede to it. The promises [sic] made to them upon the Borders of the *Arkansas* not having been fulfilled at *Saint Louis*, their Confidence is destroyed.

(Le Printems dernier le gouverneur a jugé à propos de se rapprocher de la bande osage etablie sur la riviere des Arkansas, mais tourours sans faire part à mon pere de ses projêts, il envoya Mr McFarlane second agent près les nations ozages, mon pere ni moi, n'avons aucune connoissance des instructions qui lui furent données, Mr McFarlane au nom du gouverneur fit les promesses les plus etendues aux Osages et vient d'arriver a St Louis avec les chefs de cette bande, il leur a été immediatement proposé de partir pour Washington City avec Mr McFarlane, mais les Sauvages s'y sont refusés, les promesses faites sur les rives des Arkansas n'etant point remplies a St Louis, leur confiance est detruite. [Carter, *Territorial Papers*, 14:314, 317])

See also, Clark to Eustis, September 21, 1809, *Letters Received Secretary of War, Main Series*.

35. Clemson, et al., to Eustis, July 16, 1812, Carter, *Territorial Papers*, 14: 587-90.

the river near the trading post, they became victims of attacks by northern Indians. While the fort offered little protection for the Osage, it attracted the northern Indians who hunted in the region and occasionally killed and robbed the Osage living nearby. The Osage were attacked by the Sac, Mesquakie, Iowa, and others, and the close contact with outsiders at the fort created problems. The Osage quickly learned the risks of becoming fort people, and most abandoned the area. Between 1808 and 1811, the northern bands broke into several smaller groups. Some remained around the fort, while others returned to their old villages. Despite their reluctance to live at the post, they continued to trade there and supplied most of the 29,568 deerskins, 256 otter skins, and 1,055 bearskins traded at Fort Osage in 1809.[36]

By the spring of 1812, few Osage remained about the fort, and when a group of Arkansas Osage arrived at the fort to pick up their annuities they were attacked by a group of unidentified "northern Indians." By July of 1812, there were no Osage living near the fort. "Traders are now established at the Grand Osage Villages on the river of the same name, and the inducement to their coming here to trade is trifling indeed when put into competition with the riske [sic] they run of losing life and property."[37] In June 1813, fearing an attack by the British and their Indian allies, the government closed the trading factory at Fort Osage and moved it down the river to Arrow Rock. In 1815, it was reestablished at the old Fort Osage site, but by that time only the

36. Sans-Nerf, a Big Osage *A-ki-da*, said in 1813, "We do not like Fort Clark for very good reasons, the road between that place & our Village, is nearly as long as the one to this place, & is a very dangerous one to travel—Our Enemies lay in wait for us when we go there to Trade, and have Killed Several of our People." Grey Bird, the oldest brother of Pawhuska, said, "The Bones of my oldest Brother (White Hair) are buried on the road between this place and my Village—the Bones of several of my Nation lie unburied and bleaching on the Prairie between my Village & Fort Clark—They were murdered by our enemies who lay in ambush for them when they went to trade" (Sibley to Clark, November 30, 1813, Carter, *Territorial Papers*, 14:713-14); *American State Papers: Indian Affairs*, 1:770-72.

37. Clemson, et al., to Eustis, July 16, 1812, Carter, *Territorial Papers*, 14: 587-90.

Little Osage favored northern settlement.[38] After the War of 1812, enough traders came to the Osage River, so most Osage remained at their Osage River villages and only hunted and traded in the north.

During the War of 1812, there was some fear that the Osage might join with the Sac and other northern tribes to fight for the British. These fears were unwarranted, for despite their long-time friendships with Canadian traders, the Osage would never have joined up with their former Indian enemies to fight against the United States. Osage relations with some of their northern neighbors shifted somewhat, for Governor Clark, fearing attacks by the Sac and Mesquakie, invited a group of friendly Sacs to live along the Missouri River near the mouth of the Osage River. The Osage left the Sacs in peace, despite the longstanding ill feeling toward them. The Osage did not want to disturb their peaceful relationship with the United States. They enjoyed the benefits of American trade and weapons provided through their alliance and were eager to maintain it. Therefore, the Sacs, protected by the United States, were safe from Osage attacks.[39]

Yet enmity between other Sacs and Osage continued, and when Governor Bates sent Pierre Chouteau to the northern villages in May 1813 to ask for volunteers to fight the British-Indian allies, the Osage jumped at the chance. Eager to raid their enemies with United States assistance, 500 warriors volunteered when Chouteau asked for 200. Chouteau reduced the party to 260 men and left for the north. They were about to cross the Missouri River when they received orders from a new governor, Benjamin Howard. He was uneasy about such a large group of armed Indians, and he ordered them to disband and go

38. Sibley to Clark, ibid., 712–14.

39. Frederick Bates, Licences for Indian Trade, 1815, October 1, 1816, ibid., 15:190–91; Marshall, ed., "Journals of De Mun," 188; "The Missouri Indians say, we will side with the Americans, as they are our traders. They bring us our clothing, arms and ammunition and we will keep their road open" (*Missouri Gazette*, August 13, 1814). See also, Kate L. Gregg, "The War of 1812 on the Missouri Frontier."

home. Howard also ordered Chouteau to get Osage permission to evacuate Fort Osage to a safer location downriver. Chouteau gave the Osage presents and promised to pay them the two years worth of past-due annuities. He also promised to build two block-houses at their villages. In exchange for presents, promised annuities, and blockhouses, Chouteau convinced the Osage to allow the United States to abrogate that portion of the 1808 Treaty that provided for the trading post at Fort Osage. They agreed to its closing and returned home.[40]

The War of 1812 had a significant impact upon the Osage. The British were forced to leave the region south of the Great Lakes, and Canadian traders no longer came to the Osage River villages. In the early nineteenth century, the United States did not pose an immediate threat to the Osage, but the eastern Indians did. Immigrant tribes killed the Osage's game, stole their women, children, and horses, and fought them for control of their hunting grounds. The Osage were forced to remain at peace with the white Americans in order to obtain essential arms. The United States, eager to remove the eastern Indians, took full advantage of their relationship with the Osage and demanded land from them to locate the evacuated eastern tribes. Dependent upon the United States for essential firearms and trade, the Osage reluctantly but unavoidably surrendered their tribal lands in a series of treaties with the United States. With the British evacuation, the United States assumed a new, more belligerent posture toward Native Americans. The United States, no longer fearing Canadian-armed Indians and British intervention, were less conciliatory. After the war, Native Americans had to deal with the government strictly on American terms.[41] Thus, the Osage alliance with the United States became more important, for now only through American traders could they acquire es-

---

40. Bates to Pierre Chouteau, March 4, 1813, *Letters Received Secretary of War, Main Series;* Pierre Chouteau to Armstrong, May 20, 1813, Carter, *Territorial Papers,* 14:671–72.
41. William T. Hagan, *American Indians,* 64–66.

sential arms and ammunition to restrain their neighbors and maintain their hegemony.

Despite the temporary closing of Fort Osage during the War of 1812 and the reduced market caused by the war, the Osage still hunted deer, bear, otter, bison, and various small animals, trading them with traders who came among them. After the war, the trading factory was reestablished at Fort Osage, and many traders returned to Osage country, trading with the Osage in the north and south. In 1821, the government established a subfactory along the Marais des Cygnes River close to the traditional Osage village sites which competed with a Chouteau post already there. At about the same time other traders operating out of the Arkansas Post began establishing permanent operations among the southern Osage.

Traders Hugh Glen and Nathaniel Pryor established posts at the Three Forks of the Arkansas near the southern villages, and when the government closed the factory once again at Fort Osage and Marais des Cygnes in 1822, the government trader at the Marais des Cygnes opened his own independent trading post along the Neosho River, just southwest of the Osage River. That same year, A. P. Chouteau, long active in the Osage trade, convinced most of the northern Osage to move down to his trading post along the lower Neosho at La Saline. After this move, few Osage remained along the Osage River, and soon most were living in several villages south and west of their traditional village sites.

A. P. Chouteau and his brothers established four trading posts among the Osage along the Verdigris and Neosho Rivers and encouraged Osage fur trade. In 1823, Chouteau traded for over 38,659 pounds of deerskin, plus bearskins that totalled $15,705. In 1825, Chouteau acquired 50,000 pounds of deerskins; 400 pounds of beaver skins; and bear, raccoon, and assorted skins worth $17,500.[42] The Osage did not produce all the furs, but the

42. Janet LeCompte, "Auguste Pierre Chouteau," 76–78.

close ties of the Chouteaus and Osage and the fact that all the posts were in Osage country suggests that the Osage supplied many of the furs that Chouteau and others shipped out.

After the end of the War of 1812, more eastern tribes moved west. In 1816, William Clark reported 1,300 Shawnee, 1,000 Cherokee, and 50 Peoria in Missouri. A year later he reported 1,200 Shawnee, 600 Delaware, 200 Piankashaw, 60 Peoria, and 6,000 Cherokee. At the same time, he listed 5,800 Osage in 1816 and 6,000 in 1817. This invasion of Osage country continued to grow, and slowly eastern tribes pushed the Osage west. The United States, having acquired the Osage lands in 1808, encouraged the immigration. Many eastern Indians, well before the Indian Removal Act, chose to leave their crowded, game-depleted homelands and move into what seemed to be much richer western lands. Chouteau wrote the Secretary of War William Eustis in the spring of 1810 that the Osage were angry that the rapidly growing population was destroying their game, and he reminded Eustis it was a major part of their existence.[43] The invasion continued despite Osage ire, and Richard Graham, Osage agent, wrote in February 1822, "This winter's hunt has given the emigrating Indians an idea of the great riches of the Osage Country and they openly avow their intentions of taking possession of it."[44] A little later, a missionary living among the Osage wrote of the Kickapoo who were hunting on Osage lands, "They [Kickapoo] came hither to hunt and trade, are said to be excellent hunters, and as a proof of the scarcity of game in their own country

---

43. Voget, *Osage Research Report*, 206–7. Osage complained of Indians coming into Osage territory without their permission and destroying game. See Clark to Dearborn, September 23, 1808, William Clark Papers. "Both the Osage and the Pawnee declare that the few whites who visit their country as hunters, kill more Buffaloe in one year than would support both their nations (containing 10,000 persons) for the same period. . . . The Osages complain that settlements are forming in the midst of their hunting country . . ." (*Missouri Gazette*, June 15, 1816); Pierre Chouteau to Eustis, April 26, 1810, Pierre Chouteau Letterbook.

44. Grant Foreman, *Indians and Pioneers: The Story of the American Southwest Before 1830*, 187.

to Missouri, they find good hunting ground where the Osages consider the game as nearly all destroyed."[45]

Just as the northern Osage faced increasing pressure from eastern tribes, so did the Arkansas Osage.[46] Their situation was particularly difficult, as they had to contend not only with the new Native American invasion but also with constant pressure from the United States government to move north to join their kin and open up the Arkansas River lands for the eastern tribes. John Treat, as early as 1805, noted trouble between the immigrating tribes and the Osage. He explained that the hunting grounds of the Chickasaw, Choctaw, and Quapaw were

> confin'd generally between the Waters of the Arkansa [which they seldom pass] and those of the St. Francis, and so far to North West as occasionally to fall in with the Osage Tribe . . . between this and the other Tribes there exists great animosity; and when on excursions; small parties accidentily [*sic*] meet [which the last year, was often the case] they never spare each other, probably in a short time this Tribe may not be so able, consequently less ready to attack; and therefore not to be so much dreaded, as they now are by their neighbours: should this be the case, it will not be the want of valour, but that of ammunition, and other supplies, which already they are apprehensive of.[47]

While the Osage fought all the eastern tribes, the most powerful group they had to contend with was the Cherokee. The Cherokee, living in the mountains of Tennessee, Georgia, and North and South Carolina, began appearing in the forests along the lower Arkansas as early as 1786. Small Cherokee bands hunted in the region, and in 1796, ten families, led by *Kon-ora-too,* moved

45. Voget, *Osage Research Report,* 220.

46. The *Arkansas Gazette* was filled with reports of white settlers going up the Arkansas and into the Ozarks and Indian country in the 1820s. "We learn, also, that great numbers are preparing to emigrate to this territory" (*Arkansas Gazette,* March 25, 1820). "The roads in that neighborhood are said to be literally swarming with emigrants in that country—and we learn from White river, that they are coming in from that quarter by hundreds" (ibid., November 26, 1822).

47. Treat to Dearborn, November 15, 1805, *Arkansas Trading House Letterbook.*

to the Saint Francis River. As conditions became crowded and inhospitable in the east, those Cherokee who wanted to continue their hunting life moved to the Saint Francis and White River areas. By 1806, there were about six hundred Cherokee there. These people joined the Choctaw, Shawnee, and Delaware and hunted in the Ozarks. The Osage responded to this intrusion. According to Treat, the Arkansas Osage robbed and attacked any Indians they encountered in the region.[48]

The migration of southeastern Indians grew, and by 1816 about six thousand Cherokee had settled on the lower Arkansas. These Cherokee invaders of Osage country were well armed and skilled hunters. When Cherokee and Osage met on hunting expeditions, violence ensued as both groups struggled for control of the territory. The competition over hunting grounds was the essential problem between the two peoples, but the economically motivated violence begat additional violence as individuals sought retaliation for the attacks. The cultural demands for retribution were different among the Osage and the Cherokee. The Osage accepted payment in place of blood revenge. A murderer could "cover the dead" with gifts, and this was culturally acceptable to the Osage. To the Cherokee, however, payment was never sufficient compensation for murder. Although blood revenge was sometimes avoided internally, it was always required when outsiders killed a Cherokee. A single Cherokee killing could cause an unending war.[49] Economic competition and cultural differences made any successful diplomacy between the two people difficult. No neutral zone could be created between these peoples, thereby eliminating a crucial diplomatic tool for peace.

In 1816, the Cherokee went to Saint Louis and complained to

48. James Mooney, "Myths of the Cherokee and Sacred Formulas of the Cherokees," 390–91; Treat to Shee, September 30, 1806, *Arkansas Trading House Letterbook.*

49. Reid, *Better Kind of Hatchet,* 8–9. Cherokee notions of blood revenge were especially strong among the more conservative and traditional Cherokee, and these were the Cherokee who were moving to the Ozarks in the late eighteenth and early nineteenth centuries.

Governor William Clark about Osage thefts and attacks. Clark urged the two groups to make peace, and in 1816 Cherokee agent William Lovely arranged a meeting with the Osage to settle the differences with the Cherokee. The Arkansas Osage did not have a separate agent and were to be represented by Pierre Chouteau. Clark ordered Chouteau to attend the meeting to represent Osage interests, but in June, when Lovely and the Cherokee went up to the mouth of the Verdigris to meet with Chouteau and the Osage, Chouteau had not arrived. Not surprisingly, considering his relationship with the southern bands, he failed to show up. Lovely, however, convinced the Osage to sign away more of their land.

In exchange for all claims made against them for real and alleged depredations, the Osage granted the United States a portion of land between the falls of the Verdigris River and the 1808 Treaty Line, approximately three million acres of prime prairie land. Lovely intended to get the land from the Osage in order to turn it over to the Cherokee. It is not clear what the Osage thought they were agreeing to with Lovely. Clermont II later insisted he had only consented to give up a small parcel of land, and that the Osage intended to give it to whites, not Cherokees. This 1816 cession, known as Lovely's Purchase, had not been authorized by the federal government, and Washington officials refused to approve the agreement or the land cession. It was, however, renegotiated in 1818.[50]

The Osage-Cherokee peace arranged in 1816 did not last, as economic competition escalated between the two tribes. Both nations worked to harvest the area's fur-bearing game, and violence between the Osage and Cherokee continued. In January 1817, the Cherokee, angered by Osage violence, began planning an attack on the Osage. The Arkansas Cherokee sent messen-

---

50. Crawford to Clark, et al., September 17, 1816, Carter, *Territorial Papers*, 15:173; Clark to Calhoun, October, no day, 1818, ibid., 454–55; Ina Gabler, "Lovely's Purchase and Lovely County," 31–39; Foreman, *Indians and Pioneers*, 71, 78, 156, 220–22.

gers back to the eastern Cherokee requesting aid in the proposed attack, and several boatloads of Cherokees came west.[51] In July 1817, the Cherokee wrote to Missouri Territory Governor William Clark, complaining that "they [the Osage] have stolen all our best horses, and have reduced us to work with our naked hands. [W]ith the few horses we have left, we intend to go to the Osages and hunt for those horses taken; we are going to do mischief."[52]

Although the Cherokee made their threat in July, they waited until October to attack. Knowing that most of the Osage men would be out on the plains for the fall hunt, the Cherokee moved against an Osage prairie village filled with food stored for the winter and left protected only by old men and women. Five hundred Cherokee, joined by Choctaw, Chickasaw, and "several whites," went up the Arkansas River to the Verdigris. As they approached the Arkansas Osage village, they sent a messenger urging them to send down a few Osage to meet with the "ten-to-fifteen" Cherokee that had come to visit. Since the warriors, *Ga-hi-ge, A-ki-da,* and *Non-hon-zhin-ga* were away on the fall hunt, only one old, former Osage leader went down to meet the Cherokee. The Cherokee immediately hacked him to death and then, sure that the warriors were gone, went up to the village and destroyed it. They killed thirty-eight Osage and captured over one hundred. Before leaving, the Cherokee raiders stole what they could carry, destroyed caches of food, and set fire to the village. They descended to their villages and celebrated their victory, later known as the Massacre of Claremore Mound. Osage prisoners were sent back to the eastern Cherokee as payment for their help on the raid.[53]

The southern Osage returned from their hunt and found their village destroyed. The Massacre of Claremore Mound outraged

---

51. Foreman, *Indians and Pioneers*, 47–48.
52. Cherokee Indians to Clark, July 11, 1817, Carter, *Territorial Papers*, 15:304.
53. Clark to Sibley, November 11, 1817, Sibley Papers; Foreman, *Indians and Pioneers*, 51–52.

the Osage, but the necessity of maintaining good relations with the United States prevented retaliatory attacks, for the government wanted to keep the peace. Just as with the Potawatomi's 1805 Osage River Massacre, the United States was able to prevent the Osage from responding. Troops arrived in December and started construction of Fort Smith on the south bank of the Arkansas River between the Osage and Cherokee villages to keep them apart.

The times now required a bold diplomatic move. During the summer of 1818, the Osage encouraged tribes to visit them. So intent on Cherokee revenge, the Osage invited old enemies to come and meet with them. Members of the Shawnee, Delaware, Creek, Quapaw, Kansa, and Mesquakie were guests of the Osage. The Osage gave away over one hundred horses that summer to the tribes in hopes of securing their alliance to form a strong army to attack the Cherokee. The tribes accepted the Osage horses and hospitality, but only the Mesquakie promised any help.[54]

While the Osage planned retaliation, the Cherokee worked more effectively against the Osage. After their "victory" at Claremore Mound, the Cherokee sent word of their triumph to the federal government. They insisted that because of their defeat of the Osage, they should have the Osage land. Unfortunately for the Osage, Secretary of War John C. Calhoun cared not that the victory had been only over defenseless women, children, and old men, and he noted,

> The Cherokees are anxious to have an outlet to the West to the game country, and it seems fair that the Osages, who hold the country West of their settlement, and have been beaten in the contest, should either make a concession of such portion of their country as might give the outlet, or at least to grant them as undisturbed passage to and from their hunting grounds. You will, as far

54. Nuttall, *Journal of Travels,* 207; Green, " 'We Dance in Opposite Directions.' "

as practicable, and consistent with justice, make the arrangements favorable to the Cherokees; as the President is anxious to hold out every inducement to the Cherokees, and the other Southern nations of Indians, to emigrate to the West of the Mississippi.[55]

As a result of their 1817 "defeat," the Osage were ordered to go to Saint Louis and surrender land to the Cherokee. The Arkansas Osage, wanting peace and trade with the United States and anxious not to incite white attacks, agreed to cede the land demanded. This cession was the land that had been previously relinquished to Lovely in 1816. They also agreed to allow the Cherokee access to the plains through their lands in exchange for the return of the 104 Osage prisoners taken in the 1817 massacre.[56]

It is not certain if all of the southern Osage leadership participated in the 1818 Treaty. Clermont II, the most influential, may have participated, but he never signed the treaty. Major Stephen Long, among the Osage in 1818, wrote,

[The Osage] have repeatedly solicited the Americans to settle near them, alledging [*sic*] that they sold the land under the expectation that the Americans would become their neighbours, ... Such having been their views in disposing of their Lands to the United States, they are not a little disappointed and chagrinned [*sic*], at the arrangement recently made with the Cherokees, their inveterate enemies, by which the latter are permitted to settle upon the Lands formerly owned by them and are by this means placed in a condition to annoy them exceedingly, which has been done of late, on repeated occasions.[57]

Clermont II may have not participated in the September meeting, but young Cashesegra did sign the treaty. After the meeting in Saint Louis, Clermont II complained about the land transfer. He maintained that the 1818 cession, just as the 1816 cession,

55. Calhoun to Clark, May 8, 1818, Carter, *Territorial Papers,* 15:390–91.
56. Clark to Calhoun, October, no day, 1818, ibid., 454–55.
57. Stephen Long to Thomas A. Smith, January 30, 1818, ibid., 19:4–7.

was intended to turn the land over to whites, not Cherokees. Clermont II adamantly claimed that he wanted white settlers in the region between the Osage and Cherokee. Arkansas Osage realized that non-Indian farming settlers posed less of a threat to their animal resources than did the commercially hunting Cherokee.[58] In 1819, Thomas Nuttall visited the Osage and the Cherokee and wrote, "It appeared, from what I could learn, that the Osages, purposely deceived by the interpreter, at the instigation of the Shoutous [Chouteaus], had hatched up a treaty without the actual authority of the chiefs, so that in the present state of things a war betwixt the Cherokees and the Osages is almost inevitable, unless the latter relinquish the banks of the Arkansa, as Messrs. Shoutou [Chouteau] wish them."[59]

There are curious aspects to this September meeting, for Pierre Chouteau, the only agent for both bands, spoke for all Osage, despite the animosity the Arkansas Band and Clermont II had for him. Chouteau insisted throughout the meeting that the Osage were determined to reunite themselves in one village, and furthermore, he claimed that they had asked that he remain their agent. The Osage requested, according to Chouteau, that their annuities not be distributed at Fort Osage, but be sent to the northern villages.[60]

All this sounds suspect, considering the southern Osage's attitude toward Pierre Chouteau and their repeated refusal to leave the Arkansas Valley. The northern Osage at Saint Louis, however, may have wanted all those things. By 1818, the northern bands were closely tied with the Chouteau family and showed little concern for their southern relatives. Richard Graham, a government agent for the Osage, wrote, "The long separation of this nation has given distinct views and feelings to the three

58. Nuttall, *Journal of Travels*, 239; Stephen Long to Thomas A. Smith, January 30, 1818, Carter, *Territorial Papers*, 19:4–9.
59. Nuttall, *Journal of Travels*, 239.
60. Clark to Calhoun, October, no day, 1818, Carter, *Territorial Papers*, 15:454–55.

Bands. In many respects they act as different nations. The band near the Osage river are jealous of the prosperity of the Arkansas tribe."[61]

Pierre Chouteau, whose family had a trading post at the Osage River villages, still wanted the Arkansas Osage back in the north, trading with his sons. It is reasonable to assume that he was willing to translate only what he wanted the federal government to hear. The Osage interpreter at the meeting was Paul Loise, who was either Auguste or Pierre Chouteau's Osage son. Pierre Chouteau's sons, A. P. and Paul Liguest, were competing with the Fort Osage traders, and the removal of the annuity distribution from the fort would certainly have worked against the traders there.[62] Clermont II's charges about the misleading nature of the treaty were sound ones.

The southern Osage maintained the dual moiety leadership and practiced traditional Osage diplomacy. The *Tsi-zhu Ga-hi-ge* Clermont II would have been responsible for negotiations, and his absence in Saint Louis invalidated the treaty. The northern Osage had only one leader and no *Tsi-zhu Ga-hi-ge*. Without the traditional procedures for conducting Osage diplomacy, the proper leaders participating, or tribal consensus arrived at by negotiation with the *Non-hon-zhin-ga*, the federal government had not truly negotiated a meaningful Osage treaty.

Osage along the Arkansas claimed to prefer whites as neighbors instead of Cherokee, as whites would act as an effective barrier between the Osage and Cherokee. Cherokee were aggressive, commercial hunters, and white farmers would have provided less competition than Cherokee hunters. Visitors noted that the Osage were more concerned about Indian resettlement in their area than they were about white settlement: "[I]t appeared, that they would not be unwilling to dispose of more of their lands, provided that the government of the United States

61. Graham to Calhoun, September 20, 1821, Richard Graham Papers.

62. Foley and Rice, *The First Chouteaus*, 45; Sibley to Valle, December 17, 1826, Sibley Papers.

would enter into a stipulation, not to settle it with aborigines, whom they have now much greater reason to fear than whites. . . . The Osages in a recent council said, they would have no objection to dispose of their lands, provided the whites only were allowed to settle upon them."[63] There was so much controversy surrounding Lovely's Purchase that although the Osage lost the land in 1818, the Cherokee did not officially acquire it until ten years later.[64] After negotiating the land cession, the Osage also agreed to make peace with the Shawnee, Delaware, and Cherokee. The Osage, in return for allowing Cherokee to hunt in the west, were to obtain their people captured in the 1817 massacre. The Osage were to meet with the Cherokee at Fort Smith the next spring for the return of the prisoners of war.

There was little hope for peace, however, despite Osage efforts. On the way back to the Arkansas, the southern Osage who participated in the Saint Louis treaty negotiations were attacked by a group of Cherokee who stole forty horses and killed four Osage. The Osage wanted revenge for the attack, but Nathaniel Pryor, a trader at Three Forks, convinced them to remain at peace until their prisoners were returned. Their restraint went unrewarded, as the Cherokee did not bring any prisoners back in the spring. When Clermont II returned to Fort Smith in July, again asking for the prisoners promised the year before, the Cherokee failed to show up. The commander of Fort Smith told Clermont II to return in September. In September, a full year since they had made peace in Saint Louis, and a year during which the southern Osage had kept peace, the Osage again went to Fort Smith for their prisoners. They waited ten days, and when none of the Cherokee arrived, all but Clermont II and Tally, the two *Ga-hi-ge,* returned home. On the eleventh day,

63. Nuttall, *Journal of Travels,* 193, 239.

64. Easton to Crawford, n.d. [received March 1819], Carter, *Territorial Papers,* 19:60–62; James Miller to Calhoun, March 24, 1820, ibid., 153–55; Foreman, *Indians and Pioneers,* 220–23.

some Cherokee arrived and announced that the Osage prisoners refused to go back to the Osage. The commander of Fort Smith, William Bradford, then ordered the Cherokee to meet their treaty obligations. The Cherokee finally produced a few Osage prisoners. The Osage took their people home, reminding the commander that 104 prisoners had been promised to be returned.[65]

The southern Osage, anxious to protect their homes and maintain good relations with the United States, tried to remain at peace with the Cherokee and restrain their young men. The Cherokee's continued lack of good faith caused increased anger and frustration among the Osage. The fragile peace of 1818 was broken in February 1820, when Skitok (Mad Buffalo), Clermont II's son, hunting along the Poteau River south of the Arkansas, killed three Cherokee hunters and stole their belongings. The Cherokee, outraged at the murders, went to Fort Smith and demanded the Osage turn over Skitok; the Osage refused. Shortly thereafter, Tahchee (Dutch), a Cherokee leader, came upon Skitok at Pryor's trading post at the Three Forks. Before Tahchee could kill Skitok, Pryor distracted Tahchee and helped the Osage warrior escape. When Tahchee discovered what Pryor had done, he and his men pillaged Pryor's trading post.[66] In August 1820, the Cherokee once again demanded the surrender of Skitok for the murder of the Cherokee. Although the Cherokee expressed outrage over the three Cherokee deaths, they never expressed any remorse for the thirty-eight dead Osage or the one hundred Osage who remained their captives. The Osage, accordingly,

---

65. A Tales, or Straiting Deer, son of Big Tract, a member of the Arkansas Band, signed the 1808 Osage Treaty. Tally is either *Ta-hah-ka-he* (Deer with Branching Horns) or *Ta-ha-ka-ha* (Antlered Deer). See Institute for the Development of Indian Law, *Treaties and Agreements*, 25; Burns, *Osage Bands and Clans*, 14, 52, 55; William Bradford, February 4, 1819, Carter, *Territorial Papers*, 19: 33–34; Clark to Calhoun, October, no day, 1818, ibid., 15:454–55; Foreman, *Indians and Pioneers*, 73–74.

66. Bradford to Calhoun, March 4, 1820, Carter, *Territorial Papers*, 19:151–52; Foreman, *Indians and Pioneers*, 74–76; Walter B. Douglas, ed., "Documents: Captain Nathaniel Pryor," 255–57.

refused to surrender Skitok until the Cherokee turned over the prisoners they had promised to return two years earlier.

Competition persisted between these peoples, and theft and attacks continued. In March 1821, the Osage learned that the Cherokee had announced they were at war with the Osage.[67] That April, Clermont II came to the Union Mission, newly established on the lower Neosho, and warned the missionaries that his men were going to attack the Cherokee. He assured the mission families of their safety. Shortly thereafter, Skitok and four hundred Osage warriors marched downstream to attack the Cherokee. Skitok and his men approached Fort Smith and asked to visit the fort to get ammunition. The commander, Lieutenant Martin Scott, refused to allow them to cross the river to the fort, and when some of them entered the river he ordered artillery aimed at the Osage.

The Osage party then moved downriver and crossed the Arkansas. Wandering along the Poteau River and Lee Creek, they discovered and killed three Quapaw and three Delaware. The Osage involved later claimed that they thought the Delaware were Cherokee and that they killed the Quapaw "at the instigation of a young chief to revenge the death of some of his relations in a former quarrel."[68] After breaking into several settlers' cabins, the Osage stole a few horses and returned home without attacking the Cherokee. Only days after the Skitok war party returned, Clermont II sent a message to the Cherokee calling for a cease-fire for three months. He promised to keep his young men at home if the Cherokee would reciprocate. Clermont II further insisted that he could only speak for his village and not the other bands, suggesting that northern bands also stole horses and robbed Cherokee hunters. Clermont II ended his message by stating, "He did not beg a peace because he could send an army of 1500 warriors, and that if they saw fit to carry on the

67. Bradford to Calhoun, February 10, 1821, Carter, *Territorial Papers,* 19: 264–65; Brearley to Calhoun, April 26, 1821, ibid., 285.
68. April 25, 1821, Union Mission Journal.

war he should on his part carry it on with vigor."[69] After sending the message to the Cherokee, Clermont II and his village left for the plains on their summer hunt. Because of the invasion of the Ozark forests by Cherokee, Shawnee, and Delaware hunters, there was less local game to supplement the winter diet. Thus the summer hunt took on a new and greater importance. The Osage wanted to keep the Cherokee away.

Skitok's raid had been a bluff. Eager to cow the Cherokee while avoiding trouble with the United States government, Skitok's march south to Fort Smith had been planned to insure that they would be seen and reported to the Cherokee. Worried about a possible attack by Cherokee, the Osage may have believed that Skitok's show of force would intimidate the Cherokee and prevent them from gathering others for an attack. Considering there were four hundred young warriors aching for revenge for past losses, little damage took place. Skitok and his men returned, Clermont II sent his peace initiative, and the Osage rushed out to the plains hoping for a safe hunt. If the Cherokee had accepted Clermont II's three-month offer, the Osage would have been back from the hunt before the Cherokee would attack.

The Cherokee did not accept the offer, however, and were not intimidated by Skitok's foray. A band of Cherokee went north but were unable to find any Osage village to attack. After the 1817 massacre, all Osage, even the very young and very old, went out on the plains for the summer hunt.

Failing to find any Osage, the Cherokee killed Joseph Revoir, a French-Osage trader who lived at La Saline.[70] When the Osage returned safely from their hunt in August, Clermont II went to Fort Smith and met with Captain William Bradford, the commander. Clermont II told Bradford:

> I have consulted my Warriours—They say the Cherokees shall not see their tracks on the Cherokee Land or in their Town if the Cher-

---

69. May 17, 1821, ibid.
70. June 24, 1821, ibid.; June 26, 1821, ibid.

okees will keep off our Land and out of our Town—We don't want the Cherokees to Steal what Game there is on our Land. We want it for ourselves & our Women and Children. . . . —when he [the President] sent the Cherokees on this side of the great River and gave them Land we had sold him he Certainly did not give to the Cherokees all the Beaver, Bear, Buffaloe and Deer on our Lands— we Sold him Land but not the game on our Land when the Cherokees hunt on our Land and kill our Game we will always have trouble they will steal our Horses and our young men will kill them—This has been a principal cause of our difficulties—. . . . We will not disturb the Cherokees between now and the time peace may be made if they will not disturb us.[71]

Bradford assured the Osage that an armistice was in effect and that he would prevent any Cherokee from going out against them.[72] After meeting with Bradford and being assured of United States protection, the Osage left for their fall hunt.

Almost immediately, a band of 250 Cherokee, along with some Delaware, Creek, Choctaw, Shawnee, and white men, headed west after the Osage. Bradford went out to stop them. He ordered the non-Indians to go back, and when he could not convince the Cherokee to return, he inexplicably gave them a barrel of gunpowder.[73] Unable to find the Osage at their villages, the Cherokee followed them onto the plains. The Osage had established a hunting camp for the women, children, and the old men, and after leaving about dozen warriors to watch over the camp, most of the men went out to hunt. The Cherokee split into two groups, and one discovered the camp of Osage women, children, and elderly. They killed the dozen guards and twenty-nine women and children. Capturing about ninety, they returned home. The main body of Cherokee ran into the Osage hunting party. The Osage attacked and drove the Cherokee off the plains. William Bradford observed, "I have the honor to re-

---

71. Bradford to Calhoun, October 1, 1821, Carter, *Territorial Papers*, 19: 320–21.
72. Graham to Calhoun, December 28, 1821, Richard Graham Papers.
73. Ibid.

port to you that the balance of the Cherokee Army passed by this Post yesterday, their accounts vary much, by their own tale I am under the impression that they have got flo[g]ged."[74] Once again the Cherokee successfully attacked Osage women and children. Unlike their victory of 1817, some of the Cherokee finally confronted an equal force of adult Osage warriors and were driven from the plains.

Despite the success of the Osage at driving off one of the groups, the Osage hunt had been ruined. The Cherokee destroyed the meat prepared for the winter. Missionaries reported that "they have returned with no provisions and are very poor."[75] Later it was learned that three of the Osage prisoners, one woman and two children, were murdered at the Cherokee village and thrown to the hogs.[76]

The Osage could not easily retaliate against the Cherokee who lived in the shadow of Fort Smith. Dependent still on trade with the whites for essential arms, ammunition, and other supplies, they reluctantly followed the government's wishes and again agreed to an armistice until they could meet with the Cherokee in the summer to make peace. In late July and August, the Osage met with the Cherokee at Fort Smith and agreed to peace. The Cherokee promised to bring the Osage prisoners to the fort in September. On the way to the fort, the Osage were attacked by a group of Choctaw from the Red River. They did, however, meet peacefully with the Cherokee and regained a few prisoners.[77]

The southern Osage had shown remarkable control. Placed under extreme pressure by invading Indians and suffering tremendous losses due to Cherokee attacks, they repeatedly asked for peace. With their traditional diplomatic positions and pro-

74. Bradford to Calhoun, November 18, 1821, Carter, *Territorial Papers*, 19: 355–56.
75. December 10, 1821, Union Mission Journal.
76. Graham to Calhoun, December 28, 1821, Richard Graham Papers.
77. Foreman, *Indians and Pioneers*, 120.

cedures still existent in the south, they were able to exert some control over their members. However, Clermont II, the *Tsi-zhu Ga-hi-ge,* the traditional Osage diplomatic representative, was only able to speak for and control his southern band. The principal diplomatic agents no longer existed in the north, and this lack of control prevented a unified Osage response. The Osage were not whole and responded as fragments, thus chaos continued.

Similar events were occurring among the northern Osage bands. In the fall of 1822, the Big Osage Band moved south from the Osage River. They spent the winter at La Saline, the site of Revoir's murder near the newly established trading post of A. P. Chouteau. The northern Osage had not participated in any peace negotiations with the Cherokee, so they refused to abide by them. Furthermore, Cherokee, Choctaw, Shawnee, Delaware, Creek, and others continued to hunt on Osage lands. In November 1822, a group of Cherokee hunting along the North Canadian were discovered by a group of Big Osage. A Cherokee hunter named Red Hawk, nephew of Thomas Graves, a prominent Cherokee and active leader of the 1821 attack on the Osage hunting camp, was killed. Graves, after learning of the attack, demanded revenge and refused subsequent Osage offers of payment as compensation, a traditional Osage way of dealing with murder. For years, Graves demanded revenge for the death of his nephew.

By 1824, more eastern Indians had moved to the area around the Three Forks. The Cherokee settlement continued to grow, and other groups—Delaware, Shawnee, Oto, French-Americans, and various northeastern tribes—moved into the Ozark Mountains. Breakaway bands of Kickapoo, Choctaw, Chickasaw, and Cherokee, all of whom opposed peace with the Osage, moved south of the Red River. They continued to harass Osage hunters and take their game. By April 1824, there were over two thousand French-Americans, Cherokee, Delaware, and Oto destroying Osage game.[78]

78. Voget, *Osage Research Report,* 220.

With this constantly growing encroachment, the Osage occasionally lashed out. Increased pressure of crowded settlement, reduction in game, weakened fur trade, plus the assimilative pressure of missionaries and United States soldiers—all contributed to a collective rage. In the fall of 1824, a group of Osage stole horses from a Delaware hunting party. The Delaware attempted to recapture the horses, and in the struggle a Delaware hunter was killed. He was the son of Kikthawenund (William Anderson), their chief. The Delaware launched a series of attacks to avenge his death. These attacks in turn required retaliation, and a cycle of revenge killings began that only aggravated the continued economic competition and violence that was going on in the region. The Delaware called upon the Shawnee and Kickapoo as allies against the Osage. The Osage then called for peace and asked the Delaware and Cherokee to meet them in Saint Louis in October. The Cherokee did not go to Saint Louis, but the Delaware, Kickapoo, Piankashaw, Wea, and Shawnee met and made peace with the Osage.[79]

The Arkansas Osage remained at peace with the United States despite increased competition from non-Osage hunters and the occupation of former Osage land by eastern Indians. The Arkansas Osage traded peacefully at the Arkansas Post and with traders who went to their Verdigris River villages. In general, the Arkansas Osage were not threatened by the United States directly, but the immigrating tribes, the Cherokee in particular, posed an enormous threat to the Osage, and as such the Osage bitterly fought them. The federal government intervened and attempted to establish harmony between the Osage and the immigrants because the 1805 words of Louisiana Territory Governor James Wilkinson remained true: "I have said before I believe, and I beg leave to repeat, that an indispensable preleminary [sic] to the transfer of the Southern Nations, to the West of

79. Clifton, *Prairie People*, 191; Atkinson to Gaines, October 7, 1826, Carter, *Territorial Papers*, 20:294; Foreman, *Indians and Pioneers*, 207; C. A. Weslager, *The Delaware Indians: A History*, 365.

the Mississippi is a solid peace between those nations and the Osages particularly."[80] White soldiers and settlers were not harmed. The Osage realized that an attack on any non-Indians would jeopardize their relations with the United States, stop trade, and incite an attack from the soldiers at Fort Smith. Therefore, the Osage directed their violent attacks against Native Americans who were less apt to invoke retaliation by the United States.

Soldiers had little to fear, but all hunters, Indian and non-Indian alike, were likely to be treated roughly by Osage hunters. In the fall of 1823, Skitok and a group of warriors attacked a hunting party made up of about nine white hunters and twelve mixed-blood Quapaw camped along the Blue River. The Osage attacked the camp and killed at least four of the hunters, including the white leader, Major Curtis Welborn. They wounded several others and stole thirty horses and several thousand deerskins.[81] The United States government, never overly concerned about the ongoing Cherokee and Osage deaths, was angered by the attack on the non-Indians. The commander at Fort Smith demanded the surrender of Skitok and other guilty individuals. Clermont II expressed regret and reminded the soldiers that Welborn and his party had been hunting illegally on Osage land. He returned most of the skins and twenty-one of the horses, yet he refused to surrender his son.

While the Osage waited to give up Skitok, the United States War Department decided that Fort Smith was too far away from the Osage to control them. Therefore, the Secretary of War ordered Fort Smith to be abandoned. In April 1824, Major Matthew Arbuckle and five companies of men moved up the Arkansas

---

80. Wilkinson to Dearborn, September 22, 1805, Carter, *Territorial Papers,* 13:229.

81. Arbuckle to Gaines, December 3, 1823, ibid., 19:570–71; Benjamin Bonneville to Arbuckle, December 3, 1823, ibid., 571–72; Arbuckle to Gaines, December 4, 1823, ibid., 572–73; Philbrook to Calhoun, December 9, 1823, ibid., 576; Brad Agnew, *Fort Gibson, Terminal on the Trail of Tears,* 25–26; April 28, 1824, Union Mission Journal.

River. Near the mouth of the Neosho River they began construction of a new military post, later named Cantonment Gibson.[82] The presence of United States troops on the Neosho only a few miles from their villages convinced Clermont II and the Osage to surrender those who had attacked Welborn's party. Anxious to avoid violence with the United States and intimidated by the presence of the soldiers and the fort, four thousand Osage left their villages on June 7, 1824, and approached the fort. They camped four miles away, and the next morning Clermont II and four hundred warriors approached the fort and surrendered Skitok and five other "heads of bands."[83]

The Osage could have destroyed Arbuckle and his soldiers, but they knew by 1824 that any such victory would be short-lived. They did not want to acquire another powerful enemy. The Cherokee, Shawnee, and Delaware were enemy enough, and frankly, a greater threat; so the Osage walked to Fort Gibson and surrendered their sons. After the surrender of the six warriors, Major Arbuckle and David Barber, the subagent for the Arkansas Osage, announced the establishment of a new Osage tribal organization. The new government made *Tsi-zhu Ga-hi-ge* Clermont II the president, *Hon-ga Ga-hi-ge* Tally the vice-president, and created an Osage National Council and a national guard.[84]

82. Agnew, *Fort Gibson,* 28–31; Foreman, *Indians and Pioneers,* 163–70.
83. "Our informant states, that the Osages are greatly alarmed at the removal of the U.S. troops to the mouth of the Verdigris, which is within 50 miles of their villages" (*Arkansas Gazette,* May 4, 1824). "Osages are very much alarmed at the measures which have been taken to compel them to surrender the murderers" (ibid., June 29, 1824). Crittendon to Calhoun, September 12, 1824, Carter, *Territorial Papers,* 19:691–92; Arbuckle to Nourse, November 4, 1824, ibid., 719–20; June 11, 1824, Union Mission Journal; Graves, *Osage Missions,* 62.
84. "He assures us, that the Osages are extremely anxious to maintain a good understanding with the government of the United States, and are particularly desirous off [sic] having traders come to their country, who they uniformly treat with the greatest friendship and hospitality" (*Arkansas Gazette,* September 16, 1823). The six Osage notables were taken downriver to Little Rock, where five were indicted in Arkansas territorial court. Three were found innocent, and two, Skitok and Little Eagle, were convicted and sentenced to death. Later,

The 1824 summer meeting at Fort Gibson was a turning point in Osage history, but not because of the new Osage government; after the meeting broke up, it probably survived only in the minds of Arbuckle and Barber. Instead, the meeting marked the peaceful acceptance of United States domination over the Osage nation. The Osage were forced to turn over six important Osage warriors, members of prominent families. The United States had accomplished what the French and Spanish had not been able to do—control the Osage. The control was limited, but it was more than any other non-Osage had ever possessed. Curiously, the United States had not subdued them as much as had the Cherokee and other immigrant Indians, but the peaceful surrender of Skitok and the Osage agreement with the United States, the Saint Louis Treaty of 1825, clearly demonstrated the government's control.

The federal government wanted still more Osage land to make room for eastern tribes. The presence of Cantonment Gibson and thousands of eastern Indians in Osage country prevented the Osage from resisting. Thus, when the Osage were summoned to Saint Louis in 1825, there was little they could do but accept any demands made by Missouri Territory Superintendent of Indian Affairs and Governor William Clark. In June 1825, when they normally would have been out on the plains hunting, the leaders of both the southern and northern bands, Clermont II and Pawhuska, agreed to give up more of their homelands. As a result of the 1825 Treaty, the Osage were forced to "cede and relinquish to the United States, all their right, title, interest, and

President John Quincy Adams pardoned the two Osage, and they were eventually released in May 1825. See Roane to Pleasanton, October 22, 1824, Carter, *Territorial Papers,* 19:712; Arbuckle to Nourse, November 4, 1824, ibid., 719–20; McNair to John Q. Adams, January 30, 1825, ibid., 762–63. For a description of the trial, imprisonment, and pardon, see *Arkansas Gazette,* October 19, 1824; October 26, 1824; December 21, 1824; December 28, 1824; April 5, 1825; May 3, 1825. It is interesting to note that the system created by the soldiers followed the traditional Osage form, with *Tsi-zhu Ga-hi-ge* Clermont as head chief and Tally, the *Hon-ga Ga-hi-ge,* as vice-president. See July 31, 1824, Union Mission Journal; Agnew, *Fort Gibson,* 43–44.

claim, to lands lying within the State of Missouri and Territory of Arkansas, and to all lands lying West of the said State of Missouri and Territory of Arkansas, North and West of the Red River, South of the Kansas River, and East of a line to be drawn from the head sources of the Kansas, Southwardly through the Rock Saline."[85] Having given up all their remaining land, they were assigned a fifty-mile strip of land in the north that stretched west to the western boundary of their ceded lands. Although Clermont II signed the treaty, he and his band steadfastly refused to leave their villages on the lower Verdigris. They continued to plant corn and beans and live at their old village sites, but just as the Osage were reluctant to fight the soldiers, the United States was reluctant to fight the Osage. Eager to entice the eastern Indians to move to the Arkansas Valley, they knew warfare would bring a halt to any eastern migration, and further, they knew that although the Osage were friendly, they were a formidable enemy. The government took the 1825 cession and continually urged Clermont II and his people to go north and vacate the land for the Cherokee and Creek.[86]

The United States occupation of Louisiana had an important impact on Osage relations with neighboring Native American peoples. Tribes to the south and west, no longer under Spanish trade restrictions, acquired trade goods and resisted further Osage expansion. United States settlement in the east, combined with a concerted effort on the part of the United States government to move eastern tribes onto lands west of the Mississippi, placed inordinate pressure on the Osage. The Osage, as a result of United States control of Louisiana, had to confront large, well-armed tribes from the east and west. Caught between opposing forces, the Osage continued their earlier policy of alternately seeking peace in the east while fighting in the west to retain their western hegemony. The compromises made by

85. Institute for the Development of Indian Law, *Treaties and Agreements,* 51–54; Clark to Barbour, April 19, 1825, Carter, *Territorial Papers,* 20:42–45.
86. Agnew, *Fort Gibson,* 55, 81, 175.

the southern and northern Osage in order to maintain partial control of their homelands simply would not work.

The Osage situation changed by 1824. They no longer dominated the eastern forests. Instead, they struggled to retain control of the eastern prairie hunting grounds, and their hegemony in the west would soon be challenged. Things were to be altered dramatically for the Osage; neither their adaptive culture, martial skills, or skillful diplomacy would prevent their loss of power and influence.

9.

THE END OF HEGEMONY

They are surrounded by Various tribes of Indians Upon whom they look with a jealous eye. These Indians are now overrunning the former hunting grounds of the Osages; the Osages are cramped in their means of subsistence, in fact hunting has become so laborious, that the privations and dangers they suffer in pursuing the Chase is not compensated by the sale of their skins, and as their annuity is small (only 8500 per annum to upwards of 6000 souls) they have become a poor people.

—Paul Liguest Chouteau, 1832

It is indeed humiliating and distressing to hear their complaints and charges against the people of the United States. . . . From the commencement of their transactions with them, they date a very unfavorable change in their circumstances—a great increase of diseases, the destruction of their game, and in a word, almost all their troubles are ascribed to their connection with the white people. "You have brought poverty to us. . . ."

—William Montgomery, 1833

I have reflected much upon the condition of the Osages, they are the remnant of a powerful tribe from whom the United States acquired considerable lands, for other tribes.

—William Armstrong, 1837[1]

1. Paul Liguest Chouteau to Cass, April 6, 1832, *Letters Received by the Office of Indian Affairs, 1824–1881;* "Extracts from the Journal of Mr. Montgomery," *Missionary Herald* 30 (January 1834): 23; Armstrong to Carrey A. Harris, December 27, 1837, *Letters Received Office of Indian Affairs.*

Osage hegemony was severely challenged in the 1820s and 1830s. Pressed in the east by aggressive immigrant tribes and under the steady pressure of the federal government, which was intent on moving them out of the region, the Osage grudgingly gave up control of the eastern forests and southern tall-grass prairie margins. Yet as they surrendered their influence in the east, they fought vigorously to maintain their supremacy in the west. The plains contained millions of buffalo and abundant supplies of horses, so the Osage focused their energies there, but they had to deal with other Native American groups who resisted the Osage domination of the plains. The Osage fought the Comanche, Kiowa, Wichita, and Pawnee for the first thirty years of the nineteenth century as all struggled to maintain control of the rich hunting grounds on the western plains.

The Osage changed, yet they remained the same. They skillfully and bravely exploited their resources, yet they managed to retain traditional economic elements as they eagerly adopted new ones. Symbolic of that adaptability and change within old cultural patterns was their behavior in the 1820s and 1830s. Forced to abandon the eastern forested lands and challenged out on the western plains, the Osage compromised. They continued to plant their crops, albeit along different prairie rivers, and they peacefully shared the buffalo herds with many of their old adversaries in the west. Upon completing their hunts, they conducted a lucrative trade with western tribes.

The increased warfare of the nineteenth century and the ever-present economic opportunity forever altered the traditional Osage leadership. The eighteenth-century pattern continued as disgruntled, ambitious Osage, who had no power within the traditional system, broke away and formed their own small, independent bands. Nineteenth-century accounts of the Osage reveal the ongoing division. In 1815, as French fur trapper Jules de Mun passed through upper Osage country, he noted four groups of northern Osage: the Little Osage, led by Sans Oreille; the Big Osage, led by Pawhuska; another group he referred to as Gros Côte (a branch of Big Osage); and another unnamed village gathered at Paul Liguest Chouteau's (son of Pierre Chouteau) trading post. In 1819, Thomas Nuttall, visiting the southern Osage, reported that the Osage had just returned from hunting on the plains and that ten of their villages had joined with the Kansa for common safety. In 1820, George Sibley, the Osage factor, submitted a report that described two large groups of northern Big Osage. One group was still on the Osage River, while another was west along the upper Neosho River. The Little Osage lived in three villages on the Neosho and included some members of the Missouri.[2] Sibley knew little about the southern bands, and he noted that half the entire Osage tribe was down among the Arkansas group.

An 1822 map shows Clermont's village on the lower Verdigris River and the Gros Côte village just above it. Three Little Osage villages are shown, two along the upper Neosho and one above the Gros Côte village on the Verdigris. Pawhuska's single Big Osage village is still shown on the Marmaton River. In 1826, missionaries living near the Osage reported that they were grouped in six villages, four on the Neosho and two on the Verdigris.[3]

As the Osage continued to separate into smaller villages, the quality of village life deteriorated. The Osage were divided politically and lacked the essential unity needed for successful military actions and diplomacy. The smaller villages no longer contained either a complete *Non-hon-zhin-ga* or all twenty-four clans. Secular offices and religious positions were left unfilled, and vital ceremonies that gave meaning to Osage life were altered, abandoned, or performed only when several villages came together. The traditional offices and procedures no longer existed among the northern bands. In the south, where the traditional diplomatic framework remained largely intact, the Osage

2. Marshall, ed., "Journals of De Mun," 311–25; Nuttall, *Journal of Travels,* 206; Morse, *Report to the Secretary of War,* 203–4.
3. Carter, *Territorial Papers,* 19:92–94; *Missionary Herald* 22 (September 1826): 267.

rivals were strong, skillful in manipulating the United States government, and unwilling to accept any compromise negotiated by the Osage.

The prosperity of the eighteenth century gradually faded as the Osage competed with the growing number of non-Osage hunters for animal resources. Summer and fall hunts on the plains were disrupted by violence with the Comanche and Pawnee, and winter hunts in the forest and prairies produced little as the game disappeared under pressure of the increased population in the region. Clermont II complained in 1825, "We are not happy; but must hunt hard and pay high for our goods."[4] Such complaints would only multiply in the following years.

Confronted with increased competition, the Osage abandoned any tribal sanctions against wasting game. Pressured by invading hunters, the Osage became desperate. Individual hunters were reportedly killing over one hundred deer in a five to six week period. A missionary living near the northern Osage wrote that they were killing animals only for their skins.[5] The overkill by the Osage and the invasion of outsiders ruined their fur trade and severely weakened their economy.

In 1820, a missionary group from the United Foreign Mission Society established a mission along the lower Neosho to work with the southern Osage. This first mission, named Union, was followed in August 1821 by the Harmony Mission established along the Osage River for the northern bands. These missionary groups attempted to change the life and economic base of the Osage people. Convinced that their seminomadic life and communal living was an unfortunate way of life and detrimental to their salvation, the missionaries worked diligently for over ten years to transform them from seminomadic hunters into sedentary Christian farmers. The missions and their offshoots established among the Osage had only temporary and limited success.[6]

4. *Missionary Herald* 22 (September 1826): 270.
5. Ibid.; Sarah Tuttle, *Letters on the Chickasaw and the Osage Missions,* 89, 95.
6. Graves, *Osage Missions,* 26, 39, 42, 45, 106–8; M. L. Wardell, "Early Prot-

Working to change the Osage economic system, the missionaries, first at Union and Harmony then later at Hopefield, Boudinot, and Neosho stations, established farms and attempted to convince the Osage to become farmers. Hunting, despite the scarcity of game and declining fur market, remained an important element in Osage economy and life. The Osage were willing to farm, and they had done so for centuries, yet they continued farming in their own fashion, in small, unfenced plots with the work done by women. Gardens left unattended while they hunted in the summers were an affront to the churchmen. The missionaries attempted to persuade Osage men to work in the fields and remain nearby to tend them in the summer, but cultural and economic realities were too strong. One time, the leader of the northern Osage, Pawhuska, was convinced to go into the fields, where he worked for a day. His presence had little impact on the others, and he never returned.[7]

Traditional cultural and economic patterns were too strong and successful in the minds of the Osage for the missionaries to convince them to change. In 1823, however, a few Osage and French métis families temporarily left the villages and formed a small Osage farming community known as Hopefield. Attacks by immigrant Indians, notably the Cherokee, made life dangerous for the Osage who decided to leave the safety of the village to live alone and work in the fields. Hopefield farms never produced enough food to support the Osage, and they had to resort to hunting to feed their families. The cholera epidemics of 1834–1836 finally destroyed the Indian farm experiment; many died, and the survivors fled to the plains.[8]

While the missions had little impact on Osage life, the presence

estant Missions Among the Osages, 1820 to 1838"; Carolyn Thomas Foreman, "Hopefield Mission in Osage Nation, 1823–1837"; T. F. Morrison, "Mission Neosho, The First Kansas Mission," 232–34; Mrs. W. W. Graves, "In the Land of the Osages—Harmony Mission."

7. Graves, *Osage Missions,* 126.

8. Ibid., 197–210; C. Foreman, "Hopefield Mission," 194–95; *Missionary Herald* 32 (January 1836): 25.

of Fort Gibson a few miles from Clermont's village changed the
Osage situation. With well-armed soldiers so close to Clermont's
village, the Osage for the first time acquired military supervi-
sion. As the influx of eastern Indians in the region around the
Three Forks grew, the United States government sought to move
the Osage to make room for the other groups. The 1825 Treaty
had taken almost all the land between the Canadian and Arkansas Rivers in the south and the Smoky Hill and Kansas Rivers in
the north, leaving the Osage with only a narrow strip of land in
the north. Osage living along the lower Verdigris and Neosho
Rivers were supposed to leave and join the northern bands.
While many did, Clermont's band refused to leave. Clermont II,
as his father before him, believed that once again the Anglo-
Americans were trying to force the southern Osage back under Pawhuska's political control.[9] Clermont II and his village
of about two thousand people remained on the lower Verdigris.
The United States government wanted to make room for the
Cherokee, Creek, Choctaw, Chickasaw, and other eastern tribes,
and from 1825 it constantly urged Clermont II's people to join
their kin living in the northern reservation.

Combined with the government's demands, eastern Indians
constantly challenged the Osage along the prairie and forest
edges. Shortly after the establishment of Fort Gibson in 1824,
the Cherokee and the Osage met once again to settle their differences, and again they both agreed to a temporary peace. The
Delaware, however, stinging from an Osage attack on their
hunters, continued to harass the Osage, and in January of 1826
a group of Delaware, Shawnee, and Cherokee killed five Osage
hunters on the Red River. The January attack ushered in a season of violence along the prairie. Throughout the spring, Delaware hunters looked for Osage along the Neosho and Verdigris.
In April they killed a lone Osage hunter along the Illinois River,

9. *Treaties and Agreement,* 55–56; Stokes and Schmerhorn to Cass, April 8,
1834, *Letters Received Office of Indian Affairs.*

and in May the Osage, hoping to end the violence, went to Fort Gibson to meet with the Delaware. The Delaware refused to come to the fort, but the Cherokee arrived looking for vengeance. They demanded the Osage surrender the murderer of Red Hawk to them. The Osage refused to negotiate with the Cherokee without their agent, and instead they left for the plains without resolving their differences.[10]

The summer of 1826 was a tense one along the prairies as the eastern tribes constantly preyed upon any Osage who remained in the Three Forks region. In June, a Delaware war party roamed along the lower Neosho looking for Osage, and in July, Tahchee, a Cherokee, killed and scalped an Osage at A. P. Chouteau's trading post on the Neosho. Tahchee took the scalp to the Cherokee villages, where the Cherokees danced over it. At another trading post, an old blind Osage man was killed while he sat in the yard.[11] Most of the Osage had been out on the plains during the summer, and when they returned they did not seek immediate retaliation for the killings.

Upon returning in August, they went to Fort Gibson with their new agent and sought to settle their differences with the Cherokee. Their desire for peace was such that they finally agreed to meet Cherokee demands. They brought the murderer of Red Hawk and turned him over to the commander at Fort Gibson. In return, they demanded the Cherokee give Tahchee to them for the trading-post murder. The Cherokee refused, claiming that he was from the Red River villages, and that they could not be held responsible for him, since they had no control over him. The Osage refused to accept this argument, but as a demonstration of their desire for peace they left Red Hawk's murderer with the soldiers, insisting that he remain at the fort until the Osage got Tahchee.[12]

10. Agnew, *Fort Gibson*, 44, 46.

11. Ibid., 49; Arbuckle to Butler, November 4, 1826, Carter, *Territorial Papers*, 20:301–2; *Missionary Herald* 23 (October 1827): 311.

12. Atkinson to the Adjutant General, January 9, 1827, Carter, *Territorial Papers*, 20:361–62.

Later that same fall, the Osage, still in hopes of establishing peace along the eastern prairies, journeyed to Saint Louis to meet with the Delaware, Cherokee, and other immigrant tribes living along the White River. The Cherokee did not receive word of the meeting, so they did not attend, but the Delaware and other tribes who attended finally, after some reluctance, agreed to a peace with the Osage.[13]

The Cherokee finally arrived at Saint Louis, too late for the peace negotiations but in time to complain to William Clark about Osage behavior. They demanded Clark execute Red Hawk's murderer, still a prisoner at Fort Gibson. Clark refused to order the execution, and he suggested instead an exchange of Tahchee for Red Hawk's killer. The Cherokee rejected that suggestion, so Clark submitted the issue to President John Q. Adams. While Adams deliberated, Red Hawk's killer escaped from the stockade at Fort Gibson. In February, the agent for the Cherokee, Edward DuVal, wrote a letter to Matthew Arbuckle, Commander of Fort Gibson, concerning the blood feud of the Cherokee and their continued desire for revenge. The Cherokee were sending twenty-five men against the Osage, he wrote, stating

> that they have no desire for a general War with the Osages: that a life for the life they had lost was all that they demanded, and that if that could be obtained without further bloodshed they would be satisfied. . . . It is not unlikely, however, that more than one life may be taken by this. . . . Be that as it may, good policy, I think requires that the Osages should be advised not to strike another blow if an amicable settlement of their differences can be effected. On the return of the Cherokee-party, should they accomplish this object, it will be for the Osages to say whether there shall be peace, or war.[14]

The expedition was stopped by Nathaniel Pryor and Cherokee leader Walter Webber before it reached the Osage. In May, the

---

13. Clark to Barbour, ibid., 20:357–58; Agnew, *Fort Gibson*, 49.
14. DuVal to Arbuckle, February 3, 1827, Carter, *Territorial Papers*, 20:420.

president ruled that Tahchee's murder of the Osage had settled the score between the tribes, so they should make peace.[15] The Osage, without the strong cultural demands for blood revenge, were willing to accept Adams's decision. They called for a meeting with the Cherokee in September after their summer hunt. The ruling did not satisfy the Cherokee, and they refused to discuss anything with the Osage until the Osage turned over Red Hawk's murderer. The next spring, a group of Cherokee went to Washington to appeal directly with the president to reverse his judgment.

The Cherokee's Washington visit was not successful, for Adams refused to modify his decision. Instead, bowing to white settlers' demands for Cherokee land, he persuaded the Cherokee to exchange their land in Arkansas for land in the Indian Territory. In order to make his earlier decision more acceptable, Adams included in the land cession agreement a payment to Thomas Graves for the death of his nephew.[16]

Although Graves accepted the payment, economic competition and cultural misunderstandings continued, and ill-feeling persisted between the two tribes. Tensions along the prairies increased after the Cherokee visit to Washington, because the new treaty forced the Cherokee to move out of Arkansas into country ceded by the Osage but still occupied by Clermont's band. As the Cherokee moved further west, they placed more pressure on the Osage, and Osage-Cherokee relations, already strained from years of violence and feuding, deteriorated. The Osage and Cherokee continued to meet again and again and made promises of peace, promises that were continually broken the first time rival hunters encountered one another. In the fall of 1829, a group of Cherokee, probably from the Red River bands, attacked and killed eight Osage, all members of Tally's family. Despite Tally's prominent position as *Hon-ga Ga-hi-ge* of

15. Foreman, *Indians and Pioneers,* 208; Barbour to Izard, May 21, 1827, Carter, *Territorial Papers,* 20:468–69.
16. Agnew, *Fort Gibson,* 52–53.

Clermont's village, he was persuaded not to retaliate and to accept the government's offer to "cover the dead" with eight hundred dollars worth of presents and a promise to punish the guilty parties.[17]

Such violence continued because political factionalism among the Cherokee and Osage prevented any meaningful diplomacy. The Red River Cherokee refused to abide by any agreement made by the Arkansas Cherokee, and although Clermont II could control the southern Osage, which still maintained its traditional structure, the northern Osage, with little of their traditional polity intact, dismissed any agreement negotiated by the southern band.[18] Without a polity that could conduct successful diplomacy and with an increasing, diverse, and antagonistic population competing for a shrinking supply of game, the prairie frontier remained a tense and dangerous place.

Tensions increased as more eastern tribes immigrated into the region. In the fall of 1827, over nine hundred Choctaw and Creek settlers moved into the area around the Three Forks. The southern Osage, trying to maintain old diplomatic patterns of keeping peace in the east, met with the Creek and offered friendship. Clermont II, wanting peace where his people traded and spent the winter, offered his daughter in marriage to one of the Creek.[19] This traditional method of peace by establishing kin ties with outside peoples was a tried and usually successful one. While it is not certain if Clermont II's daughter married into the

17. Ibid., 60–62; Arbuckle to McComb, May 31, 1830, *Letters Received Office of Indian Affairs.*

18. Clermont's control was demonstrated by Tally's restraint after the attack on his family.

19. "Claymore, the principal chief of that portion of the Osage nation who reside on the Arkansas, appear highly pleased with his new neighbors—proposed an [sic] union of the two nations, which will probably be acceded to—and as evidence of his sincerity, offered his daughter in marriage to the Creeks, . . . believe that union would help both tribes against the Pawnee, Comanches, and other Indians, with whom the Osages have been at variance with for many years" (*Arkansas Gazette*, February 13, 1828).

Creeks, it is likely, for there was less tension between the Osage and Creeks than with other eastern groups.

With the occupation of the Ouachita and Ozark Mountains and the Arkansas Valley by immigrant tribes and white settlers, there was no longer enough wild game to feed all the people in the area. The Osage, who had relied on wildlife along the prairies and the forest edge for food, could not find enough game during the bitter winter of 1830–1831. Unable to take deer, bear, or other game, they killed Creek and Cherokee cattle and hogs for food. In early 1831, the Osage met with Cherokee and Creek leaders and expressed their regret for killing their neighbors' cattle and swine, explaining that they had only done it to keep their families alive and offering to pay for the livestock out of their treaty annuities. Although the Cherokee and Creek were angry, they accepted the explanation and payment.[20]

With the passage of the Indian Removal Act in May 1830, the United States government began forcing eastern tribes to move into the west. Soon, thousands of Indians began settling in Osage country. These forced tribal movements pushed the Osage out of the Ozarks and Ouachitas by the early 1830s. Occasionally, the Osage reacted violently to the strangers, but the level of violence between the Osage and the eastern Indians gradually declined. The Osage simply were not strong enough to fight the United States government, eastern tribes, and western plains tribes.

While Osage were being driven from their eastern homelands by immigrant eastern Indians, they confronted strong Native American groups in their western hunting grounds. The 1830s were a distressing time for the Osage; caught between the eastern intruders and the western plains tribes, the Osage struggled in the east and west to survive.

20. *Missionary Herald* 27 (September 1831): 287–89; Pryor to P. L. Chouteau, March 5, 1831, *Letters Received Office of Indian Affairs;* Arbuckle to P. L. Chouteau, February 4, 1831, ibid.; Grant Foreman, *Advancing the Frontier, 1830–1860,* 110–11.

Osage relations in the west in the late 1820s and early 1830s were almost always violent, for the pattern of alternating peace and war seen in the east was absent in the west. As the Osage lost more and more control and influence in the east, survival became dependent upon retaining domination of the plains hunting grounds, and compromise was impossible. Thus, while the violence with old rivals on the plains continued, the Osage maintained their domination there.

Osage relations with the Wichita, Comanche, Pawnee, and Kiowa in the first thirty years of the nineteenth century were explosive. The Comanche were involved in frequent skirmishes with the Osage in the 1820s and 1830s. In the fall of 1823, as the Osage were contending with hostility in the east, they fought with Comanche in the west. The commander at Fort Gibson, Colonel Matthew Arbuckle, reported, "I am informed that a Dispute took place about 15 or 20 days since between a party of Delaware Indians who reside on the waters of the White River and a party of Osages, . . . and it has also been reported that the Comanchy [sic] Indians had a short time since killed Twenty or Twenty five Osage Warriors."[21] In August of 1824, after securing one of their temporary truces with the Cherokee, the Osage went west to fight the plains tribes:

> The ostensible motives assigned by the nation for these expeditions [to the west] is, for the purpose of procuring buffalo meat, and other game for their support; skins for trade; and to catch wild horses. This is partly the case; and their present condition requires such support. But these expeditions, which take place three or four times a year, sometimes end in disputes and skirmishes with the Pawnees and other western tribes.[22]

Not only the Comanche challenged the Osage in the west. As the Kiowa moved south and began a hunting and military alliance with the Comanche, they too became involved in struggles

---

21. Foreman, *Indians and Pioneers*, 188.
22. Graves, *Osage Missions*, 162.

with the Osage for the plains hunting grounds. In 1833, the Osage surprised a Kiowa camp on Rainy Mountain Creek west of the Wichita Mountains. Most of the Kiowa men had left on an expedition against the Ute, and the defenseless village was destroyed by Osage. Five men and a number of women and children were killed, and in an effort to intimidate the Kiowa, the Osage beheaded the dead and placed the heads in brass pails around the campsite. Stealing what they could, the Osage took two children prisoners and captured one of the sacred Kiowa medicine bundles, the *taime*.[23] This attack on a Kiowa village, reminiscent of the Cherokee attacks on the Osage, enraged the Kiowa. As a result of this bloody attack, the Kiowa and Comanche went looking for the Osage. These angry Comanche and Kiowa war parties kept the Osage from hunting along the Canadian and Cimarron Rivers that fall.

The Kiowa, aching for revenge and desperate to recover the *taime*, traveled east to the tall-grass prairie in the fall of 1833 and attacked a group of Osage near Clermont's village on the Verdigris. The Kiowa's surprise strike was unsuccessful, for a violent thunderstorm broke out in the middle of the battle and drove everyone from the battlefield. While the raid was not destructive, an attack by a plains tribe so close to Clermont's town was unexpected. Plains peoples rarely ventured that far east to fight, further evidencing the Osage's deteriorating situation.

Overall, 1833 was a bad year for the Osage. The plains summer hunt had been poor, and when they returned to the prairies not only were they assaulted by the Kiowa, but also they discovered that most of their crops had been destroyed by summer floods. Despite the threat of the Kiowa and Comanche, the Osage did not linger long in the east, but quickly returned to the plains to hunt food for the winter.[24]

23. James Mooney, "Calendar History of the Kiowa Indians," 169–70, 257–63; Mildred P. Mayhall, *The Kiowas,* 169–70.
24. Foreman, *Advancing the Frontier,* 119; *Missionary Herald* 30 (August 1833): 24.

In time, however, the Osage would sit down with the plains people and make peace with them. Curiously, the impetus for the talks came about as an indirect result of the government's removal policy. Just as the Osage faced increased challenges in the west, so did the removed tribes. The eastern tribes, also intent on hunting on the plains, were challenged by the Comanche, Wichita, and Kiowa. The government, eager to carry out the successful removal of the eastern tribes, did not want warfare in the west to impede removal. Therefore, the War Department ordered the army to go west and make contact with the plains tribes and establish peace between the plains and eastern tribes. In 1833, Colonel James Many led an expedition to the plains, but he failed to find any plains Indians. The next summer, however, the newly created dragoons, led by Osage scouts, went onto the plains. Just north of the Red River along the Wichita Mountains, the dragoons met with the Wichita, Comanche, and Kiowa. Colonel Henry Dodge, the dragoon commander, returned a Kiowa girl captured by the Osage in 1833, and the Osage scouts who accompanied the dragoons told the plains people that the Osage wanted peace. Dodge tried to convince the Kiowa, Wichita, and Comanche to come back with him to Fort Gibson to meet with the eastern peoples, but they refused, claiming they were reluctant to pass beyond the Cross Timbers.[25]

That September, however, some Kiowa and Wichita did come to Fort Gibson where they met with the Cherokee, Creek, and Choctaw. During the meeting, the Kiowa and Wichita expressed a special desire to meet with the Osage, and despite recent violence between them, the Osage, Kiowa, and Wichita agreed to

25. Agnew, *Fort Gibson,* 115–39; "Journal of Colonel Dodge's expedition from Fort Gibson to the Pawnee Pict village," *American State Papers: Military Affair,* 5:373–82; Fred S. Perrine and Grant Foreman, eds. "The Journal of Hugh Evans, Covering the First and Second Campaigns of the United States Dragoon Regiment in 1834 and 1835"; Thomas B. Wheelock, "Colonel Henry Dodge and his Regiment of Dragoons on the Plains in 1834"; Grant Foreman, ed., "Journal of the Proceedings at Our First Treaty with the Wild Indians."

stop fighting. The Osage agreed to return the Kiowa *taime* which they had stolen in 1833, and the next summer a group of Osage, led by Black Dog and representatives from the immigrant tribes, met with the Comanche, Kiowa, and Wichita at Camp Holmes, A. P. Chouteau's newly established trading post on the Canadian River.[26]

After the Camp Holmes and Fort Gibson summer councils of 1834 and 1835, the Osage and the Kiowa, Wichita, and Comanche enjoyed peaceful relations. While the peace was occasionally marred by horse thefts or killings, all three tribes worked to maintain it. In 1836, after an Osage killed a Comanche woman, the Osage sent word to the Comanche explaining that the killing had been a mistake, and they offered to "cover the dead" with presents as compensation for the killing. The Osage had "found one of the women asleep, and supposing her to be a Pawnee Mohaw, they killed her, they appeared to regret the circumstances and requested me to inform the Padokas when I saw them, that they had no hostile feelings toward them, and that it was altogether owing to a mistake that they had killed the woman and that they were willing to pay according to the Indian custom for her death." The Comanche accepted the gifts, and peace was preserved.[27]

One important reason for the continued Osage-Comanche peace was trade. After the 1830 peace conferences, the Osage began an active trade with the Comanche. The Comanche and Kiowa had long wanted trade goods. Although they had carried on trade with the Spanish and Mexicans of Texas and New Mexico, the quality and quantity of their merchandise was never as good as that from the United States. They had engaged in occasional trade with Americans, but Osage hostility had always prevented them from trading in the east. The declining fur trade

26. Harold W. Jones, ed., "The Diary of Assistant Surgeon Leonard McPhail on His Journey to the Southwest in 1835"; Agnew, *Fort Gibson*, 144–48.
27. P. L. Chouteau to Armstrong, December 12, 1836, *Letters Received Office of Indian Affairs.*

was causing an economic crisis for the Osage, so they eagerly entered into a new economic enterprise. They quickly became middlemen for the Kiowa and Comanche in the west and American traders in the east. The Osage secured manufactured goods at prairie trading posts, and during their summer hunt they took the goods to the Comanche and Kiowa. Meeting in late July at the Great Salt Plains on the Salt Fork of the Arkansas, the Osage exchanged rifles, ammunition, and other trade goods for Comanche captives, buffalo robes, horses, and mules.[28] All three tribes enjoyed the commerce and thus worked to maintain the peace.

Another important element to this plains détente was the fact that the Osage were willing to share with the Comanche and Kiowa the territory south of the Canadian River. With economic collapse in the east, the Osage were willing to share the southern hunting territory in exchange for a profitable trade with the Comanche and Kiowa. The area along the upper Canadian had never been their prime hunting territory. They had always concentrated their hunting north of the Cimarron. The Canadian region was being hunted by the Cherokee, Choctaw, Creek, and other eastern tribes, and it was crowded with Indians that the Osage could not dislodge or could ill-afford to attack, so they compromised. Forced to share the region, the Osage remained in the area, shared the hunting, and carried on their lucrative trade.

The peace that they maintained with the southwestern tribes was not enjoyed to the north. The Osage, pushed out of the east and crowded in the south, simply could not afford to lose their prime buffalo country along the upper Arkansas River, and they vigorously protected the region. Their longtime enemies, the Pawnee, pressed by the Lakota in the north, occasionally ven-

---

28. Mooney, "Calendar History of Kiowa," 242, 259; McDermott, *Tixier's Travels*, 150–54; Victor Tixier, *Voyage aux Prairies Osages, Louisiane et Missouri, 1839–1840*, 129–33.

tured south of the Saline and Smoky Hill Rivers, and the Osage dealt harshly with their intrusions.

One means of keeping the Pawnee out of Osage hunting territory was through their alliance with Kansa. The Kansa-Osage friendship was strong and had been in place since the 1760s. Osage and Kansa hunters traveled and hunted together, and their friendship was frequently noted by many early observers. In 1819, when Thomas Nuttall visited the southern Osage, they had just returned to their village from a tallow hunt "in which they had travelled not less than 300 miles up the Arkansas. . . . In this hunt, they say, that 10 villages of themselves and friends (as the Kansas, who speak nearly the same language) joined for common safety."[29] In September 1821, when the Fort Osage factor, George Sibley, went out with a band of Little Osage to hunt the buffalo, they visited the Kansa and were received with great hospitality.[30] The alliance remained true through the trying times of the 1820s and 1830s, and in the summer of 1840, while Frenchman Victor Tixier was traveling with the Osage, they came upon a large Kansa hunting camp out on the plains. "Our warriors (Osage) had been entertained by the Kansa, who . . . were living in plenty and advised us to come and share their good fortune. Our lodges were hardly covered when a messenger came in the name of the Head Chief of the Kansa to invite all the Osage warriors and the palefaces to a great banquet."[31]

This alliance was good for the Kansa and Osage. There was enough buffalo for the two tribes, and together they could keep the Pawnee north of the Smoky Hills. Osage animosity with the Pawnee was ancient, dating back to the early Osage movement onto the prairie-plains in the late seventeenth century. The long enmity persisted, and through the nineteenth century the most

29. Nuttall, *Journal of Travels,* 206.
30. Sibley Papers; *Louisiana Gazette,* May 16, 1812; ibid., May 23, 1812; Brooks, "Sibley's Journal," 173; Isern, "Exploration and Diplomacy," 89.
31. McDermott, *Tixier's Travels,* 199–200.

consistent and bitter enemy of the Osage were the Pawnee. The first forty years of the nineteenth century were filled with reports of Osage-Pawnee violence. While the whites reporting the violence did not always distinguish between the Pawnee and Wichita, often calling both groups Pawnee, it is obvious that the northwest was a scene of ongoing violence as the Osage fought to keep their buffalo country.

In April 1818, a band of four hundred Pawnee surprised a hunting party of forty-nine Osage. Although the Pawnee always had fewer guns than the Osage, their numerical advantage allowed them to kill all but one of the Osage. The missionaries at Union and Harmony repeatedly reported the almost perpetual violence between the Osage and Pawnee. Missionary William Vail wrote, "[T]he Osage, all know, have had perpetual war with these people, so that they do not sooner shoot a bear than a Pawnee and so *visa versa in toto*." Another visitor wrote, "To cut off the head of a Pawnee, or even strike him after he has fallen is a source of greater distinction than the knowledge of letters on the arts of civilized life."[32] In the fall of 1826, the Osage arrived back at their southern villages with twenty Pawnee scalps and eight captives. The Osage, in 1829, volunteered to help the United States Army fight the Pawnee and other western tribes. The government declined their offer of help, but when the Osage returned from their summer hunt of 1829, they brought back Pawnee prisoners and horses. Every summer throughout the 1830s, the Osage went out on their summer hunt, killed buffalo, and pursued the Pawnee. In the fall of 1830, three hundred Osage reportedly killed eighty to ninety Pawnee when the Osage attacked using spears and clubs. Despite their victory, they were anxious about possible Pawnee revenge, and in the spring of 1831 they established their southern villages closer to Fort Gibson. In 1831, the annual mission report noted,

32. Foreman, *Indians and Pioneers,* 244; Graves, *Osage Missions,* 140.

"Their wars with their western enemies continue with unabated fury."[33]

In June 1832, while missionaries were visiting the Osage villages, warriors organized a mourning war-party to go out and kill Pawnee to accompany the *Ga-hi-ge* Pawhuska, who had just died in April.[34] A missionary wrote, "[T]hese expeditions, which take place three or four times a year, sometimes end in disputes and skirmishes with the Pawnees . . . and often terminate in bringing in a considerable number of stolen horses."[35] Throughout the 1830s, United States officials attempted to bring peace to the region. They were able to negotiate peace between the southern plains tribes and the Osage but not with the Pawnee. When Tixier hunted with the Osage in 1840, they went searching for the Pawnee after they had killed enough buffalo. He noted, "The Pawnee-Maha, who live on the banks of the Nebraska or Platte River, are today the greatest enemies of the Osage. . . . During the summer hunting expedition of 1839 they [Osage] took from the Pawnee eleven scalps, which are now drying in the village of the Little Osage."[36]

The Pawnee-Osage struggle clearly demonstrated the nature of Osage warfare. They fought not for glory or the mere sake of violence; they fought to control their buffalo country. This was apparent in the remarks of an Osage hunter, whom missionaries reproached for going west to hunt and fight. He replied that if the missionaries would help them, the Osage "would stay at home, and then there would be no more quarrelling about the buffalo."[37] The Osage continued to quarrel about the buffalo, however, and they continued to fight Pawnee long after they

---

33. *Missionary Herald* 30 (September 1830): 287; Agnew, *Fort Gibson*, 97; *Missionary Herald* 27 (October 1831): 322; Graves, *Osage Missions*, 76.

34. *Missionary Herald* 29 (April 1833): 134.

35. Graves, *Osage Missions*, 162.

36. McDermott, *Tixier's Travels*, 221–23; Tixier, *Voyage aux Prairie Osages*, 200–203.

37. *Missionary Herald* 29 (April 1833): 134.

had made peace with other tribes in the region. Forced from the eastern forests and outnumbered on the prairies, the Osage reluctantly made peace with the immigrant and southern plains tribes because these nations did not challenge Osage control of the plains to the north. The Osage ended their fighting with the tribes in the region, but they refused to halt their war with the Pawnee. They could not, for that territory between the Smoky Hill River and Canadian River was all that remained of Osage hunting grounds. Their survival hinged on control of the western plains. There would be no compromise, and thus wars with the Pawnee continued.

The Osage were able to resist the pressure until the late 1830s. Warfare continued to provide opportunity for prestige that the Osage could not accommodate; the young hunters and warriors moved away from the older villages, and the earlier political divisions continued. By 1831, the Osage were divided into six towns: Clermont's village, two villages of White Hair (Pawhuska), Wasooches town, a Little Osage village, and the Osage mission farm at Hopefield. In 1832, missionaries noted seven: White Hair's town, a small village at the Boudinot mission, *Wa-so-shee* town, Little Osage town, the Osage community at Hopefield, Clermont's town, and a village they called Bear's town. In 1836, French traveler Louis Cortambert visited the Osage and described six villages. Two separate villages on the Neosho were obviously Big Osage villages, and one was still led by White Hair. Above these two villages were two others, one inhabited by the Little Osage and another by a group called Coeur Tranquille (Heart Stays). Two villages were situated on the Verdigris, Clermont's village and Big Hill (Gros Côte).[38]

In the summer of 1840, the young Frenchman Victor Tixier counted at least seven Osage villages. One village was attached to the American Fur Company, and its chief was Baptiste Mon-

---

38. Ibid., 27 (September 1831): 188–89; ibid., 28 (September 1832): 290–91; Chapman, "Journey to Land of Osages," 216–17.

grain, an Osage métis. A village named Naniompa (The Village of the Pipe) was led by old White Hair, and Maison Cailles was identified with Majakita, whose mother was Pawhuska's sister. The Heart Stays village was noted as the village of the Quiet Hearts, and it was under the command of *Man-Chap-Che-Mani*. *Ouachinka-Lagri* (or Belle Oiseau) led still a fifth village, and although the leaders were not mentioned, Tixier noted that the Gros Côte and La Cheniere (Clermont's band) lived in two villages above the Neosho. There may have been another village, as Tixier mentioned the Little Osage, but he never tied a village name to a Little Osage Band.[39]

The collapse of the traditional Osage political system continued, and by 1839 the Osage were living in numerous small bands that hunted independently in the same general area. The hereditary leadership and clan ties were obviously gone. There were no dual chieftains, and those who led the Osage assumed their power outside the traditional clan framework. The patrilineal, hereditary chieftainships no longer existed. Majakita, who led a large group of the Osage, was related to the former leader through his mother. One band was led by a mixed-blood Osage whose claim to power rested upon his connection with the American Fur Company. The *Non-hon-zhin-ga* still existed, yet Tixier noted that the young warriors also had a formal organization and were meeting together as did the old *Non-hon-zhin-ga*. This new council of young warriors, not a part of the traditional system, further evidenced the growing power and influence of the young hunters and warriors.[40] The Osage, however, were devastated by epidemic disease in the 1830s, and this, combined with the growing population of the eastern tribes and wars with the Pawnee, finally left them weakened and unable to resist eventual removal to the north.

Diseases had attacked the Osage before, yet it seems that

---

39. McDermott, *Tixier's Travels*, 125–29.
40. Ibid., 172–73; Bailey, "Osage Social Organization, 1673–1906," 61.

until the 1830s the Osage had avoided the devastating losses that had destroyed other tribes. For much of the year, the upper Osage River beyond the Niangua did not contain enough water for navigation, so the Osage were not visited as frequently by outsiders carrying the diseases as those tribes living along the major rivers in the west. Their seminomadic existence also limited their losses, for they did not remain year round in their large villages where contagious diseases were so devastating. They spent most of the summer and winter in small kin-groups, lessening the impact of diseases. Seventeenth-century accounts do, however, mention epidemics among the Missouri River Indians, and in 1758 smallpox was reported among their neighbors, the Kansa. The Osage, too, might have been infected, for they had apparently participated in some of the eastern campaigns of the Seven Years' War where smallpox was present, and they may have brought the disease back with them.[41]

The 1801 smallpox epidemic reportedly killed a great many of the Osage, and in 1806, after Zebulon Pike visited the Osage, about two hundred Osage died.[42] The Osage accused Pike's men of giving it to them, but it may have been brought by the Osage prisoners returned from the Potawatomi or by leaders who had just returned from Washington. By the 1820s, the Osage were no longer isolated, and more Indians and whites came among them, infecting the Osage. In 1821 and 1825, a "bilious fever" in Osage country killed some Osage. In August and September 1826, many suffered from a deadly dysentery, and in 1827 and 1828, smallpox attacked them. In 1832, the government authorized Osage vaccinations, but not all of the Osage were inoculated. The doctor went to their prairie towns during

41. Nasatir, *Before Lewis and Clark*, 1:51; Esther Wagner Stearn and Allen E. Stearn, *The Effect of Smallpox on the Destiny of the Amerindian*, 43–44.

42. Jackson, *Journals of Pike*, 2:128, 163. "They had the small pox among them in the year 1801 which destroyed about half the nation (2,000 or upward) since which time it has not visited them" (Conway to Cass, September 25, 1832, *Letters Received Office of Indian Affairs*). Conway was mistaken, for it was reported among them in 1827 and 1828.

the summer, when most were out hunting on the plains, and some of his vaccine was damaged by improper sealing and summer heat. Only a third of the Osage were vaccinated. Fortunately, smallpox did not kill more; in 1840, Victor Tixier remarked that the northern Osage were unscarred by smallpox.[43]

Vaccination saved some of the Osage from the scourge of smallpox, but nothing saved them from the terrible outbreak of cholera in the 1830s. By the 1830s, the Osage were surrounded by thousands of missionaries, soldiers, hunters, traders, and eastern Indians who had come to Osage country and brought epidemic diseases with them. Throughout the 1830s, the Osage confronted successive and sometimes simultaneous attacks by diseases. From 1829 to 1831, the Osage suffered from influenza and thus were in a weakened condition when attacked by cholera. Cholera struck the Osage in 1832, 1833, and 1834. When the Kiowa and Wichita came to Fort Gibson in 1834 to meet with the Osage, few appeared, and when they asked the soldiers where the Osage were, the soldiers told them the Osage were dying of cholera.[44] Missionaries reported that the Osage attacked by the disease fled out onto the plains to escape "the prevalence of cholera among the Osages, causing them to forsake their towns."[45] Despite their flight to the plains, over four hundred Osage died in the summer of 1834.

Weakened by disease, political division, and the destruction of the economy, outnumbered by alien and hostile Native Americans and whites, and under the constant nagging of govern-

43. *Missionary Herald* 23 (October 1827): 311; Conway to Cass, September 4, 1832, *Letters Received Office of Indian Affairs;* Conway to Cass, September 25, 1832, ibid. Conway explained that it was impossible to collect all the Osage in August and that he was only able to vaccinate 2,177 Osage. See Stearn and Stearn, *Effect of Smallpox,* 62–63; McDermott, *Tixier's Travels,* 140–41.

44. Alfred W. Crosby, Jr., "Virgin Soil Epidemics as a Factor in the Aboriginal Depopulation in America," in *The American Indian: Past and Present,* edited by Roger L. Nichols; Foreman, *Advancing the Frontier,* 121, 133, 143.

45. Graves, *Osage Missions,* 206.

ment agents and soldiers, Clermont's Osage would not abide by the 1825 Treaty and steadfastly refused to move to the north. In 1834, the United States sent a special commission to convince the Osage to leave the land assigned to the Creek and Cherokee. After weeks of negotiation, the Osage refused once again to leave, and after planting their corn and beans, they left for the summer hunt. The following winter the Osage did not agree to move, but they did agree to cede a thirty-mile-wide strip of land from their northern reservation for a sizeable annuity. Congress refused to ratify the treaty because it was expensive and considered unnecessary, for the Osage had already ceded the land in 1825. Two thousand Osage therefore remained on the Verdigris River surrounded by angry and antagonistic non-Osage.[46]

Troubles continued for the Osage, for in 1837 rumors of an Osage attack on white settlers in western Missouri convinced Missouri Governor Wilburn W. Boggs to call out the militia to save the settlers. Five hundred Missouri volunteers gathered on the Grand River and searched for the Osage raiders. Unable to find any attacking Indians, they seized several mixed-blood Osage women living at the trading post near the old Harmony Mission. These women were later saved from the Missouri soldiers when federal troops from Fort Leavenworth arrived, released the women, and ordered the volunteers to go home. The settlers' militia did not disband; instead, they searched the area until they finally found some Osage families foraging for food, whereupon they surrounded the Osage, beat them, and drove them out of the state.[47]

The following winter, with most of the prairie wildlife gone, the Osage were once again forced to take their neighbors' livestock in order to survive. The Creek and the Cherokee were

---

46. Agnew, F*ort Gibson*, 142.
47. Robert A. Glenn, "The Osage War"; Roy Godsey, "The Osage War, 1837"; Christianson, "Study of Osage," 120–28. This Osage-Missouri conflict has been mistakenly called the Osage War.

angered by the killing of their animals, and they again complained to the War Department. They demanded that the government remove Clermont's band from "their" land. Pressures
mounted in the winter of 1838–1839, for thousands of Cherokee, forced from their homes by the removal policy, were on
their way to the Three Forks. It was imperative that the Osage
leave the region, so in January Clermont II and the *Non-hon-zhin-ga*
were summoned to Fort Gibson. Weakened by disease, political
division, and almost constant violence in the northwest, the
Osage were no longer able to resist. In return for leaving the
ceded lands, the Osage were promised twelve thousand dollars
in cash, eight thousand dollars worth of goods, provisions for
twenty years, and settlement of all claims against them. They
were also granted a blacksmith, a gristmill, a sawmill, and livestock.[48]

Smallpox broke out among the Osage before they left, but
General Arbuckle sent a doctor to vaccinate the Osage to prevent any delay in their evacuation. When they missed their spring
departure date, soldiers from Fort Gibson went to the village
and compelled the Osage to leave. In March 1839, as the Cherokee were arriving from their tragic journey from Tennessee,
soldiers were driving the Osage away from their homes to vacate
land for the Cherokee. The Osage were finally forced to accept
complete United States control, for that spring the Osage left
the Three Forks for the last time. Never again would they be
allowed to return to their traditional homeland in the south.
Osage hegemony had ended.

The Osage had enjoyed tremendous power and influence
throughout most of the eighteenth century and for the first twenty-
five years of the nineteenth century. But, by 1840, the Osage,
once the most powerful Native American people of the southern
prairies, that area of flowing grass and timberlands between the
Red River in the south and the Missouri in the north, had been

48. Foreman, *Advancing the Frontier,* 109–11; *Treaties and Agreements,* 107–8.

driven from their home country and stripped of their power and independence by a nation they had never fought, but a nation which had nonetheless deprived them of their national hegemony.

As Teton and Yanktonai conquered in the north, so did the Osage in the south. The Osage occupied the prairies between the Missouri and Arkansas Rivers by 1673. Living near the Missouri, Arkansas, and Mississippi Rivers and between the French and Spanish frontiers, the Osage acquired the horse, gun, and access to the European market in the late seventeenth century. Mounted and armed, the Osage moved to defend their old hunting grounds and secure new ones. The Osage were surrounded by numerous competing Native American rivals, and their survival depended upon success in acquiring and protecting their resources. Large, well-armed tribes to the north and east threatened the Osage and limited Osage expansion in those directions, yet poorly armed tribes in the west and south could not defend their territory. Therefore, the Osage moved to the western and southern forests, prairies, and plains. The Osage attacked their neighboring tribes and pushed the Pawnee north, the Wichita and Caddo south, seizing control of their land. By the 1760s, the Osage were the most powerful tribe between the Missouri and Red Rivers.

The French, concerned largely with the economic exploitation of Louisiana rather than occupying territory, armed and equipped the Osage. The Osage brought furs, slaves, and horses to the French outposts on the Mississippi and Missouri Rivers, and they received guns, ammunition, and other trade goods, fueling Osage expansion. Spain acquired Louisiana after the Seven Years' War, and the Spanish attempted to limit Osage expansion. They occupied all of Louisiana and wanted peace and stability in their territory. The Spanish believed that by eliminating the market for slaves and livestock, they would stop Osage raids in the interior.

The Spanish could do little to control the Osage, however. Osage trade was lucrative, and the Osage made up a large nation located strategically along the frontiers of Spain's rivals. The

Spanish could not conquer the Osage, nor could they prevent foreign traders from dealing with them. Osage culture adapted well to the new conditions of the eighteenth century, as Osage subsistence economic patterns blended well with their new market economy. Osage social and political systems valued individual economic and military success and could, at least initially, accommodate the growing wealth and status of individual Osage.

The Osage withstood the invasion of the French and the Spanish. They became and remained a powerful people on the prairie-plains. Osage hegemony in the eighteenth and early nineteenth centuries rested upon Osage strength. It was not French or Spanish altruism that armed the Osage; it was economic, political, and imperial necessity. The Osage, numerically strong and strategically located, could demand and receive concessions from the Europeans. Unfortunately for the Osage, the foundations of their early power eroded. Their location and rich resources contributed to their loss, for the economic success they enjoyed as a result of their economic and political domination of the area created political chaos and destroyed their subsistence economy.

As Osage hegemony expanded, the increased raiding and economic success of the Osage eventually created changes that their political system could no longer accommodate. Increased economic expansion created political division. The traditional political framework was unable to meet the challenges posed by the European presence. Successful raiders and hunters gained status among the Osage, but the hereditary nature of the elaborate Osage political system prevented the newly successful Osage from gaining effective political power. The Osage social system adapted to the new conditions and created new social divisions, positions, and functions, but in time the compromises were inadequate, and many Osage left the parent group and formed independent bands with new leadership.

During the first quarter of the nineteenth century, those cultural elements so necessary for Osage hegemony were weakened and eventually substantially altered. Trade continued to grow after the United States occupied Louisiana in 1803, and the continued economic growth further weakened Osage society and political unity. The Osage also were confronted by stronger Native American rivals. In the west, the Pawnee, Comanche, and Kiowa acquired firearms from American traders and posed serious challenges to Osage domination. But more significantly, thousands of well-armed and powerful eastern Native American tribes moved into Osage country to live and hunt. American settlement and United States policy worked to remove tribes east of the Mississippi and place them in the west. The Osage were soon outnumbered by the immigrant tribes, and their animal resources were depleted by the new hunters. Their location, which had at one time controlled access into the interior, became the pathway of nineteenth-century western expansion. Their carefully guarded gateway of the eighteenth century became a public highway in the nineteenth century.[49]

Ironically, the most immediate and grave threat to the Osage were the Native American invaders; the United States in the early nineteenth century did not pose an immediate threat to the Osage, but the eastern Indians did. Immigrant tribes stole their women, children, and horses, fought them for control of their hunting grounds, and killed their game. The Osage had to have access to guns and ammunition to protect their territory; their survival as a people depended upon it. After the War of 1812, Canadian traders no longer came among the Osage. Therefore, they were forced to remain at peace with the white Americans in order to obtain essential arms. The United States, eager to remove the eastern Indians, took full advantage of their relationship with the Osage, and demanded land from them to locate the evacuated eastern tribes. Dependent upon the United States for essential firearms and trade, the Osage reluctantly

49. White, *Roots of Dependency*, xiii–xix, 313–23.

surrendered their tribal lands in a series of treaties with the United States.

Confronted by strong, well-armed nations in the east and powerful nations in the west, the Osage struggled throughout the 1820s and 1830s to protect their villages and hunting grounds and to maintain Osage hegemony. It was not to be, for by the late 1830s, the Osage, weakened by continued political division, disease, destruction of their economic base, and incessant Native American warfare, were no longer able to dominate the prairies. By 1840, Osage hegemony existed only in the memory of the Osage people.

BIBLIOGRAPHY

Agnew, Brad. *Fort Gibson, Terminal on the Trail of Tears.* Norman: University of Oklahoma Press, 1980.

Alvord, Clarence Walworth. *The Illinois Country, 1673–1818.* 1922. Reprint. Chicago: Loyola University Press, 1965.

Alvord, Clarence Walworth and Clarence E. Carter, eds. *The Critical Period, 1763–1765.* Springfield: Illinois State Historical Library, 1915.

American State Papers: Indian Affairs. Vols. 1 and 4. Washington, D.C.: Gales and Seaton, 1832–1834.

American State Papers: Military Affairs. Vol. 5. Washington, D.C.: Gales and Seaton, 1860.

Annals of the Congress of the United States. Expeditions of Lewis and Clark. 9th Cong., 2d sess., December 1, 1806–March 2, 1807.

Archives de la Marine. Série 3JJ: Journaux, mémoires, correspondance. Archives Nationales, Paris, France.

Archives des Colonies. Série C13A: Correspondance générale, Louisiane, and Série C11A: Correspondance générale. Archives Nationales, Paris, France.

Arkansas Gazette. Little Rock: 1820–1839.

Arthur, George W. *An Introduction to the Ecology of Early Historic Communal Bison Hunting Among the Northern Plains.* Archaeological Survey of Canada, no. 37. Ottawa: National Museums of Canada, 1975.

Atkeson, W. O. *History of Bates County, Missouri.* Topeka, Kans.: Historical Publishing Co., 1918.

Axtell, James. "Ethnohistory: An Historian's Viewpoint." *Ethnohistory* 26 (Winter 1979): 1–13.

Bailey, Garrick A. "Changes in Osage Social Organization, 1673–1969." Ph.D. diss., University of Oregon, 1970.

———. "Changes in Osage Social Organization, 1673–1906." *University of Oregon Anthropology Papers* 5 (1973): 1–122.

Baird, Donald. "Some Eighteenth Century Gun Barrels from Osage Village Sites." *Great Plains Journal* 4 (1965): 49–62.

Baird, W. David. *The Osage People*. Phoenix: Indian Tribal Series, 1972.

————. *The Quapaw Indians: A History of the Downstream People*. Norman: University of Oklahoma Press, 1980.

Bates Papers. Missouri Historical Society, St. Louis.

Bauxar, J. Joseph. "History of the Illinois Area." In *Northeast,* vol. 15 of *Handbook of North American Indians,* edited by Bruce G. Trigger, 594–601. Washington, D.C.: Smithsonian Institution, 1978.

Bearss, Edwin C. "In Quest of Peace on the Indian Border: The Establishment of Fort Smith." *Arkansas Historical Quarterly* 23 (Spring 1964): 123–53.

Berry, Brewton, and Carl Chapman. "An Oneota Site in Missouri." *American Antiquity* 7 (January 1942): 290–303.

Berry, Brewton, Carl Chapman, and John Mack. "Archaeological Remains of the Osage." *American Antiquity* 10 (July 1944): 1–11.

Boeri, David. *People of the Ice Whale: Eskimos, White Men, and the Whale.* New York: E. P. Dutton, 1983.

Bolton, Herbert E., ed. *Athanase de Mézières and the Louisiana-Texas Frontier, 1768–1780.* 2 vols. Cleveland: Arthur H. Clark Co., 1914.

Brackenridge, Henry M. *Brackenridge's Journal Up the Missouri, 1811.* Vol. 6 of *Early Western Travels, 1748–1846,* edited by Reuben Gold Thwaites. 1904. Reprint. New York: AMS Press, 1966.

Bradbury, John. *Travels in the Interior of America: In the Years 1809, 1810, and 1811.* Vol. 5 of *Early Western Travels, 1748–1846,* edited by Reuben Gold Thwaites. 1904. Reprint. New York: AMS Press, 1966.

Bray, Robert T. "The Missouri Indian Tribe in Archaeology and History." *Missouri Historical Review* 55 (April 1961): 213–25.

Brooks, George R., ed. "George C. Sibley's Journal of a Trip to the Salines in 1811." *Missouri Historical Society Bulletin* 21 (April 1965): 167–207.

Burns, Louis F. *Osage Indian Bands and Clans.* Fallbrook, Calif.: Ciga Press, 1984.

Bushnell, David, Jr. "Villages of the Algonquin, Siouan, and Caddoan Tribes West of the Mississippi." *Bureau of American Ethnology Bulletin,* no. 77, pp. 98–109. Washington, D.C.: Government Printing Office, 1922.

Caldwell, Norman W. *The French in the Mississippi Valley, 1740–1750.* Urbana: University of Illinois Press, 1941.

Callahan, Alice Anne. "The Osage Ceremonial Dance: I'n-Lon-Schka." Norman: University of Oklahoma Press, 1990.

Carter, Clarence E., ed. *The Territorial Papers of the United States.* 26 vols. Washington, D.C.: Government Printing Office, 1934–1962.

Caruso, John Anthony. *The Mississippi Valley Frontier: The Age of French Exploration and Settlement.* Indianapolis: Bobbs-Merrill Co., 1966.

Catlin, George. *Letters and Notes on the North American Indians.* Edited by Michael MacDonald Mooney. New York: Clarkson N. Potter, 1975.

Chapman, Carl H. "Culture Sequence in the Lower Missouri Valley." In *Archeology of the Eastern United States,* edited by James B. Griffin, 139–51. Chicago: University of Chicago Press, 1952.

———. "The Indomitable Osage in Spanish Illinois (Upper Louisiana), 1763–1804." In *The Spanish in the Mississippi Valley, 1762–1804,* edited by John Francis McDermott, 286–312. Urbana: University of Illinois Press, 1974.

———. "Journey to the Land of the Osages, 1835–1836, by Louis Cortambert." Translated by Mrs. Max W. Myer. *Missouri Historical Society Bulletin* 19 (April 1963): 199–299.

———. "The Little Osage and Missouri Indian Village Sites, ca. 1727–1777 A.D." *The Missouri Archaeologist* 21 (December 1959): 1–67.

———. *The Origin of the Osage Indian Tribe.* Vol. 3 of *Osage Indians,* edited by David A. Horr. New York: Garland Publishing, 1974.

———. "The Origin of the Osage Indian Tribe: An Ethnographical, Historical, and Archaeological Study." Ph.D. diss., University of Michigan, 1959.

———. "Osage Prehistory." *Plains Anthropologist* 7 (1962): 99–100.

———. "Osage Village Sites and Hunting Territory, 1808–1825." In vol. 4 of *Osage Indians,* edited by David A. Horr, 251–93. New York: Garland Publishing, 1974.

———. "A Preliminary Survey of Missouri Archaeology." In vol. 4 of *Osage Indians,* edited by David A. Horr, 9–249. New York: Garland Publishing, 1974.

———. "A Preliminary Survey of Missouri Archaeology, Part I: Historic Indian Tribes." *Missouri Archaeologist* 10 (October 1946): 1–51.

Chapman, Carl H., and Eleanor F. Chapman. *Indians and Archaeology of Missouri*. 1964. Reprint. Columbia: University of Missouri Press, 1983.

Chouteau, Auguste. "Glimpses of the Past: Notes of Auguste Chouteau on Boundaries of Various Indian Nations." *Missouri Historical Society Bulletin* 7 (October–December 1940): 12.

———. Papers. Missouri Historical Society, St. Louis.

Chouteau, Pierre. Collection. Missouri Historical Society, St. Louis.

———. Letterbook. Missouri Historical Society, St. Louis.

Chouteau Collection. Missouri Historical Society, St. Louis.

Christianson, James R. "A Study of Osage History Prior to 1876." Ph.D. diss., University of Kansas, 1968.

Clark, William. Papers. Missouri Historical Society, St. Louis.

Clark Collection. Missouri Historical Society, St. Louis.

Clifton, James A. *The Prairie People: Continuity and Change in Potawatomi Indian Culture, 1665–1965*. Lawrence: Regents Press of Kansas, 1977.

Clough, Shepard B., and Charles Woolsey Cole. *Economic History of Europe*. Boston: D. C. Heath and Co., 1941.

Cole, Charles Woolsey. *French Mercantilism, 1683–1700*. New York: Columbia University Press, 1943.

Conrad, Glen R., ed. *Historical Journal of the Settlement of the French in Louisiana*. Translated by Joan Cain and Virginia Koenig. University of Southwestern Louisiana History Series, no. 3. Lafayette: University of Southwestern Louisiana, 1971.

Coues, Elliott, ed. *The Expeditions of Zebulon Montgomery Pike*. 3 vols. 1895. Reprint (3 vols. in 2). Minneapolis: Ross and Haines, 1965.

Crane, Verner W. *The Southern Frontier, 1670–1732*. 1929. Reprint. Ann Arbor: University of Michigan Press, 1956.

———. "The Tennessee River as the Road to Carolina: The Beginnings of Exploration and Trade." *The Mississippi Valley Historical Review* 3 (June 1916): 3–18.

Cronon, William. *Changes in the Land: Indians, Colonists, and the Ecology of New England*. 1983. Reprint. New York: Hill and Wang, 1986.

Crosby, Alfred W., Jr. "Virgin Soil Epidemics as a Factor in the Aboriginal Depopulation in America." In *The American Indian: Past and Present*, edited by Roger L. Nichols, 39–46. New York: Alfred A. Knopf, 1986.

Davis, Adelle. *Let's Eat Right to Keep Fit.* 1954. Reprint. New York: New American Library, 1970.

Din, Gilbert C. "Arkansas Post in the American Revolution." *Arkansas Historical Quarterly* 40 (Spring 1981): 3–30.

Din, Gilbert C., and Abraham P. Nasatir. *The Imperial Osages: Spanish-Indian Diplomacy in the Mississippi Valley.* Norman: University of Oklahoma Press, 1983.

Dorsey, George A. "The Osage Mourning-War Ceremony." *American Anthropologist* 4 (July-September 1902): 404–11.

———. *Traditions of the Osage.* Field Columbian Museum Publication, no. 88, Anthropological Series, vol. 7. Chicago: Field Columbian Museum, 1904.

Dorsey, J. Owen. "An Account of the War Customs of the Osages." *American Naturalist* 18 (February 1884): 113–33.

———. "Migration of Siouan Tribes." *American Naturalist* 20 (March 1886): 211–22.

———. "Omaha Sociology." Bureau of American Ethnology *Third Annual Report, 1881–1882,* 211–370. Washington, D.C.: Government Printing Office, 1884.

———. "Osage Traditions." Bureau of American Ethnology *Sixth Annual Report, 1884–1885,* 377–97. Washington, D.C.: Government Printing Office, 1888.

———. "Siouan Sociology." Bureau of American Ethnology *Fifteenth Annual Report, 1893–1894,* 205–44. Washington, D.C.: Government Printing Office, 1897.

———. "The Social Organization of the Siouan Tribes." *Journal of American Folk-Lore* 4 (October–December 1891): 331–42.

Douglas, Walter B. *Manuel Lisa.* Edited by Abraham P. Nasatir. New York: Argosy-Antiquarian, 1964.

Douglas, Walter B., ed. "Documents: Captain Nathaniel Pryor." *American Historical Review* 24 (January 1919): 253–65.

Dunbar, John B. "Massacre of the Villazur Expedition by the Pawnees on the Platte, in 1720." *Kansas State Historical Society* 11 (1909–1910): 397–423.

Eccles, William J. *The Canadian Frontier, 1534–1760.* 1969. Rev. ed. Albuquerque: University of New Mexico Press, 1983.

———. "The Fur Trade and Eighteenth-Century Imperialism." *William and Mary Quarterly* 40 (July 1983): 341–62.

Edmunds, R. David. *The Potawatomis: Keepers of the Fire.* Norman: University of Oklahoma Press, 1978.

Eggan, Fred. *The American Indian: Perspectives for the Study of Social Change.* Chicago: Aldene Publishing Co., 1966.

Ellis, Richard N., and Charlie R. Steen, eds. "An Indian Delegation in France, 1725." Translated by Charlie R. Steen. *Journal of Illinois State Historical Society* 67 (September 1974): 385–405.

Euler, Robert. "Ethnohistory in the United States." *Ethnohistory* 19 (Winter 1972): 201–7.

Ewers, John C. "Symbols of Chiefly Authority in Spanish Louisiana." In *The Spanish in the Mississippi Valley, 1762–1804,* edited by John Francis McDermott, 272–84. Urbana: University of Illinois Press, 1974.

Faye, Stanley. "The Arkansas Post of Louisiana: French Domination." *Louisiana Historical Quarterly* 26 (July 1943): 633–721.

———. "The Arkansas Post of Louisiana: Spanish Domination." *Louisiana Historical Quarterly* 27 (July 1944): 629–716.

———. "Indian Guests at the Spanish Arkansas Post." *Arkansas Historical Quarterly* 4 (1945): 93–107.

Featherstonhaugh, George William. *Excursion Through the Slave States, From Washington on the Potomac, to the Frontier of Mexico; with Sketches of Popular Manners and Geological Notices.* New York: Harper and Brothers, 1844.

Fenton, William. "Ethnohistory and Its Problems." *Ethnohistory* 9 (Winter 1962): 1–23.

Fessler, W. Julian, ed. "Captain Nathan Boone's Journal." *Chronicles of Oklahoma* 7 (March 1929): 58–105.

Finiels, Nicolas de. *An Account of Upper Louisiana.* Edited by Carl J. Ekberg and William E. Foley. Translated by Carl J. Ekberg. Columbia: University of Missouri Press, 1989.

Fitzgerald, Mary Paul. *Beacon on the Plains.* Leavenworth, Kans.: Saint Mary College, 1939.

Fitzpatrick, W. S., ed. *Treaties and Laws of the Osage Nation, as Passed to November 26, 1890.* Cedar Vale, Kans.: Press of the Cedar Vale Commercial, 1895.

Fletcher, Alice C., and Francis LaFlesche. *The Omaha Tribe.* 2 vols. 1911. Reprint. New York: Johnson Reprint Corporation, 1970.

Flores, Dan L. "The Red River Branch of the Alabama-Coushatta Indians: An Ethnohistory." *Southern Studies* 16 (Spring 1977): 55–72.

Flores, Dan L., ed. *Journal of an Indian Trader: Anthony Glass and the Texas Trading Frontier, 1790–1810.* College Station: Texas A & M Press, 1985.

Foley, William E. *A History of Missouri: Volume I, 1673 to 1820.* Columbia: University of Missouri Press, 1971.

Foley, William E., and C. David Rice. "Compounding The Risks: International Politics, Wartime Dislocations, and Auguste Chouteau's Fur Trading Operations, 1792–1815." *Missouri Historical Society Bulletin* 34 (April 1978): 131–39.

———. *The First Chouteaus: River Barons of Early St. Louis.* Urbana: University of Illinois Press, 1983.

———. "Pierre Chouteau, Entrepreneur as Indian Agent." *Missouri Historical Review* 72 (July 1978): 365–87.

Folmer, Henri. "Etienne Veniard de Bourgmond in the Missouri Country." *Missouri Historical Review* 36 (April 1942): 279–98.

———. *Franco-Spanish Rivalry in North America, 1524–1763.* Glendale, Calif.: Arthur H. Clark Co., 1953.

———. "French Expansion Toward New Mexico in the Eighteenth Century." M.A. thesis, University of Denver, 1939.

Foreman, Carolyn Thomas. "Hopefield Mission in Osage Nation, 1823–1837." *Chronicles of Oklahoma* 28 (Summer 1950): 193–205.

Foreman, Grant. *Advancing the Frontier, 1830–1860.* Norman: University of Oklahoma Press, 1933.

———. *Indians and Pioneers: The Story of the American Southwest Before 1830.* 1936. Reprint. Norman: University of Oklahoma Press, 1967.

———. *The Last Trek of the Indians.* Chicago: University of Chicago Press, 1946.

———. "Nathaniel Pryor." *Chronicles of Oklahoma* 7 (June 1929): 152–63.

———. "Our Indian Ambassadors to Europe." *Missouri Historical Society Collections* 5 (February 1928): 108–28.

Foreman, Grant, ed. "Journal of the Proceedings at Our First Treaty with the Wild Indians." *Chronicles of Oklahoma* 14 (December 1936): 393–418.

Gabler, Ina. "Lovely's Purchase and Lovely County." *Arkansas Historical Quarterly* 19 (Spring 1960): 31–39.

Garraghan, Gilbert J. *Chapters in Frontier History: Research Studies in the Making of the West.* Milwaukee: Bruce Publishing Co., 1934.

————. "Fort Orleans of the Missoury." *Missouri Historical Review* 35 (April 1941): 373–84.

Giraud, Marcel. *The Reign of Louis XIV, 1698–1715.* Vol. 1 of *A History of French Louisiana.* Translated by Joseph C. Lambert. Baton Rouge: Louisiana State University Press, 1974.

Giraud, Marcel, ed. "Etienne Veniard De Bourgmont's 'Exact Description of Louisiana'." Translated by Mrs. Max W. Myer. *Missouri Historical Society Bulletin* 15 (October 1958): 3–19.

Glenn, Robert A. "The Osage War." *Missouri Historical Review* 14 (January 1920): 201–10.

Godsey, Roy. "The Osage War, 1837." *Missouri Historical Review* 20 (October 1925): 96–100.

Graham, Richard. Papers. Missouri Historical Society, St. Louis.

Graves, W. W., Mrs. "In the Land of the Osages—Harmony Mission." *Missouri Historical Review* 19 (April 1925): 409–19.

Graves, William W. *The First Protestant Osage Missions, 1820–1837.* Oswego, Kans.: Carpenter Press, 1949.

Green, Frederick. *Eighteenth-Century France: Six Essays.* London: J. M. Dent and Sons, 1929.

Green, Michael D. "'We Dance in Opposite Directions': Mesquakie (Fox) Separatism from the Sac and Fox Tribe." *Ethnohistory* 30 (1983): 129–40.

Gregg, Josiah. *Josiah Gregg's Commerce of the Prairies.* Vol. 20 of *Early Western Travels, 1748–1846.* Edited by Reuben Gold Thwaites. 1905. Reprint. New York: AMS Press, 1966.

Gregg, Kate L. "The History of Fort Osage." *Missouri Historical Review* 34 (July 1940): 439–88.

————. "The War of 1812 on the Missouri Frontier." Parts 1–3. *Missouri Historical Review* 33 (October 1938–July 1939): 3–22, 184–202, 326–48.

Gregg, Kate L., ed. *Westward with Dragoons: The Journal of William Clark on His Expedition to Establish Fort Osage, August 25 to September 22, 1808.* Fulton, Mo.: Ovid Bell Press, 1937.

Griffen, James B., ed. *Archaeology of the Eastern United States.* Chicago: University of Chicago Press, 1952.

Grove, Nettie Thompson. "Fort Osage, First Settlement in Jackson County." *Missouri Valley Historical Society* 1 (October 1921): 56–70.

Hackett, Charles W., ed. *Pichardo's Treatise on the Limits of Louisiana*

and Texas. 4 vols. 1931. Reprint. Freeport, N.Y.: Books for Libraries Press, 1971.

Hagan, William T. *American Indians.* 1961. Reprint. Chicago: University of Chicago Press, 1979.

———. *The Sac and Fox Indians.* Norman: University of Oklahoma
Press, 1958.

Haines, Francis. "The Northward Spread of Horses Among the Plains
Indians." *American Anthropologist* 40 (July–September 1938): 429–37.

———. "Where Did the Plains Indians Get Their Horses?" *American
Anthropologist* 40 (January–March 1938): 112–17.

Hamilton, T. M. "Concluding Comments and Observations." *Missouri Archaeologist* 22 (December 1960): 207–9.

———. "The Gunsmith Cache Discovered at Malta Bend, Missouri."
Missouri Archaeologist 22 (December 1960): 150–71.

———. "Some Gun Parts From Eighteenth-Century Osage Sites."
Missouri Archaeologist 22 (December 1960): 120–49.

Hanson, Jeffery R. "Bison Ecology in the Northern Plains and a Reconstruction of Bison Patterns for the North Dakota Region." *Plains
Anthropologist* 29 (May 1984): 93–113.

Harner, Joe. "The Village of the Big Osage." *Missouri Archaeologist* 5
(February 1939): 19–20.

Harper, Elizabeth Ann. "The Taovayas Indians in Frontier Trade and
Diplomacy, 1719–1768." *Chronicles of Oklahoma* 31 (Spring 1953):
268–89.

———. "The Taovayas Indians in Frontier Trade and Diplomacy,
1719–1835." *Panhandle-Plains Historical Review* 23 (October 1953):
1–32.

———. "The Taovayas Indians in Frontier Trade and Diplomacy,
1769–1779." *Southwestern Historical Quarterly* 57 (October 1953):
181–201.

———. "The Trade and Diplomacy of the Taovayas Indians on the
Northern Frontier of New Spain." M.A. thesis, University of Oklahoma, 1951.

Hauser, Raymond E. "The Illinois Indian Tribe: From Autonomy and
Self-Sufficiency to Dependency and Depopulation." *Journals of the
Illinois State Historical Society* 69 (May 1976): 127–38.

Hennepin, Louis. *Father Louis Hennepin's Description of Louisiana:
Newly Discovered to The Southwest of New France by Order of the*

King. Translated by Marion Cross. Minneapolis: University of Minnesota Press, 1938.

———. *A New Discovery of a Vast Country in America.* Edited by Reuben Gold Thwaites. 1698. Reprint. Chicago: A. C. McClurg and Co., 1903.

Henning, Dale R. "Development and Interrelationships of Oneota Culture in the Lower Missouri Valley." *Missouri Archaeologist* 32 (December 1970): 146–67.

———. "The Osage Nation, 1775–1818." In vol. 4 of *Osage Indians,* edited by David A. Horr, 295–325. New York: Garland Publishing, 1974.

Hill, Ed C. "Has the Site of Fort Orleans Been Discovered?" *Missouri Historical Society Collections* 4 (1914): 367–69.

Hodge, Frederick Webb, ed. *Handbook of American Indians North of Mexico.* 2 vols. Bureau of American Ethnology Bulletin, no. 30. Washington, D.C.: Government Printing Office, 1907–1910.

Holder, Preston. "The Fur Trade as Seen from the Indian Point of View." In *The Frontier Re-examined,* edited by John Francis McDermott, 129–39. Urbana: University of Illinois Press, 1967.

———. *The Hoe and the Horse on the Plains: A Study of Cultural Development among North American Indians.* 1970. Reprint. Lincoln: University of Nebraska Press, 1974.

Horr, David A., ed. *Osage Indians.* 5 vols. New York: Garland Publishing, 1974.

Horsman, Reginald. *Expansion and American Indian Policy, 1783–1812.* Lansing: Michigan State University Press, 1967.

Houck, Louis A. *A History of Missouri.* 3 vols. Chicago: R. R. Donnelley and Sons, Co., 1908.

Houck, Louis A., ed. *The Spanish Régime in Missouri.* 2 vols. Chicago: R. R. Donnelley and Sons, Co., 1909.

Hunter, William A. "History of the Ohio Valley." In *Northeast,* vol. 15 of *Handbook of North American Indians,* edited by Bruce G. Trigger, 588–93. Washington, D.C.: Smithsonian Institution, 1978.

Hyde, George E. *Indians of the High Plains: From the Prehistoric Period to the Coming of Europeans.* 1959. Reprint. Norman: University of Oklahoma Press, 1976.

———. *Indians of the Woodlands: From Prehistoric Times to 1725.* 1962. Reprint. Norman: University of Oklahoma Press, 1975.

———. *The Pawnee Indians.* 1951. Reprint. Norman: University of Oklahoma Press, 1974.

Hyde, Hanford Montgomery. *John Law: The History of an Honest Adventurer.* London: Home and Van Thal, 1948.

Indian Claims Commission. *Commission Findings on the Osage Indians.* Vol. 5 of *Osage Indians.* Edited by David A. Horr. New York: Garland Publishing, 1974.

Indian Papers. Missouri Historical Society, St. Louis.

Institute for the Development of Indian Law. *Treaties and Agreements of the Eastern Oklahoma Indians.* Washington, D.C.: Institute for the Development of Indian Law, 1975.

Isern, Thomas D., ed. "Exploration and Diplomacy: George Champlin Sibley's Report to William Clark, 1811." *Missouri Historical Review* 73 (October 1978): 85–102.

Jackson, Donald, ed. *The Journals of Zebulon Montgomery Pike: With Letters and Related Documents.* 2 vols. Norman: University of Oklahoma Press, 1966.

———, ed. *Letters of the Lewis and Clark Expedition with Related Documents, 1783–1854.* 2 vols. Urbana: University of Illinois Press, 1978.

James, Lewis Edwin, comp. *Account of an Expedition from Pittsburgh to the Rocky Mountains Performed in the Years 1819 and 1820, By Order of the Hon. J. C. Calhoun, Secretary of War, Under the Command of Maj. S. H. Long.* Vols. 14–17 of *Early Western Travels, 1748–1846.* Edited by Reuben Gold Thwaites. 1905. Reprint. New York: AMS Press, 1966.

Jennings, Francis. *The Invasion of America: Indians, Colonialism, and the Cant of Conquest.* New York: W. W. Norton and Co., 1976.

John, Elizabeth A. H. "Portrait of a Wichita Village, 1808." *Chronicles of Oklahoma* 60 (Winter 1982–1983): 412–37.

———. *Storms Brewed in Other Men's Worlds: The Confrontation of Indians, Spanish, and French in the Southwest, 1540–1795.* 1975. Reprint. Lincoln: University of Nebraska Press, 1981.

Johnson, J. B., ed. *History of Vernon County, Missouri.* 2 vols. Chicago: C. F. Cooper and Co., 1911.

Jones, Harold W., ed. "The Diary of Assistant Surgeon Leonard McPhail on His Journey to the Southwest in 1835." *Chronicles of Oklahoma* 18 (September 1940): 281–92.

Kavanagh, Thomas Whitney. "Political Power and Political Organization: Comanche Politics, 1786–1875." Ph.D. diss., University of New Mexico, 1986.

Kellogg, Louise Phelps, ed. *Early Narratives of the Northwest, 1634–1699.* New York: C. Scribner's Sons, 1917.

Kinnaird, Lawrence, ed. *Spain in the Mississippi Valley.* Vols. 2 and 3 of *Annual Report of the American Historical Association for the Year 1945.* Washington, D.C.: Government Printing Office, 1946.

Knight, James E. "Basics of Muzzleloading." New Mexico State University, Cooperative Extension Service Circular, no. 500. Las Cruces: New Mexico State University Press, 1985.

Kroeber, Alfred L. "Cultural and Natural Areas of North America." *University of California Publications in American Archaeology and Ethnology* 38, pp. 74–85. Berkeley: University of California Press, 1939.

LaFlesche, Francis. "Ceremonies and Rituals of the Osages." Smithsonian Institution *Miscellaneous Collections* 63, pp. 66–69. Washington, D.C.: Government Printing Office, 1914.

———. *Dictionary of the Osage Language.* Bureau of American Ethnology Bulletin, no. 109. Washington, D.C.: Government Printing Office, 1932.

———. "Ethnology of the Osage Indians." Smithsonian Institution *Miscellaneous Collections* 76, pp. 104–7. Washington, D.C.: Government Printing Office, 1924.

———. "Osage Marriage Customs." *American Anthropologist* 14 (1912): 127–30.

———. "Osage Songs and Rituals." Smithsonian Institution *Miscellaneous Collections* 65, pp. 78–81. Washington, D.C.: Smithsonian Institution, 1915.

———. "Osage Tribal Rites, Oklahoma." Smithsonian Institution *Miscellaneous Collections* 72, pp. 71–73. Washington, D.C.: Smithsonian Institution, 1920.

———. "The Osage Tribe: Rite of the Chiefs; Sayings of the Ancient Men." Bureau of American Ethnology *Thirty-sixth Annual Report, 1914–1915,* 37–601. Washington, D.C.: Government Printing Office, 1921.

———. "The Osage Tribe: Rite of Vigil." Bureau of American Ethnology *Thirty-ninth Annual Report, 1917–1918,* 31–636. Washington, D.C.: Government Printing Office, 1925.

————. "The Osage Tribe: Rite of the Wa-xo'-be." Bureau of American Ethnology *Forty-fifth Annual Report, 1927–1928,* 523–833. Washington, D.C.: Government Printing Office, 1930.

————. "The Osage Tribe: Two Versions of the Child-naming Rite." Bureau of American Ethnology *Forty-third Annual Report, 1925–1926,* 23–164. Washington, D.C.: Government Printing Office, 1928.

————. "Right and Left in Osage Ceremonies." In *Holmes Anniversary Volume: Anthropological Essays,* edited by F. W. Hodge, 278–87. Washington, D.C.: J. W. Bryan Press, 1916.

————. "The Symbolic Man of the Osage Tribe." *Art and Archaeology* 9 (February 1920): 68–72.

————. "Tribal Rites of the Osage Indians." Smithsonian Institution *Miscellaneous Collections* 68, pp. 84–90. Washington, D.C.: Government Printing Office, 1918.

————. *War Ceremony and Peace Ceremony of the Osage Indians.* Bureau of American Ethnology Bulletin, no. 101. Washington, D.C.: Government Printing Office, 1939.

————. "Work Among the Osage Indians." Smithsonian Institution *Miscellaneous Collections* 66, pp. 118–21. Washington, D.C.: Government Printing Office, 1917.

Lange, Charles H. "Relations of the Southwest with the Plains and Great Basin." In *Southwest,* vol. 9 of *Handbook of North American Indians,* edited by Alfonso Ortiz, 201–5. Washington, D.C.: Smithsonian Institution, 1979.

Lauber, Almon Wheeler. *Indian Slavery in Colonial Times Within the Present Limits of the United States.* Studies in History, Economics and Public Law, vol. 54. Williamstown, Mass.: Corner House Publishers, 1970.

LeCompte, Janet. "Auguste Pierre Chouteau." In vol. 9 of *The Mountain Men and the Fur Trade of the Far West,* edited by LeRoy R. Hafen, 63–90. Glendale, Calif.: Arthur H. Clark Co., 1972.

Letters Received by the Office of Indian Affairs, 1824–1881. Osage Agency, 1824–1880. Record Group 75. M234. National Archives, Washington, D.C.

Letters Received by the Secretary of War, Main Series, 1801–1870. Record Group 107. M221. National Archives, Washington, D.C.

Letters Received by the Secretary of War Relating to Indian Affairs, 1800–1823. Record Group 75. M271. National Archives, Washington, D.C.

Lewis, Anna. "Du Tisné's Expedition into Oklahoma, 1719." *Chronicles of Oklahoma* 3 (December 1925): 319–23.

———. "La Harpe's First Expedition in Oklahoma, 1718–1719." *Chronicles of Oklahoma* 2 (December 1924): 331–49.

Lewis, Oscar. *The Effects of White Contact Upon Blackfoot Culture, with Special Reference to the Roles of the Fur Trade.* Monographs of the American Ethnological Society, no. 6. Seattle: University of Washington Press, 1942.

Limerick, Patricia Nelson. *The Legacy of Conquest: The Unbroken Past of the American West.* New York: W. W. Norton and Co., 1987.

Lindenwood Collection. Missouri Historical Society, St. Louis.

Loomis, Noel M., and Abraham P. Nasatir. *Pedro Vial and the Roads to Santa Fe.* Norman: University of Oklahoma Press, 1967.

Louisiana Gazette. Saint Louis: 1809–1812.

Lowie, Robert H. *Indians of the Plains.* 1954. Reprint. Lincoln: University of Nebraska Press, 1982.

Lucas Collection. Missouri Historical Society, St. Louis.

Lurie, Nancy Oestreich. "Ethnohistory: An Ethnological Point of View." *Ethnohistory* 8 (Winter 1961): 78–92.

McCoy, Isaac. *Annual Register of Indian Affairs within Indian Territory.* Shawanoe Baptist Mission House, Indian Territory: J. G. Pratt, 1835–1838.

McDermott, John Francis. "Auguste Chouteau: First Citizen of Upper Louisiana." In *Frenchmen and French Ways in the Mississippi Valley,* edited by John Francis McDermott, 1–14. Urbana: University of Illinois Press, 1969.

———. "Cadet Chouteau, An Identification." *Missouri Historical Review* 31 (April 1937): 267–71.

———. "The Myth of the 'Imbecile Governor'—Captain Fernando de Leyba and the Defense of St. Louis in 1780." In *The Spanish in the Mississippi Valley, 1762–1804,* edited by John Francis McDermott, 314–405. Urbana: University of Illinois Press, 1974.

McDermott, John Francis, ed. *Frenchmen and French Ways in the Mississippi Valley.* Urbana: University of Illinois Press, 1969.

———, ed. *The Frontier Re-examined.* Urbana: University of Illinois Press, 1967.

———, ed. *The Spanish in the Mississippi Valley, 1762–1804.* Urbana: University of Illinois Press, 1974.

———, ed. *Tixier's Travels on the Osage Prairies.* Translated by Albert

J. Salvan. 1940. Reprint. Norman: University of Oklahoma Press, 1968.

———, ed. "The Western Journals of Dr. George Hunter, 1796–1805." *Transactions of the American Philosophical Society* 53 (July 1963): 1–133.

———, ed. *The Western Journals of Washington Irving.* Norman: University of Oklahoma Press, 1964.

McNickle, D'Arcy. Review of *The Long Death,* by Ralph Andrist and *The Lost Universe,* by Gene Weltfish. *The Nation,* September 17, 1965, 165.

Margry, Pierre, ed. *Exploration des affluents du Mississipi et découverte des Montagnes Rocheuses, 1679–1754.* Vol. 6 of *Découvertes et établissements des Français dans l'ouest et dans le sud de l'Amérique Septentrionale (1614–1754).* 1888. Reprint. New York: AMS Press, 1974.

———, ed. *Voyages des Français sur les Grands lacs et découverte de l'Ohio et du Mississipi: 1614–1684.* Vol. 1 of *Découvertes et établissements des Français dans l'ouest et dans le sud de l'Amérique Septentrionale (1614–1754).* 1888. Reprint. New York: AMS Press, 1974.

Marriott, Alice. *Osage Research Report and Bibliography of Basic Research References.* Vol. 2 of *Osage Indians.* Edited by David A. Horr. New York: Garland Publishing, 1974.

Marshall, Thomas Maitland, ed. "The Journals of Jules De Mun." Parts 1 and 2. Translated by Mrs. Nettie H. Beauregard. *Missouri Historical Society Collections* 5 (February 1928): 167–208; (June 1928): 311–26.

———. *The Life and Papers of Frederick Bates.* 2 vols. St. Louis: Missouri Historical Society, 1926.

Martin, Calvin. *Keepers of the Game: Indian-Animal Relationships and the Fur Trade.* Berkeley: University of California Press, 1978.

Mathews, John Joseph. *The Osages: Children of the Middle Waters.* 1961. Reprint. Norman: University of Oklahoma Press, 1982.

———. *Talking to the Moon.* 1945. Reprint. Norman: University of Oklahoma Press, 1945.

———. *Wah'Kon-Tah: The Osage and the White Man's Road.* Norman: University of Oklahoma Press, 1932.

Mayhall, Mildred P. *The Kiowas.* 1962. Reprint. Norman: University of Oklahoma Press, 1971.

Miller, Walter B. "Two Concepts of Authority." *American Anthropologist* 57 (April 1955): 271–89.

Minton, Robert. *John Law, The Father of Paper Money*. New York: Association Press, 1975.

Missionary Herald. Boston: American Board of Commissioners for Foreign Missions, 1819–1838.

Missouri Gazette. Saint Louis: 1808–1809, 1812–1815, 1816–1817.

Missouri Gazette and Illinois Advertiser. Saint Louis: 1815, 1818.

Mooney, James. "Aboriginal Population of America, North of Mexico." Smithsonian Institution *Miscellaneous Collections* 80, 1–40. Washington, D.C.: Government Printing Office, 1928.

———. "Calendar History of the Kiowa Indians." Bureau of American Ethnology *Seventeenth Annual Report, 1895–1896*, 141–444. Washington, D.C.: Government Printing Office, 1898.

———. "Myths of the Cherokee and Sacred Formulas of the Cherokees." Bureau of American Ethnology *Nineteenth Annual Report, 1897–1898*, 3–548. Washington, D.C.: Government Printing Office, 1900.

Morfi, Juan Augustin. *History of Texas, 1673–1779*. 2 vols. Edited by Carlos Eduardo Castañeda. 1935. Reprint. New York: Arno Press, 1967.

Morris, Wayne. "Traders and Factories on the Arkansas Frontier, 1805–1822." *Arkansas Historical Quarterly* 28 (Spring 1969): 28–48.

Morrison, T. F. "Mission Neosho, The First Kansas Mission." *Kansas Historical Quarterly* 4 (August 1935): 227–34.

Morse, Jedidiah. *A Report to the Secretary of War of the United States on Indian Affairs*. New Haven, Conn.: S. Converse, 1822.

Murphy, Robert F. "Matrilocality and Patrilineality in Mundurucú Society." *American Anthropologist* 58 (June 1956): 414–34.

Nasatir, Abraham P. "Anglo-Spanish Frontier on the Upper Mississippi, 1786–1796." *Iowa Journal of History and Politics* 29 (April 1931): 155–232.

———. "Anglo-Spanish Rivalry on the Upper Missouri." *Mississippi Valley Historical Review* 16 (December 1929): 359–82; (March 1930): 420–39.

———. "Ducharme's Invasion of Missouri: An Incident in the Anglo-Spanish Rivalry for the Indian Trade of Upper Louisiana." Parts 1–3. *Missouri Historical Review* 24 (October 1929): 3–25; (January 1930): 238–60; (April 1930): 420–39.

———. Manuscript Collection. San Diego, Calif. Entitled "Imperial Osages: A Documentary History of the Osage Indians During the

Spanish Regime," this extensive collection is referred to in the notes as "Nasatir Papers" to distinguish it from Gilbert C. Din and Abraham P. Nasatir's book, *Imperial Osages.*

Nasatir, Abraham P., ed. *Before Lewis and Clark: Documents Illustrating the History of the Missouri, 1785–1804.* 2 vols. St. Louis: St. Louis Historical Documents Foundation, 1952.

Nash, Gary. *Red, White, and Black: The Peoples of Early America.* 1974. Reprint. Englewood Cliffs, N.J.: Prentice-Hall, 1982.

Nett, Betty R. "Historical Changes in the Osage Kinship System." *Southwestern Journal of Anthropology* 8 (Summer 1952): 164–81.

————. "Osage Kinship." M.A. thesis, University of Oklahoma, 1951.

Newcomb, W. W., Jr. *The Indians of Texas: From Prehistoric to Modern Times.* Austin: University of Texas Press, 1961.

Newman, Tillie K. *The Black Dog Trail.* Boston: Christopher Publishing House, 1957.

Norall, Frank. *Bourgmont, Explorer of the Missouri, 1698–1725.* Lincoln: University of Nebraska Press, 1988.

Nuttall, Thomas. *A Journal of Travels into the Arkansas Territory during the Year 1819.* Edited by Savoie Lottinville. Norman: University of Oklahoma Press, 1980.

Oglesby, Richard E. *Manuel Lisa and the Opening of the Missouri Fur Trade.* Norman: University of Oklahoma Press, 1963.

Peake, Ora Brooks. *A History of the United States Indian Factory System, 1795–1822.* Denver: Sage Books, 1954.

Pease, Theodore, and Ernestine Jenison, eds. *Illinois on the Eve of the Seven Years' War, 1747–1755.* Springfield: Illinois State Historical Library, 1940.

Pease, Theodore, and Raymond C. Werner, eds. *The French Foundations, 1680–1693.* Springfield: Illinois State Historical Library, 1934.

Perrine, Fred S., and Grant Foreman, eds. "The Journal of Hugh Evans, Covering the First and Second Campaigns of the United States Dragoon Regiment in 1834 and 1835." *Chronicles of Oklahoma* 3 (September 1925): 175–215.

Priestly, Herbert I. *France Overseas through the Old Régime: A Study of European Expansion.* New York: D. Appleton-Century Co., 1939.

Reid, John P. *A Better Kind of Hatchet: Law, Trade, and Diplomacy in the Cherokee Nation during the Early Years of European Contact.* University Park: Pennsylvania State University Press, 1976.

Rich, E. E. "Trade Habits and Economic Motivation among the Indians of North America." *Canadian Journal of Economics and Political Science* 26 (1960): 35–53.

Riddell, William R., ed. "Last Official French Report on the Western Posts." *Journal of the Illinois State Historical Society* 24 (October 1931): 578–84.

Roe, Frank G. *The North American Buffalo.* Toronto: University of Toronto Press, 1970.

Rorabacher, J. Albert. *The American Buffalo in Transition: A Historical and Economic Survey of the Bison in America.* Saint Cloud, Minn.: North Star Press, 1970.

Rosenberg, Charles E. *The Cholera Years: The United States in 1832, 1849, and 1866.* Chicago: University of Chicago Press, 1962.

Rowland, Dunbar, and A. G. Sanders, eds., comps., and trans. *Mississippi Provincial Archives, French Dominion, 1701–1743.* 3 vols. Jackson: Press of the Mississippi Department of Archives and History, 1927–1932.

Rowse, Edward F. "Auguste and Pierre Chouteau." Ph.D. diss., Washington University, 1936.

Royce, Charles C. "Indian Land Cessions." Bureau of American Ethnology *Eighteenth Annual Report, 1896–1897,* 2:521–964. Washington, D.C.: Government Printing Office, 1899.

Russell, Carl P. *Firearms, Traps, and Tools of the Mountain Men.* Albuquerque: University of New Mexico Press, 1967.

Ryan, Harold W., ed. "Jacob Bright's Journal of a Trip to the Osage Indians." *The Journal of Southern History* 15 (November 1949): 509–23.

Sahlins, Marshall D. "The Segmentary Lineage: An Organization of Predatory Expansion." *American Anthropologist* 63 (April 1961): 322–43.

Sauer, Carl O. *The Geography of the Ozark Highland of Missouri.* 1920. Reprint. New York: Greenwood Press, 1968.

Secoy, Frank R. *Changing Military Patterns on the Great Plains (17th Century through early 19th Century).* Monographs of the American Ethnological Society, no. 21. Locust Valley, N.Y.: J. J. Augustin Publisher, 1953.

———. "The Identity of the 'Paduca': An Ethnohistorical Analysis." *American Anthropologist* 53 (October 1951): 525–42.

Sheehan, Bernard W. *Seeds of Extinction: Jeffersonian Philanthropy and the American Indian.* Chapel Hill: University of North Carolina Press, 1973.

Shelford, Victor Ernest. *The Ecology of North America.* Urbana: University of Illinois Press, 1963.

Sibley Papers. Missouri Historical Society, St. Louis.

Simmons, Eva Mary. "Cherokee-Osage Relations: 1803–1839." M.A. thesis, University of Oklahoma, 1940.

Smith, Bruce D. "Middle Mississippian Exploitation of Animal Populations." Anthropological Papers, Museum of Anthropology, University of Michigan, no. 57. Ann Arbor: University of Michigan Press, 1975.

Smith, Ralph A., ed. and trans. "Account of the Journey of Bénard de la Harpe: Discovery Made by Him of Several Nations Situated in the West." Parts 1–4. *Southwestern Historical Quarterly* 61 (July 1958): 75–86; 61 (October 1958): 246–59; 62 (January 1959): 371–85; 62 (April 1959): 525–41.

Snyder, J. F. "Were the Osages Mound Builders?" *Annual Report of the Board of Regents of the Smithsonian Institution to July 1888,* 587–95. Washington, D.C.: Government Printing Office, 1890.

Speck, F. G. "Notes on the Ethnology of the Osage Indians." *Transactions of the Free Museum of Science and Art of the University of Pennsylvania* 2 (1907): 159–71.

Spencer, Robert F., and Jesse D. Jennings, et al. *The Native Americans.* New York: Harper and Row, 1977.

Springer, James Warren, and Stanley R. Witkowski. "Siouan Historical Linguistics and Oneota Archaeology." University of Minnesota Publications in Anthropology, no. 1, pp. 69–79. Edited by Guy E. Gibbon. Minneapolis: University of Minnesota Press, 1981.

Stearn, Esther Wagner, and Allen E. Stearn. *The Effect of Smallpox on the Destiny of the Amerindian.* Boston: Bruce Humphries, 1945.

Steck, Francis Brogia. *The Jolliet-Marquette Expedition, 1673.* Glendale, Calif.: Arthur H. Clark Co., 1928.

Stipes, M. F. "Fort Orleans, The First French Post on the Missouri." *Missouri Historical Review* 8 (April 1914): 121–35.

Strickland, Rennard. *Five and the Spirits: Cherokee Law from Clan to Court.* Norman: University of Oklahoma Press, 1975.

Sturtevant, William C. "Anthropology, History, and Ethnohistory." *Ethnohistory* 13 (Winter–Spring 1966): 1–51.

Surrey, Nancy M. Miller. *Calendar of Manuscripts in Paris Archives and Libraries Relating to the History of the Mississippi Valley to 1803.* 2 vols. Washington, D.C.: Carnegie Institution of Washington, 1926–1928.

———. *The Commerce of Louisiana during the French Régime, 1699–1763.* New York: Columbia University Press, 1916.

Swanton, John R. "Siouan Tribes and the Ohio Valley." *American Anthropologist* 45 (January–March 1943): 49–85.

Thomas, A. B. "The Massacre of the Villasur Expedition at the Forks of the Platte River, August 12, 1720." *Nebraska History* 7 (July–September 1924): 67–81.

Thorne, Tanis Chapman. "The Chouteau Family and the Osage Trade: A Generational Study." In *Rendezvous: Selected Papers of the Fourth North American Fur Trade Conference, 1981,* edited by Thomas C. Buckley, 109–19. St. Paul, Minn.: North American Trade Conference, 1983.

Thwaites, Reuben Gold, ed. *Early Western Travels, 1748–1846.* 32 vols. 1904–1907. Reprint. New York: AMS Press, 1966.

———, ed. *The French Regime in Wisconsin, 1634–1727.* Vol. 16 of *Collections of the State Historical Society of Wisconsin.* Madison: State Historical Society of Wisconsin, 1902.

———, ed. *Lower Canada, Mississippi Valley, 1696–1702.* Vol. 65 of *The Jesuit Relations and Allied Documents: Travels and Explorations of the Jesuit Missionaries in New France, 1610–1791.* New York: Pageant Book Co., 1959.

———, ed. *A New Discovery of a Vast Country in America, by Father Louis Hennepin.* 1698. Reprint. Chicago: A. C. McClurg, 1903.

———, ed. *Ottawa, Lower Canada, Iroquois, Illinois: 1689–1695.* Vol. 64 of *The Jesuit Relations and Allied Documents: Travels and Explorations of the Jesuit Missionaries in New France, 1610–1791.* New York: Pageant Book Co., 1959.

Tixier, Victor. *Voyage aux Prairies Osages, Louisiane et Missouri, 1839–40.* Paris: Clermont-Ferrand Chez Perol, Libraire-Éditeur, 1844.

Truteau, Jean Baptiste. "Journal of Jean Baptiste Truteau on the Upper Missouri, 'Premiere Partei,' June 7, 1794–March 26, 1795." *American Historical Review* 19 (January 1914): 299–333.

Tuttle, Sarah. *Letters on the Chickasaw and Osage Missions.* Boston: T. P. Marvin for the Massachusetts Sabbath School Union, 1831.

Union Mission Journal. Missouri Historical Society, St. Louis.

U.S. Office of Indian Trade. *Arkansas Trading House Letterbook, 1805–1810.* Record Group 75. M142. National Archives, Washington, D.C.

Unrau, William E. *The Kansa Indians: A History of the Wind People, 1673–1873.* Norman: University of Oklahoma Press, 1971.

Usner, Daniel H., Jr. "The Frontier Exchange Economy of the Lower Mississippi Valley in the Eighteenth Century." *William and Mary Quarterly* 44 (April 1987): 165–92.

Villiers, Baron Marc de. *La Découverte du Missouri et l'histoire du Fort D'Orléans (1673–1728).* Paris: Librairie Ancienne Honoré Champion, 1925.

Vissier, Paul. *Histoire de la Tribu des Osages.* Paris: Chez C. Bedet, 1827.

Voget, Fred W. *Osage Research Report.* Vol. 1 of *Osage Indians.* Edited by David A. Horr. New York: Garland Publishing, 1974.

Wallace, Anthony F. C. *The Death and Rebirth of the Seneca.* 1969. Reprint. New York: Vintage Books, 1972.

Wallace, Ernest, and E. Adamson Hoebel. *The Comanches: Lords of the South Plains.* 1952. Reprint. Norman: University of Oklahoma Press, 1976.

Wardell, M. L. "Early Protestant Missions Among the Osages, 1820 to 1838." *Chronicles of Oklahoma* 2 (September 1924): 285–97.

Washburn, Wilcomb. "Ethnohistory: History 'In the Round.' " *Ethnohistory* 8 (Winter 1961): 31–48.

Wedel, Mildred Mott. "Claude-Charles DuTisné: A Review of His 1719 Journeys." Parts 1 and 2. *Great Plains Journal* 12 (Fall 1972): 5–25; 12 (Spring 1973): 147–73.

———. "The Deer Creek Site, Oklahoma: A Wichita Village sometimes called Ferdinandina, An Ethnohistorian's View." In *The Wichita Indians, 1541–1750: Ethnohistorical Essays.* 1981. Reprint. Lincoln, Nebr.: J & L Reprint Co., 1988.

———. "The Identity of LaSalle's *Pana* Slave." *Plains Anthropologist* 18 (August 1973): 203–17.

———. "J.-B. Bénard, Sieur de la Harpe: Visitor to the Wichitas in 1719." *Great Plains Journal* 10 (Spring 1971): 37–70.

———. "The Wichita Indians in the Arkansas River Basin." In *Plains Indian Studies: A Collection of Essays in Honor of John C. Ewers and Waldo R. Wedel.* Smithsonian Contributions to Anthropology, no. 30, pp. 118–34. Edited by Douglas H. Ubelaker and Herman J. Viola. Washington, D.C.: Smithsonian Institution, 1982.

Wedel, Waldo R. "An Introduction to Kansas Archeology." Bureau of American Ethnology Bulletin, no. 174, pp. 54–59. Washington, D.C.: Government Printing Office, 1959.

———. *Prehistoric Man on the Great Plains.* Norman: University of Oklahoma Press, 1961.

Wedel, Waldo R., and Mildred M. Wedel. "Wichita Archaeology and Ethnohistory." In *Kansas and the West,* edited by Forrest R. Blackburn, et al., 8–20. Topeka: Kansas State Historical Association, 1976.

Weslager, C. A. *The Delaware Indians: A History.* New Brunswick, N.J.: Rutgers University Press, 1972.

Wheelock, T. B. "Colonel Henry Dodge and His Regiment of Dragoons on the Plains in 1834." *Annals of Iowa* 17 (January 1930): 173–97.

White, Richard. "The Cultural Landscape of the Pawnees." In *The American Indian: Past and Present,* edited by Roger L. Nichols, 194–203. New York: Alfred A. Knopf, 1986.

———. *The Roots of Dependency: Subsistence, Environment, and Social Change among the Choctaws, Pawnees, and Navajos.* Lincoln: University of Nebraska Press, 1983.

———. "The Winning of the West: The Expansion of the Western Sioux in the Eighteenth and Nineteenth Centuries." *Journal of American History* 65 (September 1978): 319–43.

Wiggers, Robert. "Osage Culture Change Inferred from Contact and Trade with the Caddo and the Pawnee." Ph.D. diss., University of Missouri, 1985.

Will, George F., and George E. Hyde. *Corn Among the Indians of the Upper Missouri.* St. Louis: The William Harvey Miner Co., 1917.

Williams, Amelia W., and Eugene C. Barker, eds. *The Writings of Sam Houston, 1813–1836.* 8 vols. Austin: University of Texas Press, 1938–1943.

Williams, Robert L., ed. "Founding of the First Chouteau Trading Post in Oklahoma at Salina, Mayes County." *Chronicles of Oklahoma* 24 (Winter 1946–1947): 483–91.

Wilson, Terry. *Bibliography of the Osage.* Metuchen, N.J.: Scarecrow Press, 1985.

Windell, Marie George, ed. "The Missouri Reader: The French in the Valley." *Missouri Historical Review* 41 (October 1946): 77–106.

Wishart, David. *The Fur Trade of the American West, 1807–1840: A*

Geographical Synthesis. Lincoln: University of Nebraska Press, 1979.

Wissler, Clark. "The Influence of the Horse in the Development of Plains Culture." *American Anthropologist* 16 (January–March 1914): 1–25.

Wood, W. Raymond, and Margot Liberty, eds. *Anthropology on the Great Plains.* Lincoln: University of Nebraska Press, 1980.

INDEX